CALLING
JESUS
NAMES

PUBLISHED VOLUMES

Bruce J. Malina and Jerome H. Neyrey, *Calling Jesus Names*

CALLING
JESUS
NAMES

THE SOCIAL VALUE OF

LABELS IN MATTHEW

BRUCE J. MALINA

&

JEROME H. NEYREY

SONOMA, CALIFORNIA

To John H. Elliott
for support and encouragement
and for being a good friend

Library of Congress Cataloging-in-Publication Data

Malina, Bruce J.
  Calling Jesus names.

  (Foundations & facets. Social facets)
  Bibliography: p.
  Includes index.
  1. Jesus Christ—Name. 2. Bible. N.T. Matthew—Criticism, interpretation, etc. 3. Sociology, Biblical.
I. Neyrey, Jerome H., 1940– . II. Title.
III. Series.
BT590.N2M35   1988   226'.2067   88–5821
ISBN 0-944344-05-4 (pbk.)

Printed in the United States of America

Contents

Foreword to the Series

Foundations & Facets: New Testament has two major divisions as indicated by the title.

Much of the more creative biblical scholarship on the contemporary scene is devoted to *Facets* of biblical texts: to units of the text smaller than canonical books, or to aspects of the New Testament that ignore the boundaries of books and canon. In one sense, *Facets* refers to any textual unit or group of units that does not coincide with the boundaries of canonical books. In another sense, *Facets* refers to aspects of the biblical materials that are being addressed by newly emerging biblical disciplines: literary criticism and its partner, narratology, and the social sciences in various guises. These two senses of *Facets* produce the second major division of the series with its two subdivisions: Literary Facets and Social Facets.

The creative and innovative impulses in current scholarship are also linked to the creation of new study instruments and tools, based on emerging new methods in biblical criticism or to the reconception of old ones. These instruments are shaping the first division of the series: *Foundations*.

Together, the two divisions of *Foundations & Facets* will form the basis for the next phase of biblical scholarship.

Polebridge Press
Sonoma, California 1987

Robert W. Funk, *editor*

Preface

Calling Jesus Names is about several things. While it focuses on Christology, it treats only one document, the gospel of Matthew. It specifically examines the negative and positive assessments of Jesus in conflictual situations. In regard to these Christological conflicts, we will interpret them from the viewpoint of the social sciences. We focus, then, on interpreting from a social science perspective the conflict over the correct evaluation of Jesus in the gospel of Matthew.

Let us be more specific about the perspective and task of this book. To begin with, our enterprise is one of *textual interpretation*, which is always the task of those who study biblical documents. What textual interpretation entails will be briefly described below (section 0.4 below). Second, our specific textual focus will be *the gospel of Matthew*, in particular the accusation from the triple tradition in chapter 12 of demonic possession, along with the account of Jesus' arrest, trial and execution in chapters 26–27. Third, our approach will be one of conflict analysis, since *conflict* is the stuff of this gospel. From start to finish, the whole gospel is one extended account of Jesus' conflicts, from the genealogy in chapter 1 that legitimates Jesus' familial standing as one of honor, to Herod's quest for the life of the child in chapter 2, to the battle between Jesus and Satan in chapter 4, to Jesus' fight with the Pharisees in chapter 12, eventually to his confrontation with the Chief Priests in chapter 21–27. Chapters 12 and 26–27, however, are particular areas of conflict that require special treatment. Fourth, the perspective for analyzing this conflict comes from the *social sciences*. In order to interpret the conflictual dynamic whereby Jesus and the Pharisees trade accusations of demon possession, we propose to use a model of witchcraft from cultural anthropology. Then, to explain how Jesus was ultimately branded a blaspheming pretender and executed, we will turn to labelling and deviance theory. The perspective throughout this book, then, is social science modeling. Finally and ultimately, this book is about *Christology*. As a rule, Christology considers the honorific titles attributed to Jesus of Nazareth as Christ. We, however, would look upon Christology as a process whereby Jesus of Nazareth was either acclaimed by his followers as a prominent person or defamed by his enemies as a deviant. Yet Christology in this book is not the standard study of Jesus' self-consciousness or his titles, "historically" considered. Rather it is an instance of Christology "from the side."

0.1   Christology "From the Side"

While this book is about Christology, it is not about Christology "from above" or "from below" (Lane 1975: 14–18). Christology "from above" describes the assessments of Jesus that developed in fourth- and fifth-century conciliar debates. In those debates churchmen formulated a doctrine about Jesus as the divine Word of God descending from heaven and incarnated on earth, so that Jesus was confessed by the Church as "true God" and "true man." Christology "from below" refers to contemporary descriptions of Jesus based mainly on the synoptic gospels, where the focus is squarely on the humanity of Jesus, i.e., how he was like us in all things, even as the perfection of our humanity.

The contrasting of Christology as "from above" and/or "from below" implies a vertical perspective (e.g., heaven to earth or earth to heaven). This is often expressed in highly complex philosophical terms dealing with the metaphysical personhood and the psychological constitution of the person Jesus in terms of that metaphysical personhood. And, because it is an instance of vertical classification, this perspective is chiefly, if not exclusively, concerned with power or force (Malina 1986: 71, 82–83). In one form or another, Christology "from above" and "from below" focuses on the person of Jesus in terms of power symbols. Jesus is viewed in relationship to God, either descending from God's right hand faithfully to carry out God's preordained plan, or attempting to reach God while remaining faithfully subject to him in obedience, within the constraints of the human condition.

Christology "from above" reflects Christian tradition only after the time of Constantine, when hierarchy became the expressive social structure, with power or force a primary concern (see Mayer 1983: 61–213). Christology "from below" expresses twentieth-century concerns with the relationship of natural and supernatural and the possibility of transcendence in a secular world. Both of these views express Jesus' vertical relationship to God and would be rather anachronistic for an adequate understanding of New Testament views of Jesus, even though the question of Messiah with power was a concern of early Christian groups.

Yet within Christian groups before Constantine, the chief expressive social dimension for non-Roman and Roman non-elite Christians was not vertical, but horizontal—"from the side." This is the human perspective and social arrangement marked by the relation of inside and outside, center and periphery. It was in terms of this sort of social structure that early Christian groups were organized and thus perceived their fundamental ideology. This perspective is expressed in language with the terminology of faith and trust, of commitment, loyalty and solidarity. In line with these dimensions, our task will be to describe Christology as it was articulated from the outside and from the inside, that is, how Jesus was evaluated by his enemies and his followers. This is Christology "from the side." In short, the focus is on the social processes whereby Jesus, as described in the gospel of Matthew, was acclaimed or defamed by members of his society who took him seriously and interacted with him as an equal.

0.2   Christology

Christology, as the word is used in the jargon of theologians, is about the positive assessments of Jesus of Nazareth in terms of the Jewish role and status of Messiah or Christ as presented in gospel and subsequent traditions. In *Calling Jesus Names* we shall focus on positive as well as negative assessments of Jesus, specifically in the gospel of Matthew and its sources, but always from the perspective of the social sciences.

Recent, significant essays indicate an abiding scholarly interest in Christology (see most recently Keck 1986), as well as the relatively recent issue of *Semeia* dedicated to "Christology and Exegesis: New Approaches" (Jewett *et al*: 1985, predated to 1984:30), and the reaction to James D. G. Dunn's recent work, *Christology in the Making* (1980). That reaction, along with Dunn's rebuttal to his critics, was presented in a recent article (Dunn 1985) in which the author takes his critics to task by noting:

> In each case I have the same complaint: they have not taken seriously enough what I regard and repeatedly stressed to be basic axioms of exegetical method. What I have in mind can be summed up in two phrases—"historical context of meaning" and "conceptuality in transition." Unless these principles are taken with full seriousness a proper exegesis is rendered impossible (Dunn 1985:296).

Dunn explained the first principle, "historical context of meaning," as follows:

> To achieve a proper exegesis of a NT text we must ask what the writer intended his first readers to hear—that also means, what he could have expected his readers to understand by the language he used, given the way words and concepts were understood individually and in combination within the broader context of thought at that time and within the particular context of the situation in which or for which the text was written. Only when we have some reasonably clear idea of the context of meaning in which the NT texts were initially understood can we have any hope of recognizing the distinctive and unique features of these texts which caused them to be treasured and preserved (Dunn 1985:296).

And the second principle, "conceptuality in transition," refers to the following assumed "fact":

> Words change meaning, fresh concepts emerge and develop, others degenerate or disappear, and so on. The consequence is that to ask after historical context of meaning in another culture and age involves a careful locating of words and ideas within the *movement* of the thought of the time. . . . a relatively short span of decades saw the emergence of a whole new religion of

international significance (Christianity itself), not to mention the emergence of rabbinic Judaism as the enduring form of the Jewish religion. On any count, all this must have involved a substantial movement of thought, a shaping of concepts and remoulding of categories (Dunn 1985:298).

Obviously, Dunn is correct in seeing the genius of contemporary biblical interpretation in the acute and consistent sense of history that informs most trained biblical scholars. However, it does not seem that he in fact does justice to how human beings go about making sense of their experience. His descriptions of both "historical context" and "conceptuality" are simply abstractions that do not relate to the human groups whose experience they seek to describe. After all, "historical context" basically refers to a group of interacting people in a given time and place. To speak of "historical context" is to describe and explain the behavior of group members, not disembodied ideas or concepts. Christology, if truly "historical," will be Christology "from the side." It must take into account the human evaluative process.

This point needs to be even more sharply underscored relative to Dunn's description of his second principle, "contextuality," for at bottom it is not words and concepts that change but rather the experience of people interpreted in terms of social systems realized by and encoded in these words and concepts. As most people enculturated in the U.S. realize, reality is not socially constructed, it is socially interpreted (see Borhek and Curtis 1975), and it is these interpretations of experience, as well as the experiences themselves, that change.

0.3   Social Sciences

The goal of social science is to develop an understanding of the processes that involve the creation, maintenance and change of social relations that invariably occur in patterned ways. Such patterns are usually called structures or frameworks, and these in turn mediate and realize values. Primary focus in social science analysis may be on *how and why the structures work the way they do* (functionalism); here behavior and its determinants are underscored. Or analysis may be focused on *how and why the structures are as they are* (conflict theory); conflicting persons and their motives are thus highlighted. Or finally, analysis may look to *how and why the structures mediate the meanings that they do* (symbolic or interpretative approaches); attention is then brought to bear on human actions and their sense. In this later perspective, human meanings are developed in and as social relations.

If human meanings are rooted in social relations, it follows that language ultimately and simply encodes aspects and items of human social relations. Communication, too, would be a form of such social relations in which language is the mediating material, the channel. While not a few biblical scholars study the languages of their sources, such study of language rarely takes the social sciences seriously, as grammars and grammatical analyses of biblical languages evidence. In this book, on the other hand, we propose to take the social sciences quite seriously and in a positive way, for we assume that cultural anthropology, ethnography, sociolinguistics and, in its own way, sociology are essential for understanding the meanings of the languages that encode social relations by means of texts. We intend, then, to set forth some of the appropriate and commonly known social science models that we have found useful for people interested in Christology.

0.4   Presuppositions

As in good social science method, we make known our major presuppositions before we begin. First, by "Christology" we mean the interpretation and assessment of Jesus of Nazareth as Christ, hence as a socially meaningful figure for some groups of people in the first century C.E. in the eastern Mediterranean area. Evidence for this interpretation and assessment emerges in language as a scattergram of titles and behaviors ascribed to Jesus and noted by that set of groups called the "early Church." Further, the existence of that set of groups is itself evidence and will be treated as such from a social science point of view. Granted the existence of such groups and their writings, how can we interpret them in a fair and testable way so as to understand *their* interpretation and assessment of Jesus? This entails three further presuppositions: one having to do with reading, one with language and a third with social science methodology.

0.4a Reading.   Since by and large our evidence for early Christology consists in texts and entails reading and interpreting written language, it is important to have some verifiable theory of how reading takes place (this point is entirely overlooked by Chouinard 1987). We use a model commonly called a scenario model, if only because there is evidence to indicate that people actually read in terms of scenarios (Sanford and Garrod 1981). Interpreting anything indicates that some information necessary for understanding is lacking. What the interpreter does is provide this information so that the person or thing being interpreted can be readily understood.

All human beings carry on an interpretative enterprise. As a rule, people carry in their heads one or more models of "society" and "human being" that greatly influence what they look for in their experiences, what they actually see and what they eventually do with their observations by way of fitting them into a larger scheme of explanation along with other facts. In this respect, every human being is no different from any scientist in our society (Garfinkel 1967: 262–83). Every scientist, like every other human being, holds some general conception of the realm in which he or she is working, that is, some mental picture of how it is put together, how it works and how one ought to feel about it. Of course, the same is true of the biblical interpreter, professional and non-professional.

The scenario model of reading begins with the assumption that every reader has a full and verifiable grasp of how the world works, which awareness the reader brings to a text. In the linguistic interchange that follows, an author presents some distinctive sets of scenarios of how the world works that in effect rearrange the scenarios the reader brings to the reading. The considerate author attempts to deal with the scenarios shared by his or her readers.

Of course, by this standard, the biblical authors are all inconsiderate, for they neither know our modern view of the world nor make any attempt to explain their ancient world in terms we might understand. But given historical constraints, we instead are asked to be considerate readers and so bring a set of scenarios proper to the time, place and culture of the biblical author. Granted the need to be a considerate reader, how do the squiggles on a page get to have meaning as language?

0.4b Language.   Another presupposition concerns the nature of language. We adopt the perspective of sociolinguistics, specifically that of the neo-Firthian tradition as articulated by Michael A. K. Halliday (1978; see Cicourel 1985). This material might seem overly complex, but we consider it important to clarify certain aspects of this theory of language that have a bearing on the project of *Calling Jesus Names*.

First, in this tradition the chief social purpose of language is to mean, and the purpose of meaning is to have some social effect. Language, moreover, is a three-tiered affair consisting of (1) soundings/spellings that (2) realize wordings that (3) realize meanings. But where do the meanings realized in language come from? They come from and in fact constitute the social system. Thus, the three-tiered model of language would have the Bible reader ask, What social system or meaning is expressed in the wordings realized in the spellings of biblical "texts"?

What, moreover, is "textual" interpretation? In this sort of sociolinguistics "text" means several things. "Text" is a meaningful configuration of language intended to communicate. And "text" is the unit of interpretation, whereas "sentences," which are individual units of thought, realize meaning. The gospel of Matthew is our "text," within which we will examine two "text segments," Matthew 12 and 26–27. As regards "interpretation," interpreting anything indicates that there is some non-understanding or misunderstanding. The interpreter provides the necessary information so that the person or thing being interpreted can be readily understood. What is lacking for a historical interpretation of ancient texts are sets of scenarios that might facilitate reading in terms of the meanings familiar to the original audience of those texts. Reading and language theory, then, indicate that in this book we concern ourselves with understanding the social system of those who evaluated Jesus, and so come to a scenario adequate for understanding the gospel of Matthew.

Calling Jesus Names, then, is about the models of "society" and of "human being" that persons normally bring to their negative and positive interpretation of what they read in the New Testament about Jesus and his titles. Interpersonal communication requires some shared universe of discourse, some shared acceptance of how the world works, even if this acceptance be hypothetical. Thus, the question posed by historically informed biblical interpretation is how must one imagine the world to be working to understand the human interactions described in the New Testament. This is spelled out in further questions: what information is lacking to make a text understandable; i.e., what needs to be studied to produce the required information; in this study, what questions have to be asked and how should they be asked; finally, what procedure ought to be followed in interpreting and assessing the answers thus obtained? Here we hope to present some such alternate models of how the world and its peoples work so as to facilitate a historical appreciation of what concerned the people who wrote the biblical texts.

Our project differs substantially from other treatments of Christology, conflict and the gospel of Matthew because it formally addresses the problem of gospel interpretation from a social science perspective. This becomes apparent from the very way we conceive of the task of biblical interpretation. This book is primarily intended to provide contemporary readers of the gospel of Matthew with a set of scenarios to facilitate their reading and understanding of the titles or labels appended to Jesus in that gospel. Meanings realized in texts inevitably derive from some social system. Thus, to interpret the originally intended meanings set out in various New Testament texts the contemporary reader must have access to the social system(s) available to the original audience of those texts. To recover those social systems, we believe it is essential to employ adequate, explicit social science models.

0.4c Scientific method. Of course, in the interpretations that follow, we follow the general canons of the scientific method: (1) postulate a model; (2) test the model against the real-world experience to which it relates; (3) modify the model in terms of the outcome of the test to reduce divergence by detecting errors of omission or commission. These steps are meant to safeguard against the usual pitfalls of thought: superficiality and inaccuracy. In themselves these steps in learning are quite commonsensical (Garfinkel 1967), perhaps even transcultural, in that they describe general abstract thinking. However, where the "scientific" method runs onto the reefs of cultural specificity and self-fulfilling prophecy is in the area of the "Western" values (see Smart 1983) that often permeate it as applied in U.S. experience. These values emerge in the following postulates, often identified as *the* "scientific method" itself: (1) the world exists; (2) the world is knowable; (3) the world is knowable through our senses; (4) the elements comprising the world are related in terms of cause and effect (see Goode and Hatt 1952:20).

These postulates, of course, are based on a specific world view and lead us to assume that reality is in fact just as the postulates determine. These postulates derive from what is called the "paradigm of fact" (see Pfuhl 1980: 4-15; and as espoused concretely, e.g., by Gager 1983). This paradigm presumes that all knowledge is objective, totally outside the head and experience of the knower. In our estimation, this presumption is quite ethnocentric and is simply not the whole story. While there are indeed objects totally outside the head and experience of the knower, they cannot be known as objective or anything else without a knower, and this knower gets to know due to and in accordance with a socially shared learning process. In this sense, all knowledge is social, totally within the shared paradigms and accumulated experiences of a group of knowers, a social group.

On the basis of this corrective, our postulates turn out as follows: (1) we learn to perceive that the world exists in a certain way; (2) this socially perceived world is knowable, specifically in ways most adequate to the meaningful survival of our human social group; (3) the world is knowable through human interaction; and (4) the elements comprising the world are related in terms of the assigned meanings and motives of human social groups and their agents. In this perspective, the "law of cause and effect" is a social product, deriving from group motives and maintained because of its utility for an adequately meaningful human existence within a given physical and social environment.

Given these different postulates, it follows that either in society at large or in smaller social groups nothing is simply "objective" and nothing socially significant operates impersonally. Behind everything that occurs are persons with their choices and motivations, their biographies and standpoints. While there are objects and things in the human environment, these objects and things have their meaning, utility and value precisely because of human interpretations, hence due to personal choices and motivations. The fundamental question in interpretation, then, becomes "who" and not "what." Consequently, while there may be actions good or bad in themselves, they can be known as such only through the social process of defining those actions as good or bad by, within and often for a given social group. The perspective described here might be called "definitional" (Pfuhl 1980:15–25) or symbolic.

In this approach, meaning derives from the socially perceived and appreciated lines that human groups draw around the self, others, nature, time, space and some All. This set of lines produces a system, a set of interrelated parts with a place for everything and everyone. Things out of place are dirty, since dirt is matter out of place. Persons out of place are equally unclean, since deviance is a person out of place. Knowledge out of place is occult or "metaphysical," even "supernatural." In this definitional perspective, then, the crucial concern is who draws lines, for what purpose, for whose benefit and the like. Hence, Christology "from the side" attends precisely to the interpretations of Jesus by those who assessed him in terms of the socially perceived and appreciated lines that produced the culture of Jesus and Matthew.

0.5   Mediterranean Culture

While the Christology described in this book will derive from a set of social science models, we are painfully aware that the beneficial application of such models requires some overall awareness of the cultural particularities of the Eastern Mediterranean (Gilmore 1982), as well as the historical idiosyncrasies of first-century Palestine and its surroundings. Hence, while this book presents a piece of social science theory and its New Testament application, and while most readers will be sufficiently aware of New Testament history, most will be innocent of first-century Mediterranean culture and its values. To facilitate a quick orientation with these values, we have drawn up a comparative set of perceptions and listed these in the Appendix, Table 1. The information in the table is meant to serve as the wider frame of reference within which to situate the models and consequent interpretations that follow. For the reader's convenience, we have also provided a table of all the negative labels in the gospel of Matthew (Appendix, Table 2) followed by all the positive labels (Appendix, Table 3).

0.6   Technical Phraseology

To avoid confusion resulting from an overly theological understanding of social terminology, we consider it appropriate to establish and specify the meaning of several key terms in our approach to Christology "from the side." Throughout we will make a distinction between the Jesus "movement" and the Jesus "movement group." This perhaps sounds clumsy at first, but it may also prove to be a conceptually useful distinction, both in social science analysis and in theology (we follow Snow *et al.* 1980:787). (1) The Jesus "movement" refers to that *set of opinions and beliefs* developed and diffused by Jesus of Nazareth and held by first-century Mediterranean populations that represent preferences in support of or in opposition to social change. (2) Concerning the Jesus "movement group," "group" refers to a *social unit of restricted membership* (we-ness versus they-ness or you-ness) determined by specific criteria that define the restrictions for acceptance for a given process. The Jesus "movement group," then, would include those who espoused the opinion and beliefs articulated by Jesus. A primary group consisted of those who accompanied Jesus, while a secondary group included those who espoused the movement but did not travel around with Jesus.

"Groups" are always involved in processes, in a series of regularly repeated activities directed to some specific end or purpose. Since groups are end- or purpose-specific, there will always be different groups engaged in different processes that may overlap or be coterminous when the same individuals belong to different groups whose purposes they fulfill at the same time (e.g., Paul the Jew and follower of Christ). Consequently, the Jesus "movement group" is defined as a group that identifies its ends or purposes with the preferences of the Jesus "movement" and attempts to implement those ends and purposes.

In a similar vein, it might be useful to note that the Jesus "movement" might also be called the Jesus "community." Here a community is (1) a *set of values, interests and relationships* shared by (2) *people who are a group set off or set apart from others*, with the result that those people perceive a sense of oneness, of fictive kinship (i.e., brotherhood and/or sisterhood). Kinship terminology, ranging from family terms to neighbor terms, is quite normal for a community group.

Finally, while the Jesus "movement" was spread to many groups throughout various regions by persons traditionally called "missionaries" on a "mission," we have refrained from using the terminology of mission, if only because it is too familiar and charged with freight it did not bear in the first century. Instead, we speak of "change agents," since the end or purpose of the Jesus movement group was change.

0.7 Plan of the Book

The first focus in this Christology "from the side" is an analysis of Matthew 12, the accusation against Jesus of demonic possession. For this purpose the anthropological model of witchcraft developed by Mary Douglas, among others, can serve as an adequate vehicle for interpreting the conflictual scenario that culminated in the Mediterranean phenomenon of an accusation against Jesus of demonic possession. The second chapter will go back over the same text-segment, but from the perspective of labelling and deviance theory. The advantage of this redundant interpretation is the appreciation of two complementary social science models for analyzing conflictual process.

Chapters 3 and 4 will focus on the conflict embodied in Jesus' arrest, trial and execution in Matthew 26–27. That text-segment will be studied first from the perspective of labelling and deviance theory, for Jesus' shameful execution appears to be a clear example of a successful status degradation ritual. But as Jesus was labelled a deviant by his enemies and rivals, the same labelling process served as an apt occasion for his followers to acclaim him a prominent. Thus, the last chapter will review Matthew 26–27 from the perspective of prominence labelling. The prominence-labelling model defines the process whereby Jesus ceases to be acknowledged as a criminal who suffered a just recompense for his evildoing, and is acclaimed as the true son of God who assumed kingship, glory and power through his death on the cross.

Bruce J. Malina
Jerome H. Neyrey

ESUS

THE WITCH

Jesus the Witch

Witchcraft Accusations in Matthew 12

1.1 The Evidence: Accusations

Matthew's gospel is remarkable in that it contains numerous accusations of demonic possession and/or collaboration. To begin with, the Pharisees' accusations against Jesus are quite familiar. Twice they interpret Jesus' healing actions negatively: "He casts out demons by the prince of demons" (9:34) and "It is by Beelzebul, the prince of demons, that this man casts out demons" (12:24). They even call him "Beelzebul," a terrible accusation that extends also to Jesus' disciples: "If they have called the master of the house Beelzebul, how much more will they malign those of his household" (10:25). Further, John the Baptizer is dismissed as an imposter with this slur: "He came neither eating nor drinking, and they say he has a demon" (11:18). In turn, members of Matthew's community accuse the Pharisees and other enemies of being possessed by demons. The inimical Pharisees, who were once exorcised of a demon, are accused of being repossessed by that demon and "seven others more evil than itself" (12:43–45). They are identified as the tares among the wheat, "the sons of the evil one" (13:38), because "the enemy who sowed them is the devil" (13:39). They are more fearsome than those who cause physical pain and misfortune because they also kill and so "destroy both life and person (=soul and body) in Gehenna" (10:28). And when they find a proselyte, they make of him "twice a child of Gehenna" as themselves (23:15). Finally, Jesus himself is alleged to have called Peter "Satan," perhaps metaphorically, but perhaps not (16:23). The point is that accusations of demon possession and/or collaboration pervade the gospel, reflecting not just the Pharisees' label for Jesus and his followers, but also the reaction of members of Jesus' group to the Pharisees and other non-members.

Comparable accusations are made in John's gospel as well. We are all familiar with the verbal affront to Jesus: "Are we not right that you are a Samaritan and have a demon?" (8:48) and "Now we know that you have a demon" (8:52). In another place, a charge is made against Jesus: "He has a demon, and he is mad" (10:19). But Jesus himself is credited with accusing his opponents of the same thing: "You are of your father the devil, and your will is to do your father's desires" (8:44). The accusations, then, are mutual, and they continue among adherents of the Johannine tradition (see 1 John 3:8–10). Thus, the gospels do not have a monopoly on this sort of labelling.

Paul, too, was accustomed to attacking opponents such as the "super apostles" in 2 Corinthians 11 with a similar charge (Neyrey 1986a). Regarding rival preachers in Corinth, Paul remarked:

3

> For such men are false apostles, deceitful workmen, disguising themselves as apostles of Christ. And no wonder, even Satan disguised himself as an angel of light. So it is not strange if his servants also disguise themselves as servants of righteousness (2 Cor 11:13–15).

Whatever the circumstances of Paul's accusations, he considered his rivals as demonic figures who were seducing the pure bride of Christ, just as the serpent deceived Eve by his cunning (11:3).

Although this study will concentrate on the accusations in Matthew's story of Jesus, it is evident that followers of Jesus charged others—even other members of various Jesus groups—with the same charge of demonic possession and/or collaboration with which they were charged. Such accusations were a recurring phenomenon in the time and place occupied by the persons described in the New Testament.

How can readers of the New Testament understand and interpret the experience of those persons? It is the purpose of this discussion to suggest a set of models developed in the field of cultural anthropology that can offer an adequate scenario for a reader to interpret this evidence. The charges mentioned above may be labeled "witchcraft accusations," a technical anthropological term that concretely points to a specific situation in a village or small group where a charge is made that (1) one's enemies or rivals are actually the forces of evil or are demonically controlled by them, (2) they are thoroughly evil and so (3) should be expelled from the village or group. The "witchcraft accusation," then, while it focuses on the charge of demonic possession, implies much more. For example, it implies a social script based on enemies in constant conflict, on the perception of enemies as fully evil and friends as totally good, on exile and expulsion as the main forms of extreme punishment. Furthermore, the way the witch works, his sources of power and the nature of his attack all relate to an image of the community, the way it works, the sources of power that control it and the kind of attack to which community values are subject. Thus, the evidence of witchcraft accusations implies that the charge arises from a specific type of social script and that it serves to maintain meaningful behavior for persons living according to that sort of script.

What is needed for appreciating the import of these witchcraft accusations is a set of models that might provide insight into the cultural directives of the group in which the accusations occur. The models would thus serve to explain the meaning of such accusations within that context. We turn first to the works of the British anthropologist Mary Douglas for a model that will deal with the general social context within which witchcraft might be understood in a comparative way. This model has two parts. First, Douglas argues that witchcraft accusations occur within a certain type of cultural system (1982: viii–ix, 107–24). Accurate description of that system, then, is an integral part of the model. Second, within that cultural system, it is possible to describe who or what is a "witch," how this figure is perceived, and how a "witchcraft accusation" functions in that system. Subsequently, we shall consider another model that deals with the process by means of which persons are labelled as "witch" or "demon-possessed." Such titles, once successfully attached, serve to identify the whole personhood of the one thus labelled. Since such negative labelling is part of a degradation process by means of which a person is judged to be deviant, the model within which these elements fit is called a deviance model. We will present a deviance model in chapter 2 apropos of this same text-segment.

The reason for mentioning these models here is that accusations of deviance along with the labelling process and accompanying rituals are part and parcel of what goes on when one accuses or acclaims. Hence, they have always been part and parcel of traditional Christology. We begin here with those typically Mediterranean accusations of witchcraft (Murdock 1980:21).

1.2 Text and Data

Before we begin our anthropological study of the gospel, there is a technical, historical problem to be dealt with. It concerns the text of Matthew itself and the proper data for this study. It is common knowledge that a document such as Matthew presents what an anonymous author says that people before him said that Jesus said and did. The Lukan prologue (Luke 1:1–4) spells this out in detail. The time lag between Jesus' actual career and the writing of the document called Matthew might be some fifty to sixty years. During that period, information about Jesus was "traditioned," i.e., selectively remembered and forgotten, successfully applied to new situations and perhaps even misrepresented. While all this is nothing new in historical gospel scholarship, we are suggesting that the witchcraft accusations are found primarily in a stage of Matthew's history considerably earlier than its final form produced by the anonymous evangelist we call "Matthew." New Testament criticism can identify many of the sources of this gospel: a Q tradition, Mark's gospel, and special M materials, some of which come from the final author/editor but by no means all, for some of the special M materials may be very early. It is necessary to discriminate among these sources, as failure to do so might produce a homogenized view of the gospel as either overly faction-conscious or overly inclusive of Jews and non-Jews alike. This seems to have been the case with an earlier attempt to use Douglas's witchcraft material vis-a-vis Matthew (Pamment 1981:98–106).

In the sources of Matthew, we can clearly discern radically different attitudes to key topics such as law (5:18–19 versus 12:7), sin and forgiveness (18:15–17 versus 18:21–32), mission (10:5–6 versus 28:19), and the like (Neyrey 1985a:67–94). The differences in attitudes can be credited to different sources or layers of tradition in the gospel that in turn reflect different experiences and interpretations of those experiences. The final edition of the gospel clearly presents a more inclusive, less perfectionistic view of the ideology of the

Jesus group than the earlier materials represented in the Q stratum of the gospel traditions. In the final edition Jesus breaks down restrictive traditions by touching the unclean, eating with sinners, preferring mercy to sacrifice, urging love and forgiveness, and accepting all people, good and bad, as his followers.

Yet as we have noted, this is not the only profile of Jesus in the gospel. There are other text-segments in the same gospel that portray Jesus as strengthening Torah, urging separation from sin and sinners, pronouncing judgment, and restricting the mission only to Jews. It is in text-segments belonging to this level that we find witchcraft accusations. These restrictive, factional actions attributed to Jesus are found primarily in the Q traditions. The differences between the two layers of tradition may be summarized in the following chart.

Early Matthean Tradition	Later Matthean Tradition

1. Mission and Membership

(a) Jews only	(a) Jews and non-Jews
(b) the few, worthy ones	(b) good and bad, clean and unclean, saints and sinners

2. Interpretation of Scripture

(a) OT as legal document	(a) OT as prophetic document
(b) hedged about by tradition and customs	(b) rejection of custom and tradition
(c) all OT laws in force	(c) essential Law of Love in force

3. Eschatological Perspective

(a) imminent and sure judgment	(a) future, distant judgment
(b) prophetic judgment of the church and by the church	(b) all judgment put in Jesus' hands, not the church's

4. Ethical Directives

(a) virtue: perfection and total separation from sin	(a) virtue: mercy and forgiveness
(b) vice: hypocrisy and scandal	(b) vice: lack of charity

5. Group Self-Understanding

(a) the reformed, authentic covenant group	(a) a new, different covenant group
(b) based on the Mosaic model of covenant	(b) based on the promises made to Abraham and David

These distinctions have a direct bearing on this project, because the premier passage in which witchcraft accusations are made about Jesus and by Jesus himself comes from the earlier, more faction-focused stratum of the traditions contained in Matthew's gospel. Although the episode is found in Mark 3:21–

30, the account of it in Matthew (and Luke) reflects a different and fuller telling of the story, a version that can be identified as stemming from the Q source, as the following argument indicates.

The version of the mutual accusations of witchcraft in Matthew and Luke share notable, additional points that are not found in the Markan version of the episode:

1. Matt 12:22//Luke 11:14 locate the charge of demon-possession after the cure of a "dumb demoniac," which is not the case in Mark.
2. Matt 12:25//Luke 11:17 preface the apology of Jesus to the accusation of demon possession with the important remark that "Jesus knew their thoughts . . ."
3. Matt 12:27//Luke 11:18–19 record a counteraccusation from Jesus: "If I cast out demons by Beelzebul, by whom do your sons cast them out?"
4. Matt 12:28//Luke 11:20 record a reinterpretation of Jesus' exorcism: "But if it is by the Spirit (or finger) of God that I cast out demons, then the kingdom of God has come upon you."
5. Matt 12:30//Luke 11:23 conclude the defensive strategy of Jesus with the dualistic statement that divides the world into irreconcilable camps, believer versus unbeliever, good versus bad: "Who is not with me is against me, and who does not gather with me scatters."

The Matthean version of the episode must be identified with the Q source and not with Mark's text.

The material subsequent to the episode of mutual accusations of demon possession is also supportive of this perspective. It too comes from the Q source and appears to have been originally linked to 12:22–32, as its identical content and location in Luke's gospel illustrate:

6. Matt 12:38–42//Luke 11:29–32 record a strong judgment leveled against unbelievers, especially those who "seek a sign." Jesus' exorcism ought to be the sign indicating his agency from God (see Matt 12:28//Luke 11:20), but it is rejected by "an evil and adulterous generation." Such unbelievers will be judged by the men of Nineveh and the Queen of the South, true "outsiders" who became "insiders" because they acknowledged God's prophets and wise men.
7. Matt 12:43–45//Luke 11:24–26 tell a parable about a person once rid of a demon but later repossessed by it and seven others more evil than the first. In the context this contains a charge that those who accuse Jesus of demon possession are themselves possessed.

The importance of these observations on the stratum of the text-segment and the proper data for this study lie in the advantage they yield, for they enable us to come to this material with some clear ideas about the kinds of issues considered important at this stage and the positions the people involved then took. The episode in which the witchcraft accusations are found belongs to a tradition in which factional self-consciousness was high, where judgmental language was common and strident, where hypocrisy and conspiracy were feared, where perfection was prized and where boundaries were clearly and sharply drawn.

1.3   The Model: Part One
Cultural Cosmology of Witchcraft Societies

Douglas has been concerned throughout her research with describing the degree of control or non-control that is exercised over a social body. In describing social systems, she has set off two variables, which in her jargon are called "group" and "grid" (over the years she has readjusted the meanings of the group and grid variables; we follow the model in Malina 1986a:1–97). Social systems in general exert varying pressure on their members to conform to societal norms. This degree of pressure to conform is what Douglas means by "group"; it may be *strong* or *weak*. Strong "group" indicates a high degree of pressure to conform to societal norms, as well as a strong degree of pressure for order and control. Where there is strong group pressure, the body is imaged as a bounded, controlled system; entrances and exits are guarded; order and discipline are valued; individuals always think of themselves as group members first; hence, group values take precedence over individual desires. Weak "group" indicates a low degree of pressure to conform to societal norms. Where this pressure is weak, the body is not perceived as a controlled system but as a means to ends chosen by individuals, who are ever in charge of themselves; entrances and exits are left to individual discretion; norms and discipline are not valued; and personality tends to be individualistic.

Douglas's model of social description contains a second variable, "grid," which refers to the degree of assent given to the norms, definitions and classifications of a cultural system. "Grid" may be *high* or *low*. High "grid" indicates a high degree of fit and compliance between an individual's experience and societal patterns of perception and expectations. Individuals will perceive the world as coherent, consistent and intelligible in its broadest reaches. Low "grid" indicates a poor degree of fit and match between individual experiences and stated societal patterns of perception and experience. When "grid" is low, the world seems incomprehensible or fraught with conflict and contradictions.

According to the variables, a possible typology of social systems emerges:

    (a) strong group/high grid
    (b) strong group/low grid
    (c) weak group/high grid
    (d) weak group/low grid

The cosmology or world view of each of these types can be rather carefully delineated according to a set of categories that anthropologists and others concerned with social meanings consider significant: (1) purity, (2) ritual,

(3) personal identity, (4) body, (5) deviance, (6) cosmology and (7) suffering and misfortune. If we follow the grid and group variables, there will be four distinct social scripts or cosmologically rooted social systems. The type that interests us is that of strong group/low grid, which may be briefly described as follows.

Purity is about systematic classification. The existence of dirt, for example, points to purity. Dirt is matter "out of place." For there to be dirt, there must be a system of places sufficiently marked off so that matter can be assessed to be "out of place." Dirt entails a system of related places so that everything can be seen to belong some place. Cleaning a place is a purification process in which things are returned to where they belong. Thus, dirt is "removed." If "dirt" points to and implies disorder, then "purity" points to and implies order/system. The existence of purity concerns is revealed in the existence of societal classifications and the "law and order" deriving from them.

In strong group/low grid, there is a strong concern for an ordered society, with clear classification of persons and things, sexual and role differentiation (Malina 1981:37–41; Neyrey 1986b:92–105). Yet this concern is more a desideratum than anything realizable, for the ordered, "pure" social body is perceived to be under attack. Pollution, the actual or possible state of disorder, of mixed and blurred classifications, is present, and purification rituals are ineffective for expelling the threat. The social body as well as the individual body are perceived to be under siege.

Ritual is behavior concerning the lines that make up the purity or societal system. Line crossings are called *rites*, while the celebration of lines and of those within is called a *ceremony* (Malina 1986:139–43). In strong group/low grid, the group's ritual activity is focused on the making and maintenance of boundaries for the rather unsure purity system. This involves the development of tests for outwardly determining who is "in" and who is "out" of the group and for internally ordering and ranking people according to desirably clear roles. The threat to boundaries in this script indicates that social energy will be focused there. This means that effort will be expended (1) to identify pollutants that are invading the ordered group and (2) to seek their expulsion from the threatened system. Identifying the invader, however, constitutes one of this group's major problems because the group's internal lines of classification— especially the lines defining the authority structure of the group, the roles and the social ranking of its members—are chronically ambiguous. Who can act as spokesperson for the ordered system so as to know who is true and who is false or what is or is not in place?

Personal identity refers to the way individual humans perceive themselves relative to others in primary group settings. In strong group/low grid, the individual is enculturated to perceive himself or herself as always embedded in a group. Thus, personal identity is dyadic, assessed in terms of others, located primarily in group membership, with individual roles being ill-defined, even confused. As awareness of the threat to the system grows, there is a corresponding awakening to the divergence between the external appearance of things and people and their internal states. Things are not as they seem; deceit is at work everywhere. And because evil is disguised as good, it is very difficult to detect.

Body, that is, the individual physical body, is perceived as a microcosm of the social body. As the social body is carefully ordered and structured, so the physical body is tightly controlled. And as the social body is under attack, so the physical body is experiencing assault: invaders and pollutants have broken through the bodily boundaries, especially the oral or sexual orifices. The body, which ideally ought be considered a symbol of life, is now a battleground where disguised and corrupting pollutants are threatening attack.

Deviance refers to the behavior of persons out of place in a negative way. In traditional theological language, deviance is sin. The perception of deviance in this script might surface in two ways. A group with a strong sense of "purity" tends to be concerned with order and system, that is, with formal rules, the violation of which constitutes deviant behavior, a sin or a crime. But as people with this script perceive themselves under threat of attack from a corrupting force, sin will also be understood as pollution, evil or disease within persons and society. In other words, perceptions of some abiding "original sin," "original corruption," "evil impulses in the heart" and the like are typical. Since one cannot trust external appearances, concern will tend to be focused on a person's interior, to see if the heart or intention is still pure and in line.

Cosmology refers to world view, to common beliefs about how the world works. This group's world view is profoundly dualistic, as it perceives the cosmos peopled with warring forces of good and evil. This world, moreover, is anthropomorphic. This means that human or humanlike forces are perceived to stand behind success, as well as illness and failure. The operative question is "Who did this to me?" Yet, this world is under attack by disguised, evil personal forces, so that ultimate victory may not be apparent.

Suffering and misfortune are meted out quite unjustly. Punishment does not automatically follow transgression, but may well be the result of malevolent forces attacking and harming the ordered world. Suffering, moreover, becomes especially the lot of the good, since they are the natural enemies of the attacking evil forces. Suffering is simply part and parcel of life; it cannot be eliminated but perhaps can be alleviated for awhile.

There seems little doubt that the strong group/low grid social script served as the cultural milieu in which the early Matthean group lived, for this much is evidenced by the information presented in the basic strata of Matthew. These strata are undoubtedly representative of early traditions that made up the original gospel story as remembered and interpreted by some of the first members of the Jesus-movement group. To realize this point, simply consider that information provided by these strata in terms of the previous classification.

1.3a Purity. In a social group the concern for order and system indicates what is permitted or proscribed (Malina 1981:122–52). A strong emphasis on purity and its opposite, pollution, suggests a highly ordered social group with clear boundaries, a clear classification system, and clear standards of ortho-doxy and orthopraxis. The text of Matthew makes this evident. A strong sense of purity is linked, in the first place, with a "perfect" keeping of the Law. Total purity demands a radical keeping of all the commandments: Jesus will not relax one iota, one dot of the Law: "Whoever relaxes one of the least of these commandments . . . will be called least in the kingdom" (5:18–20; see Luke 16:17). The demand for obedience extends beyond mere external observance of the commandments to both interior attitudes and derivative behavior. The genuine keeping of "Thou shalt not kill," for instance, is abstention not just from homicide, but from anger and abusive language (5:21–22); to refrain from sexual challenges to another's honor entails abstention from lust for his wife in one's heart, as well as in actual behavior (5:27–28). Group members are not only informed about the meaning of genuine obedience to Torah (5:21–47), but are also given an exalted ideal: "Be perfect as your heavenly Father is perfect" (5:48; see Luke 6:36), a command analogous to Lev 11:44–45, "Be holy as I am holy." In short, the ordering of life according to the principle of Torah is complete and systematic, as hedges are constructed around the Law and every ambiguity or detail fully accounted for.

The demand for order and purity is total; even partial evil, or "darkness," makes the whole body into darkness. Hence, a pure and perfect "eye" is demanded; if it is sound, "your whole body will be full of light," but if there is pollution in the eye, then "your whole body will be full of darkness" (6:22–23//Luke 11:34–36). In this regard, the group is explicitly contrasted with hypocritical Pharisees, who cleanse only the outside of the cup and plate, but neglect the inside (23:25–26//Luke 11:39–41). Members of the Jesus group must be clean within and without. It is evident, then, that this early stage of Matthew's community strongly emphasized purity, and that this purity was identified with the radical and reformed keeping of Torah as this was inter-preted by Jesus and his followers and not by the Pharisees. Called to be perfect, they must be so in every area of life.

But in accordance with the witchcraft perceptions indigenous to the Medi-terranean area (Murdock 1980:58), the social and physical bodies are under attack in the Jesus faction as well. These attacks come from the outside and the inside: (1) *From without*—the Jesus-movement group is challenged by another Jewish reform group, the Pharisees, whose members disparage allegiance to Jesus and his teaching. (2) *From within*—some members are perceived as not living up to Torah perfection, and behavior rooted in undisciplined enthusiasm threatens to displace Torah observance as the group's ideal. Against these it must be affirmed that it is not those who say "Lord, Lord," nor those who "prophesy in my name and do mighty works" who will enter the kingdom, but only those "who do the will of my father who is in heaven" (7:21–23//Luke 6:46 and 13:25–27). The system, then, is under siege from within and without.

1.3b Ritual. The typical or characteristic activity of this society is bound-ary making and boundary maintenance (Douglas 1966:114, 123–24; 1982:viii–ix, 113). Consequently, it seems normal to find great concern with boundaries in the sources of Matthew and in the final text itself, where the world is completely divided between friends and enemies, typical of strong group/low grid:

Q Matt 5:43–48:   *On the positive side:* neighbor, those you love, those you pray for, the good, the just, those you greet, brothers
   And on the negative side: enemy, those you hate, those who persecute you, the wicked, the unjust, tax collectors, non-Jews

M Matt 7:6:   Dogs, swine (fit on the negative side)

M Matt 7:15:   False prophets, inwardly ravenous wolves

Q Matt 7:16–17:   *On the positive side:* grapes, figs, good fruit
   On the negative side: thorns, thistles, bad fruit

M Matt 7:18–20:   *On the positive side:* sound tree, good fruit
   On the negative side: bad tree, evil fruit
   Note: thrown into the fire for not bearing good fruit (compare preaching of John the Baptist in Q 3:10: identical)

M Matt 10:17–25:   *On the one side:* "you," members of Jesus' household, through whom the Spirit of your Father speaks, hated, persecuted, disciples below their teacher, servants below their master, the maligned for Jesus' name sake
   On the other side: "they," fellow Jews with their councils and synagogues, with their kings and governors, along with non-Jews, persecutors and executors, those who label Jesus Beelzebul

Q Matt 12:34:   *On the positive side:* good treasure (of the heart), good things
   On the negative side: evil treasure (of the heart), evil things

The initial action that creates boundaries for those Jews who made up the Jesus-movement group is the alternative group awareness deriving from the group's preaching. Believers are the insiders who accept the preaching and the preacher, and by "change of heart" restore those limit markers setting off sin from behavior befitting God's coming kingdom. Fellow Israelite unbelievers, who reject the preacher and the preaching, are the outsiders who do not enter the kingdom but go down to destruction. By preaching, then, boundary distinctions are constantly being made. For example, John the Baptizer preaches about Jesus, describing him as a boundary maker with a winnowing fork in his hand to clean his threshing floor. The wheat (believers/insiders) will be gathered into the granary, while the chaff (unbelievers/outsiders) will be cast out and burned in the furnace (3:12//Luke 3:17).

Jesus likewise preaches in such a way as to continue this boundary-making distinction in passages such as 12:38–42 (//Luke 11:29–32): this wicked and illegitimate generation will be confronted by Nineveh and the Queen of the South. Those former outsiders have been transformed into insiders because "they repented at the preaching of Jonah" and "they heard the wisdom of Solomon." They will judge Jesus' unbelieving audiences who refuse to listen to the preaching of one who is "greater than Jonah and greater than Solomon." As a whole, the people of Chorazin, Bethsaida and Capernaum, too, rejected Jesus' preaching and so find themselves on the wrong side of the boundary of judgment. Instead of being "exalted to heaven," they will be "cast down to Hades" (11:23//Luke 10:15). Jerusalem, which was invited to come "inside" as a chick under a hen's wing, refused and remained outside, even desolate (23:37-38//Luke 13:34-35).

Becoming a member of the new Jesus faction itself produces boundaries. In the instructions that Jesus is said to have delivered to those who would promote his name, he states that he came to force people to cross boundaries and to shift allegiances. He does not bring "peace on earth . . . but a sword," to set "a man against his father, a daughter against her mother, a daughter-in-law against her mother-in-law" (10:34-35//Luke 12:53). Conversion to the new group, then, will split families and set members on different sides of the boundary. Converts cross family boundary lines—perhaps even expelled by their families (10:21)—and so become outsiders. But they become insiders in that they enter the new, fictive family of the Jesus-movement group (12:46-50), and so boundaries are maintained all around.

The ideology of the Jesus movement, as articulated in the teaching of group leaders, also makes boundaries. When it is contrasted with scribal teaching on Torah in the "Antitheses" of the Sermon on the Mount (5:21-47), the teaching of the Jesus faction establishes clear boundaries distinguishing the two groups. One will never "enter the kingdom of God" unless one's righteousness in Torah observance exceeds that of the scribes and Pharisees (5:20). The attack on the "leaven" of the Pharisees (16:6, 11-12) and the long list of woes against their teaching (chapter 23) also serve to draw sharp boundaries between them and the followers of Jesus.

The metaphors used to describe how members of the Jesus movement understood themselves indicate the extent of their appropriation of the boundaries that have been made. Jesus' followers are the "few who are chosen" out of the many Israelites who were called (22:14); they enter through the narrow gate where the way is hard, while the many go through the wide gate that leads to destruction (7:13-14//Luke 13:23-24). They are the sheep among wolves (10:16//Luke 10:3); they are the wheat growing in a field with tares (13:24-30); they are the obedient sons who go to work in the father's vineyard in contrast to sons who said that they would go, but did not (21:28-31). They are the houses built on rock that survive floods and winds, unlike the houses built on sand (7:24-28//Luke 6:47-49). All of these metaphors point to the clear distinction between those Jews who belonged to the Jesus movement group and all other Jews. They underscore how these followers of Jesus have been singled out from the others who do not share their convictions and their purity.

Yet, boundary lines are likewise drawn to assess pollution within as well as to keep outsiders from entering. Should pollution be found within the group, then the rite appropriate to this condition is the expulsion of the contami-

nating member. The procedure here was a process of (1) prophetic identification of sin, especially if it were disguised, (2) judgment of it and (3) expulsion of the offender from the group. For example, should some evil occur in
the group because of one of its members, it was apparent that the purity
boundary had been breached. The group immediately sought to contain and
expel the pollutant (18:15–18//Luke 17:3), first by individual action that
unmasked the evil, then by the help of two or three other holy members who
interpreted and judged the sinner, and finally by submission of the problem to
the entire group. If no correction took place (that is, if the polluting person
were not purified), then the errant member himself was declared an outsider, "a
non-Jew and a tax collector," and removed across the group's borders.

This group, in fact, had "the keys of the kingdom," exercising power both to
enable some to cross into the group and to compel others to cross out of it
(18:18, see 23:18). The principle of such action is clear: "If the salt loses its
saltiness it is good for nothing but to be thrown out" (5:13//Luke 14:34–35).
Evil had to be identified as such and expelled. For example, enthusiasts who
might even make the correct confession ("Lord, Lord"), but who did not
subscribe to Torah perfection were especially singled out. They were judged
"unknown" and ended up outside the house where the feast went on (7:23//
Luke 13:27), just as the person without a wedding garment at the king's
banquet was dishonored in turn by being "cast out into the outer darkness"
(22:13).

The horror of pollution extended even to temptations (18:6–9//Luke 17:1–
2). Violent remedies were proposed to offset the results of disloyalty that such
tests entailed. Those who caused fellow group members to deviate from the
group's ideology were better removed from the group and cast into the depths
of the sea. Contaminating temptations might enter by border areas of the body
such as the eye, ear, hand or foot, which are in unavoidable contact with the
corrupt "outside." Such temptations must be dealt with at once by amputation
of the contaminated organ, which is the radical redrawing of the boundaries to
exclude the pollutant.

Such judgment was exercised from within the group according to strict
standards. The group's would-be judges were told, "First take the log out of
your own eye, and then you will see clearly to take the speck out of your
brother's eye" (7:5//Luke 6:42). Be sure, in effect, that you yourself are within
the boundaries of the group's ideology before you accuse anyone else of being
outside.

The enemy without is dealt with in an analogous way. Since membership in
the Jesus-movement group at this stage was quite small, group members would
be in no position to expel their enemies from the boundaries of village and
synagogue, which they held in common. Yet their judgment language against
such majority outsiders made it clear that God, at least, would expel them from
his kingdom. Israel's unbelief would cause "the sons of the kingdom" to be
"thrown out into the outer darkness" (8:11–12//Luke 13:28). In this vein, we
note how the judgment parables consistently use boundary language: a sepa-

ration will take place, and what is good will be gathered inside, while the bad will be thrown out, as in the example of the wheat and the chaff already cited. The wheat will be gathered into God's barn, but the tares thrown out and burned (13:30). The wise will enter into the bridegroom's house for the feast, while the foolish remain outside (25:1–13). The profitable servants remain in the master's house and are given greater riches, while the unprofitable are "cast out into the outer darkness" (25:30). The sheep will be welcomed "into eternal life," while the goats are told to "depart" and to "go into eternal punishment" (25:46).

The obvious outcome of such boundary-marking activity is space set off as exclusive to the group. But because boundaries are rather porous, such "sacred space" (also a ritual concern) becomes highly privatized and fluid. Purity and holiness cannot be tied to any regularly acknowledged ritual practice or place, such as a synagogue or temple, but are found in the holy interior of the group itself. Thus, piety was best practiced not in public or in the synagogue, as the Pharisees did (23:6), but "in secret" (6:1–18). Temple sacrifice was less important than the maintenance of single-mindedness in the "heart" of believer and group (5:23–24). The group's preachers, as they carried out their mission, were not to go to the official sacred space of the village, the synagogue, but to seek private houses containing the few "worthy" people (10:11–13), for sacred space is where group members gather for group functions, as in: "Where two or three are gathered (to decide a case), there am I" (18:18; see Derrett 1979).

1.3c Personal identity. Individuals in this Mediterranean society are dyadic personalities (Malina 1981:51–60). They are anti-introspective, not psychologically minded at all. Consequently, persons are known according to stereotyping in terms of locale, trade or class, but especially according to the family, clan or faction in which they are embedded. For example, as regards place, the Simon who carried Jesus' cross was sufficiently identified as "Simon from Cyrene" (Matt 27:32); Peter was identified as a Galilean because of his accent (Matt 26:73); and Saul was always that fellow from Tarsus (Acts 22:3). "Cretans," moreover, were identified as "liars, evil beasts, lazy gluttons" (Tit 1:12). As regards trade or class, Joseph was always "the carpenter" (Matt 13:55); Peter and Andrew were "fishermen" (Matt 4:18). As regards family, it was sufficient to identify Jesus as "son of Joseph" (Matt 13:55) or "son of God," whereas Simon was "son of Jonah" (Matt 16:17) and James and John were "sons of Zebedee" (Matt 4:21; 10:2; 20:20; 26:37 and 27:56).

As regards Jesus himself, the fact that studies of the titles of Jesus in the gospels evidence little agreement among scholars, aside from the fact that there are titles, simply points to the conditions typical of strong group/low grid. Since individual roles are ill-defined and even confused, in this social arrangement the linguistic encoding of those roles in titles will reveal ill-defined, even confused, job characteristics.

In the gospel of Matthew, if Jesus embodied any social role, it surely was that of faction founder. The personal identity of individuals in this faction consisted in their group membership as followers of Jesus, the recruiter of the faction. As his followers, they were the salt of the earth and the light of the world (5:13-14//Luke 14:34-35). Since their allegiance placed them in conflict with their natural families, they were described as members of Jesus' new family of "brothers" (5:22-24; 7:3-5; 18:15; 23:8; 25:40) whose father is God. Thus, they formed a fictive kin group, male-centered with females embedded in males, with fictive kin rights and obligations and with an abiding relationship between father and son. In other words, this fictive kin group undoubtedly mirrored the arrangements of the "natural" kin group typical of the first-century Mediterranean.

These "brothers" were the unique recipients of heavenly revelation: blessed are their eyes and ears, which see and hear (13:16-17//Luke 10:23-24). For God hid from the wise and understanding what he revealed to the "babes" of this group (11:25-26//Luke 10:21-22). The few, the wheat, the sheep, the wise, the obedient—these were the designations that gave group members their identity. The internalization of specific roles within the group could not give personal identity, if only because there do not seem to have been any specific roles.

It would seem that all of the "brothers" had equal competence in hearing cases of members against each other, for all received the authority to bind and to loose (18:18). Yet, there were conflicting claims to authority. Focal figures who articulated the reformed teaching on Torah were in considerable tension with enthusiastic figures who presumed self-authenticating authority (7:21-23//Luke 6:46). Some of these later were classified within the group as "false prophets" who seduced the group from Torah perfection (7:15). Even recognized prominent figures were distinguished from their rivals, the Pharisees, by the titles with which they were addressed. Although the teachers of the Jesus-movement group and Pharisaic teachers both explained the Law for their respective groups, the former were not to be called "teacher" or "master" like the Pharisees, but rather "servant" (23:8-9). That title, of course, masked the difficult tasks that the central figures in Jesus factions had to perform, such as to define purity and pollution and to erect and maintain boundaries. It is difficult to say, on the basis of explicit statements in the gospel tradition, how such persons gained prominence within Jesus factions, how they derived their authority and how they were replaced. It is difficult, then, to sort out authoritative social roles at this stage of Matthew's community. Although the need for such central figures is obvious, it would seem that the inside/outside conflict absorbed the energy required to establish internal group structures.

Once boundaries are duly established, their continued utility depends on the group's ability to judge an individual's actual state of "holiness," i.e., whether a given individual is within or outside, a state based on any perceivable degree of commitment to or solidarity with the group. Ordinarily, one would look to external actions as indicators of heart and intention, but not here. On the contrary, it is critically important to be able to distinguish external appearances, which may be deceptive, from internal realities. The existence of witchcraft accusations indicates that this capacity to distinguish would have been well developed. Consequently, the group could readily identify the primary fault of its enemies as "hypocrisy," that is, deviant posturing and play acting, and hence the sin of only appearing to be holy. Such hypocrisy was a great dishonor to God, since it relied upon truly non-existing relationships with God to gain social prominence. These enemies loved external show and the appearance of righteousness; they prayed in public so as to be seen, seeking acclaim for their almsgiving and exaggerating their fasting (23:5–7; 6:1, 2, 5). They aimed to deceive others, not to please God. They were zealous to make converts, but they taught only surface (and so deficient) piety. And so their converts became "twice as much a child of Gehenna" as they themselves were (23:13–15) because they thought that externals substituted for true interior piety. They cleansed only the outside of the cup (23:25–26//Luke 11:39–41) as they cleansed only their own outsides (e.g., washed their hands); hence, they were like whitewashed tombs, "outwardly they appear righteous, but within they are full of hypocrisy and wickedness" (23:28).

If hypocrisy was the worst sin, the highest virtue was integral righteousness. Such righteousness was revealed in right actions accompanied by a pure heart, a correct internal attitude. This combination is best exemplified by the "Antitheses" (5:21–47), which demanded internal control of eye, tongue and heart, as well as avoidance of the "external" dishonoring of others in behavior such as murder, adultery and false swearing. To make discernment of these inner states possible, group members were counseled to judge the tree by its fruits and not merely by its foliage (7:16–20; 12:33//Luke 6:43–45). They were put on their guard against "false prophets who come in sheep's clothing but inwardly are ravenous wolves" (7:15). Extracting the beam from one's own eye before proceeding to judge a sinner (7:2–5//Luke 6:41–42) was another safeguard against hypocrisy and another example of wholeness between inside and outside.

1.3d Body. Douglas's model presupposes a correlation of the physical body and the social body (Douglas 1982:65–81; Neyrey 1986c). Care of the body, concern about its entrances and exits, attention to socially permitted and forbidden behavior attendant with bodily functions—these are windows into the workings of the social body as well. In witchcraft societies (1) the social and physical body are tightly controlled; and yet, (2) invaders have broken through bodily boundaries. The concern for boundaries that we noted above is replicated in the concern for the boundaries of the individual physical body. Entrances and exits are carefully guarded—the tongue, for example, from anger and abusive language, which endangers the inner heart (5:22). Likewise, one must guard the eye, the entrance to the heart (6:22–23//Luke 11:34). And one must beware of dishonoring one's brother through adultery, by which the genital orifices of the body (5:28) symbolize, in traditional Mediterranean fashion, male honor and female modesty (see Malina 1981:42–43).

If pollutants do invade the entrances of the body, the advice is simple: get them out! If the eye, hand or foot is an abiding source of dishonorable, unclean behavior, radical amputation is called for (5:29-30; 18:7-9). Much of the boundary language we have seen applied to such situations of endangered purity is, of course, "body" language as well.

1.3e Deviance. Consistent with these preoccupations, deviance in this group is not rooted in ignorance, human failure or the violation of formal rules, but rather in some abiding source of corruption. When deviance occurs, it pollutes and contaminates the whole organism; there is no such thing as a slight sin or a minor imperfection. If the eye of the lightsome body is darkened, "how great is the darkness" (6:23//Luke 11:34-35). If it is admitted, the "leaven" of the Pharisees will corrupt the whole batch of flour (16:11-12). A bad tree cannot bear good fruit (7:18); evil people out of their evil treasure bring forth evil (12:35//Luke 6:45). Nothing good can come from what is utterly polluted: "Either make the tree good and its fruit good or make the tree bad and its fruit bad" (12:33//Luke 6:43). There is no grey area, no middle ground.

Again, deviance is determined by inner reality, not outward adherence to rules. In this connection, we have already noted the group's concern for interior purity, both of individuals and of the group, as well as its horror at the hypocritical disguising of an impure interior by exterior piety. Correct piety, then, led to concern about the motivation behind interpersonal behavior between the individual and God, as well as its value when done in public (6:1-18). In contrast, the corrupt Pharisees were concerned rather with such rules as tithing and so neglect "the weightier matters . . . justice, mercy, and faith" (23:23//Luke 11:42).

The preference for internal states over formal rules is shown most clearly in Matthew's treatment of the exceptions to the Law allowed by the Pharisees. They evidently allowed for divorce (5:31-32; 19:3-9) and swearing and oath-taking (5:33-39; 23:16-22), all of which were rejected by Matthew's group as deviant behavior. Once admitted, such behavior would contaminate the whole and weaken the perfect keeping of Torah. Matthew's own exception to the divorce law (5:33; 19:9), however, demonstrated how this perfection was to be interpreted. Divorce was a matter of exterior social organization. Since interior states take precedence over rules for behavior, divorce *must* be allowed in cases in which a person is dishonored because someone had sexual union with his wife. For a husband to stay married after such dishonor would point to lack of concern for his honor, that is, to conduct typical of a procurer, hence to an inwardly polluting sin. Thus, it is clear again that at this level of the tradition, the principle of maintaining the group's internal purity supersedes adherence to external rules, even Torah in its most stringent form.

1.3f Cosmology. The constant distinction between insiders and outsiders points to how members of this group would look at the world from a dualistic perspective. People are either good or bad fish, wheat or chaff, wise or foolish maidens, profitable or profitless traders, sheep or goats, good or bad trees. "Who is not for us is against us; who does not gather with us scatters!" (12:30//Luke 11:23).

In keeping with the establishment of new and clear boundaries, the group emphatically distinguishes itself from the Pharisees. For the Pharisees were not just rivals of these Jewish followers of Jesus with respect to the reform of Torah. They are the enemy, "a wicked and adulterous generation" (12:39; 16:4//Luke 11:29) and "a brood of vipers" (12:34; see 3:7//Luke 3:7). It is here that the accusations of witchcraft possession against the Pharisees come into their own to identify these opponents as an altogether evil group, possessed by Satan. They were the "sons of the evil one," whom the devil, the enemy, sowed among the good wheat (13:28, 38–39).

Yet the new and clear boundaries often prove to be the stuff of unrealizable ideals, for the boundaries surprisingly and sporadically develop holes; they fade, become porous or leave room for doubt. The wicked prosper, the good suffer, injustice is rife. Because of this, the believer knew that the universe was unjust and would not reward the good nor requite the evil as they deserved in this world. God's prophets and messengers have always been rejected, from Abel to Zechariah (23:34–35//Luke 11:49–51); the messengers with invitations to the wedding feast were maltreated (22:5–6//Luke 14:17–21). The members of this group, moreover, expected and experienced the same rejection and hostility (5:11–12//Luke 6:22). But this world is, nevertheless, governed by a principle of personal causality, not fate or some impersonal and unpredictable rule. Conformity to the group's classification system was important and will be rewarded eventually "in heaven," that is, by God (6:4, 6, 18). Enduring the hostility of unbelievers (5:12), making proper professions of allegiance (10:32; 12:36), receiving a prophet (10:41)—all bring their eventual reward. The reward would not necessarily be experienced now in an unjust age when Satan and his minions prowled about, but rather in the future when God's judgment finally prevails.

1.3g Suffering and misfortune. The members of this group primarily endured hostility, rejection, failure in their mission (10:14–16//Luke 9:5), and conflict within their synagogue from Pharisees. But these things came to them not as retribution for their wickedness but because of their faithfulness, for doing right (see "on my account," 5:11 and "for my name's sake," 10:18, 22).

Because it was unlikely that the confrontation with the Pharisees would cease, since the group's claims to righteousness would not allow it to compromise and since the Pharisees could not be quickly expected to look kindly on this Jewish faction focused in Jesus, the result was a series of incidents causing suffering for members of the Jesus-movement group. Such ostensibly unjust suffering might be alleviated by several strategies, such as through a special interpretation of the phenomenon of suffering, notably through an appeal to the classical Israelite social critics of the past—the prophets. Sent by God with a reforming message and with judgment, the prophets were all rejected and persecuted (23:32–35, 37–38//Luke 11:49–51; 13:34–35). So John the Baptizer! So Jesus! Conflict that arose from the reforming and radical posture of the group was to be expected, for Scripture and tradition tell us that prophets suffered. In fact, rejection served as a sort of touchstone of authenticity for the group: this was how they knew that they were right (5:11–12//Luke 6:22). Since the agents of the suffering were unbelievers, sons of the evil one, oppression from them was another proof of the righteousness of the group's position.

In summary, the Jesus-movement group, which accused the Pharisees of being possessed, looked as follows: It was a small group of Jews who were recruited directly or indirectly by Jesus and who considered themselves as participants in the true reform movement within a Judaism marked by a number of such movements (we thus agree with the intuition of Theissen 1977:80–87). Considering purity and perfection their chief hallmarks, they established boundaries that distinguished outsiders from insiders. There can be no ambiguity: "Who is not with us is against us" (12:30//Luke 11:23). But within these clear lines of demarcation, group members were, of course, still living side by side with other Jews in a Jewish village, still sharing the general symbolic world of Judaism, especially centered in the keeping of Torah. Their reform stance and positive acclamation of Jesus brought them into conflict with a rival reform movement, the Pharisees, whom they considered as hypocrites for failure to espouse total purity of action and heart. Most of their energy was spent maintaining the boundaries between themselves and their rivals. Since they perceived the world through dualistic glasses, all that was not totally pure (that is, in proper time and place in keeping with *their* interpretation of Torah) was evil and corrupt, and this included the Pharisees, their reform ideology notwithstanding. They cast judgment not only upon the rival Pharisees but also upon imperfect members of their own group whose imperfection threatened to pollute the whole group. And so, the group remained tightly controlled and vigilant against the pollution that constantly threatened its boundaries.

1.4 The Model: Part Two
Witches and Witchcraft Accusations

Apart from the movement group revealed in the Fourth Gospel (Malina 1985; 1986a:37–44), perhaps all of the other communities represented by the various New Testament traditions can rightly be said to share many aspects of the cosmology just outlined. Since those communities were all Mediterranean groups, they would have the distinctive features typical of a Mediterranean "witchcraft society" to a lesser or greater extent (Murdock 1980:42). Inasmuch as we are focussing on Christology "from the side," i.e., how members of his society labelled Jesus or successfully accused him, it seems useful to consider how a strong-group type of individual might typically assess others. Two preliminary points need to be made: the first pertains to how stereotyping is characteristic of Jesus' world and the second looks to how Jesus' mobility would be labelled as deviance. After clarifying these two points, we will be better able to proceed to a direct examination of the anthropological meaning of accusations of witchcraft.

The strong-group persons described in the pages of the gospels, all typical first-century Mediterraneans, thought about themselves and other persons in a way best described as "sociological" (see *Personal identity*, 1.3c above). The gospel discussion of witchcraft and demon possession is quite difficult for Americans to follow because whenever anyone starts talking about some individual or other, the inevitable frame of reference in that scenario is psychological. First-century Mediterraneans did not understand the individual as such. They were not concerned with psychological personality, with the person as a unique, individualistic and incommunicable being. Hence, they would find psychological explanations extremely irrelevant and strange. Rather their basic unit of social analysis was the group-oriented person, the dyad, the person considered as embedded in some other person or some other group of persons.

To think of and describe individual persons in terms of the groups to which they belong strikes us as stereotyping, and indeed it is, for every person is judged according to features typical of the group to which she/he belongs. But the kind of stereotyping involved here is far more refined and complex, since it covers constantly verified self-stereotypes along with stereotypes of other individuals in terms of their family, place of origin, place of habitation, sex, age and distinctive features, all correlated and fixed onto some concrete person. And this concrete person, as a rule, agrees with the stereotypical assessment, assuming it as valid self-stereotype.

Contrast, for example, someone living in today's United States and anyone in the first-century Jesus-movement group. The U.S. person will dwell upon inferences about another person's psychological dispositions and could well summarize by saying something such as "He isn't all there," or "She is very neurotic." Even a word such as "together," which in formal speech refers to social relations par excellence, can take on psychological significance, as in "He's very together." The first-century Palestinian follower of Jesus would say "He is a sinner," "He submits to the Prince of this world," or "She has a demon." That would not mean that the person in question disregarded some law or commandment of Torah, which behavior she or he personally had the ability to refrain from (although that might be true). And it would equally not mean that that person participated in demon worship (although that might be true also). Rather that the first-century person, with his or her accusation of demon possession and sin, would mean that the accused "is in an abnormal position because the matrix of relationships in which he is embedded is abnormal" (Selby 1974:15). In other words, the person is accused of being a deviant.

Consequently, a type of "sociological" awareness pervades people following the strong group/low grid cultural script. The most significant way in which they differ from typical U.S. people hinges upon "their predisposition to regard offenses against the social order or conditions that bring about social disorder as being preeminently deviant" (Selby 1974:16). Naturally, the social order in question is that of Roman-controlled Israel, of the aristocratic, Sadducee-controlled temple, of Palestinian towns and villages and of various associations within these units.

Within this cultural scenario, it is not surprising that all the Jesus-movement groups who tell the story of their origins witness to the fact that their central characters clearly behaved as deviants. For if we consider Jesus or the Twelve or Paul from the perspective that boundary making produces interpretations that result in social meaning, we can see that all *acted outside of their inherited social roles and ranks*. A first indication of such social activity is to be found in physical mobility; that is, in the fact that Jesus, his followers and Paul travelled around in socially unexpected and unusual ways. Such physical mobility replicates the social behavior that rejects ascribed status and intimates willingness to be deviant.

Travel on pilgrimage or business, as well as visits to relatives and the like, would be expected, usual and non-deviant. Such travel presupposes a return home, a return to a solid and stable base from and around which boundaries of geographical stability are drawn. However, general geographical mobility, random wandering and moving from place to place all symbolize a break with previous social location and rank. The meaning symbolled by this sort of wandering life, this sort of geographical mobility, would be negatively perceived by first-century Mediterraneans precisely because for them, stability, roots, sedentary living and a stable center were the ideal. These people shared great aversion to geographical mobility that would make one a stranger and foreigner to others (Elliott 1981; Malina 1986c). Continued geographical mobility except in the case of forced movement, such as enslavement and exile, or necessity, such as emigration due to famine, war or some other calamity, was a deviant type of behavior. Perhaps the severest sort of punishment at the time, even worse than death, was exile. Consequently, geographical mobility or a wandering way of life would be a social problem requiring comment.

The wandering life undertaken by Jesus within the confines of Palestine, by Paul and others in the Mediterranean basin, or by Cynic and Stoic philosophers in the same area, all symbolize a break with inherited social role and rank. Hence, a wandering lifestyle would call for some sort of social verdict on the part of the publics confronted by wandering persons. In the gospels, it was the sedentary public that assessed Jesus and his first group of wandering followers with such traditional designations as "prophet," "teacher" and "disciple." Others, including Jesus' own family from Nazareth, assessed them variously: as imbalanced, possessed by demons, in the service of Beelzebul, seditionists and the like. Witchcraft accusations belong within this sort of scenario. What plausibly triggered them was the deviance involved in attempting change by means of roving agents of change, Jesus included.

With an understanding of stereotypical thinking as typical and mobility as deviant for first-century Mediterraneans, we are ready to probe formally into the meaning of witchcraft accusations. In line with our initial intention, we focus on the early Matthean community. To understand that group from the perspective of witchcraft, we turn again to Douglas's works to complete the model. She provides us with three important elements: (a) a list of specific characteristics of witchcraft societies, (b) a definition of a "witch" and (c) a description of the function of witchcraft accusations.

1.4a Specific characteristics of witchcraft societies. Douglas identifies six specific characteristics of witchcraft societies. These features are simply more developed aspects of the cosmology discussed in section 1.3 above. They include clearly drawn external boundaries, confused internal relations, close and continual interaction, poorly developed tension-relieving techniques, weak authority and disorderly but intense conflict. We consider each in turn:

(1) External boundaries clearly marked: In a genuine witchcraft society, external boundaries are clearly marked (Douglas 1982:113). As we noted previously, in Matthew's group there is no ambiguity over who is "in" or who is "out," for the primary ritual concern of this group is the building and maintenance of clear boundary lines to remove that ambiguity. Group members undoubtedly had a rite to mark the passing from outside to inside. Perhaps, given their high assessment of John the Baptist, they borrowed John's repentance washing and adapted it for their own form of line crossing and boundary maintenance. Be that as it may, group members were found in small Jewish villages where movement in and out was restricted. Jewish distinctiveness kept non-Jews at arm's length, and Jews stayed close for purposes of identity.

Matthew's group, moreover, clearly distinguished itself from other Jewish groups in the village by its radical teaching on Torah observance and its polemic against rival groups. Followers of Jesus, at least, can be told from Pharisees and other people in the synagogue. This group found ways to distinguish itself, often accentuating minor differences between itself and other rival reform groups such as the Pharisees (Theissen 1977:77–87).

(2) Confused internal relations: Internal relations both in the village and in the group are confused (Douglas 1982:111–14, 119). *Within the synagogue*: Since Judaism in the first century was a religion embedded in kinship, members of the Jesus faction would necessarily continue to believe themselves to be Jews. The Jesus movement that they espoused was a particularistic reform of post-exilic Judaism, meant for Jews alone. Hence, those committed to Jesus' reform knew themselves to be authentic members of the covenant, devoted to

the valid reform of contemporary Judaism. In fact, they were, as Jesus said, the salt of the earth and the light of the world. But their claims to be *the* authentic reform movement were not so appreciated by their equally zealous Jewish neighbors, some of whom (the Pharisees) claimed the same distinction. And there was no socially approved mechanism to test these conflicting claims in some public way. Roles within synagogue and village were undifferentiated: the leadership of the synagogue was vague, for no priest of Levitical pedigree, no student of Hillel or Shammai presided there.

Within the Jesus-movement group: Even within the Jesus-movement group there was role confusion. Leading figures were prohibited from being labelled "teacher," "rabbi" or "master" (23:8–10); but when they functioned within the group, they exercised just such roles. They claimed to know and to teach the correct way of interpreting the Scriptures and the authentic way of living the Torah. They were told to be "humble" and "servants" of the group (23:11–12); they were told that beatitude lies in being meek and humble (5:5; 11:29). Yet they stood in judgment of deviants and those who misled others both within the group and without. They were, after all, leaders of reform and critics of the unreformed. They have, then, ambiguous roles that are impossible to fulfil.

⸳ Even within the group, teachers of Torah clashed with prophetic figures who cry "Lord, Lord" but do not do God's will as the reform teachers would define it (7:21–23). This clash of reformed and prophetic leaders points to further role confusion within the group because the process of aspiring to a lead role, as well as the criteria for that role, were obscure. Given the low level of organization in this society, no machinery existed within the synagogue or the Jesus faction, or beyond both groups, to settle the question of authority or of conflicting claims to competence.

(3) Close, unavoidable interaction: Yet this was a *small* world, where social interaction is unavoidably close (Douglas 1982:109–14; Mair 1969:207–13). The Jewish members of the Jesus faction were not numerous; they were the few worthy figures who lived in fractured households. Prospective group members likewise tended to remain in their households in ever-growing tension with their families as a result of their new ideology (10:34–35//Luke 12:51–53). Indicative of this is the passage that warns "A man's enemies are those of his own household" (10:36; see 10:21).

(4) Tension-releasing techniques underdeveloped: Techniques for distancing, regulating and reconciling these conflicts were little developed here. Because of the crisis in leadership in both synagogue and Jesus faction, the Pharisees could not expel those members who followed Jesus nor could the latter resolve the issue by expelling the Pharisees. Neither group was apparently able to validate its claims to the satisfaction of the other or the rest of the people in the village. There was no procedure for regulating the intense confrontation, adjudicating the rival claims or even separating the parties from one another in village, synagogue or household. And reconciliation would be

possible only with the complete capitulation of one side, which was most unlikely, given the loss of honor involved.

(5) Weak authority: The ability to control the behavior of others effectively was obviously not available to village groups (Douglas 1970:xviii; 1982:iii). While the Pharisees seemed to dominate the local synagogue and were admitted to be zealous for the traditional faith, they were not clearly accepted by all as spokespersons for Judaism itself, let alone by a rival reform group that looked to Jesus as Messiah. Leadership in the Jesus group likewise had no authority to settle doctrinal issues with the Pharisees or to establish its reform praxis as village norm. Even within the Jesus groups there was a crisis of authority: we hear of one wing that insists on strict Torah observance, criticizing those who boast of prophetic activity. The procedure for being invested with leadership positions within the Jesus group is not even hinted at in our traditions, another indication of weak authority.

(6) Intense, disorderly competition: Witchcraft accusations are likely in groups best characterized as experiencing intense and disorderly confrontations (Douglas 1982:109–12; Mair 1969:208). Jesus' followers versus Pharisees! True Israel versus false Israel! Torah-observing Christians versus Torah-bypassing Christians!

The social environment in which Matthew's group functioned seems fully to meet the criteria of a genuine "witchcraft society." It consisted of groups concerned with purity and boundaries, small in size, harboring intense and disorderly confrontations, in unavoidably close interaction with rival reform movements. It had no techniques for regulating disputes, settling claims or confirming authority.

1.4b Definition of a witch. In general, we might define witchcraft itself as the ascription of some personal misfortune "to the suspected voluntary or involuntary aggressive action of a member of a special class of human beings believed to be endowed with a special power and propensity for evil" (Murdock 1980:21). A "witch," moreover, is best defined in terms of the misfortune such a person is said to cause and the context in which such misfortune appears. In the gospels, accusations of witchcraft appear in a context of sick care, hence of healing and sickening, of demon possession and demon expulsion. It is rather curious to note in this regard that witchcraft accusations in a health-care context seem typical of the Mediterranean region (Murdock 1980: 42, 57–63).

More specifically, according to Douglas's model, "witches" appear in groups dominated by a dualistic point of view (Douglas 1982:114): "Who is not with me is against me; who does not gather with me scatters" (12:30//Luke 11:23). Only insiders are good, with good fruit, while all outsiders are evil, with only evil fruit (12:33//Luke 6:43). The insiders perceive that they are under attack, especially from hostile outsiders who would condemn it, poison it or seduce it. Lastly, the human wickedness that the group experiences takes on a cosmic dimension: what is bad is all bad and it comes from the Evil One. The "witch" is a figure who sums up all of the above sense of dualism, cosmic evil and hostility to the group.

According to Douglas's analysis, the "witch" will be described as having the following characteristics (Douglas 1970:xxvi–xxvii, 1982:113):

1. The witch is one whose inside is corrupt;
2. the witch has a perverted nature, a reversal of the ways things ought to be; it is a deceiver whose external appearance does not betray its inner nature;
3. if the witch is seen as living within the group, it attacks the pure and innocent by life-sucking or by poison.

Examining the Christian accusations against the Pharisees, these characteristics are plainly evident. (1) The Pharisees' insides were said to be corrupt; they were like whitewashed tombs, which "outwardly appear beautiful but within they are full of dead men's bones and all uncleanness" (23:27//Luke 11:44). They cleansed the outside of cup and plate, but "inside they are full of extortion and rapacity" (23:25//Luke 11:39). Even though they appeared righteous, within they were "full of hypocrisy and iniquity" (23:28).

(2) Their hypocrisy, moreover, in concealing this inner corruption was considered their chief sin. They claimed to teach and practice a reformed Torah; they claimed to build a fence around it; even their name meant "the Separated Ones." But they only "preach and do not practice" (23:3). They were, therefore, deceivers whose external appearance "whitewashed" the death within, whose external show of piety covered up their actual faithlessness (23:23//Luke 11:42).

(3) Their attacks were those of witches living within the group. When they made converts, they effectively destroyed the interior of their proselytes, making them twice as much children of hell as themselves (23:15). This happened because they taught the proselytes to worry about externals and not about the core of the Torah, motivation or integrity. The interior was effectively sucked dry. They also spread about a poisonous "leaven" (16:6, 11, 12), their false teaching, which corrupted and polluted the whole pure batch with which it came in contact. The overall description of the Pharisees, then, is fully consistent with the typology of a witch in a witchcraft society.

It is the nature of the Gospels that we have basically Christian evaluations of Jesus, not those of his opponents. This means a scarcity of data about others' opinions of Jesus, which is never more evident than in assessing the accusation that Jesus is himself a "witch." The gospel tersely records in 12:24 the accusation by the Pharisees that Jesus is a "witch," an accusation repeated in 9:34 and 10:25. This is the only datum we have from these opponents with which we might understand the full scenario that makes these accusations plausible.

The gospel of John, however, does give us particulars concerning a Jewish accusation that Jesus is demon-possessed. He is regularly called a sinner (John

9:24), a corrupt person. His opponents regularly accuse him of "deceiving" the crowds (7:12, 47). They regularly expose his duplicity to the crowds. His teaching, then, cannot be from God, for he does not keep God's commandments, in particular the observance of the Sabbath; that teaching must be a poison.

The example of the gospel of John might help us to piece together disparate comments about Jesus in the gospel of Matthew that allow us to see the anthropological understanding of a "witch" operative there. In addition to several public accusations such as 12:24; 9:34 and 10:25, Matthew records charges that Jesus was a "deceiver" who worked "deception" on the people (27:63–64). The accusation in 12:24 was made precisely as a criticism of Jesus' Sabbath observance, suggesting that his opponents claimed to see through his behavior as a masquerade for his basic wickedness. They too could read hearts; they could discern the essential evil in him. Although the evidence is meagre, we are warranted in postulating a scenario in which Jesus' opponents considered him as "witch" when they accused him of demon possession in 12:24. After all, we have demonstrated amply from this text how the Christian assessment of the Pharisees is fully intelligible according to the same scenario.

As we noted earlier, in a group that sees evil disguised as good and discerns a discrepancy between external appearances and internal states, it is to be expected that some in the group will claim the ability to see beyond appearances so as to unmask the disguised evil. One would expect this skill to be highly developed in such a context, and it is. For example, John the Baptizer, the discerning prophet and hero of this group, could read hearts so as to unmask wickedness disguised as repentance. When John saw "many of the Sadducees and Pharisees coming for baptism," he was not fooled by this display of sincerity, but discerned hypocrisy and deception: "You brood of vipers! Who warned you to flee from the wrath to come?" (3:7). Baptism, a mere external show of repentance, is not what they required to make them clean: "Bear fruit that befits a change of heart" (3:8), that is, a total reform of life, inner and outer, a reform that would include acceptance of Jesus as God's designated reforming prophet.

It is in this vein that Jesus was said to be able to read hearts. On the one hand, he could "see faith," that is, commitment within people (9:2). But he was especially skilled in "knowing their (evil) thoughts": "Jesus, *knowing their thoughts*, said: 'Why do you think evil in your hearts?'" (9:4); "*Knowing their thoughts*, he said: 'Every kingdom divided against itself . . .'" (12:25). Jesus was so skilled at this that he could tell (1) when people merely "honor God with their lips, but their heart is far from God" (15:8) and (2) when people are self-deceived (22:29), deceive others (24:4–5, 24) or act as false prophets (7:15; 24:11, 24). John the Baptizer and Jesus both claimed to have to a high degree this skill of reading hearts so as to unmask deception and hypocrisy.

1.4c Function of witchcraft accusations. According to Douglas's profile, the characteristic activity of this kind of society focuses on discernment and eradication of the witch. In the world of Palestinian Jews under consideration, witchcraft concerns relativize "righteous" behavior, for "righteousness" was not to be sought in traditional, external behavior directed at interpersonal relationship with God. Instead, focus is on behavior directed at one's fellow, to have impact on them. Thus, acts of piety, such as prayer, fasting or sacrifice are put in the service of witch hunting and witch cleansing. Public prayer, fasting and almsgiving are protestations of innocence and prominence in a witch-ridden world.

On the other hand, the primary act in the process of coming to grips with personal, group-felt misfortune is the "witchcraft accusation." With this accusation, the two-faced witch is identified and the threat to the boundaries of the group is revealed. This item points up an important feature, namely, the function of witchcraft accusations in this type of social group. In a highly contentious society marked by strong rivalry and strong ambition, the accusation functions to "denigrate rivals and pull them down in the competition for leadership" (Douglas 1970:xviii; 1982:114). Such accusations are, in short, "an idiom of control." On this point Douglas echoes the consensus of anthropologists on the social function of witchcraft accusations (Mair 1969:203, 216; Goody 1970:211).

As regards the situation in Matthew's early community, in the intense and disorderly contentiousness over reform of Torah, accusations of demonic possession served to denigrate the Pharisees, who were rivals of the Jesus faction, by showing that they were not reformers at all but corrupters of Torah purity. This, then, is the proper background of the extensive polemic that Matthew's gospel recorded. For example, Jesus' followers developed a polemic against the Pharisees that amounts to a complete dishonoring of their rivals. They were a "brood of vipers," "an evil and adulterous generation," "hypocrites," "whitewashed tombs," and the like. And they were accused of being demonic and in the service of Satan; they were possessed of seven demons worse than the first that once was successfully expelled from them (12:43–45//Luke 11:24–26). How can they be teachers of Torah, being evil? Christian witchcraft accusations against the Pharisees, then, served to discredit these rivals for leadership.

Alternately, the Pharisees were wont to criticize every action of Jesus in terms of his orthopraxis: he ate with sinners (11:19//Luke 7:34); he did not wash before eating (15:1–10); he violated the Sabbath (12:9–13). How could a person so lax about purity be a true reformer of Torah? And so his exorcisms served as occasions for his enemies to claim that he performed them because he was in league with the Prince of demons. According to them, Jesus only appeared to observe Torah and teach its proper observance, but in fact he was evil and in league with Satan to corrupt the synagogue. The accusation of demon possession against Jesus, then, was intended to dishonor and discredit him.

Witchcraft accusations have two possible effects. If successful, they will lead to the expulsion of the witch from the village, which action could then end the tension of this ongoing conflict. But often the political resources of the accusing party are insufficient to bring about this expulsion, and in this case the accusations might lead instead to "fission" (Douglas 1970:xviii; 1982:114). The accusers themselves cannot remain in a polluted world that threatens them so acutely. Hence, they voluntarily withdraw from the conflict under the guise of maintaining their standard of purity. One thinks of the Qumran community in this regard. Expulsion or fission—in either case the group remains small and disorganized. Generally speaking, then, such groups prove unable to assimilate any lessons in conflict management from their experience.

As regards the desired effects of witchcraft accusations against rivals in Matthew, both Christians and Pharisees would expel each other if they could! But the followers of Jesus were too few in the small villages to expel the Pharisees. Furthermore, as a minority, they lacked recognized authority. On the other hand, neither could the Pharisees get rid of those Jews who followed Jesus, distributed as they were in individual households and claiming to be true members of the covenant. The reason for this was that the Pharisees' authority was not unanimously accepted in the synagogue. Of course, after the destruction of Jerusalem in 70 c.e. and with the spread of Judaean elites to the north, the particularistic Judaism of the Pharisaic sort would gain the ascendancy and become more successful in excommunicating Christians (see John 9:22, 34; 12:42; 16:2 as evidence of this later phenomenon).

There is some evidence to suggest that on occasion "fission" took place in the tense situations where the followers of Jesus and the Pharisees engaged in reciprocal witchcraft accusations. The ritual of erecting boundaries and distinguishing inside from outside served in some cases to set the members of Jesus-movement groups apart from their own neighbors and households. Furthermore, their deep appreciation of their own holiness and the threats to it from all the surrounding pollutions made it finally impossible to maintain the status quo. Some of these followers of Jesus seem voluntarily to have gone into exile. We can track their footsteps in the advice given them: "If anyone will not receive you or listen to your words, shake the dust from your feet as you leave that house or town" (10:14//Luke 9:5). Yet, it is hard to determine whether this action was self-imposed exile or whether it represented the success of Pharisaic accusations resulting in expulsion: "When they persecute you in one town, flee to the next" (10:23; see 5:11–12).

At least those agents commissioned to preach about the Jesus movement were able to "shake the dust from their feet" and "flee." But for most of Jesus' followers in so small a society, both leaving and capitulating were alternatives as impossible as forcing their enemies to do the same. Another path seems to have been taken. We have a window on it in the parable of the wheat and the tares: tension-filled tolerance (13:24–30, 36–43). According to the parable, the polluting tares are found living in threatening proximity to the pure wheat. Jesus is credited with making clear the source of this evil in a genuine witch-craft accusation: "The enemy who sowed them is the Devil" (13:39). The group's leaders would like to uproot (i.e., expel) the tares, but this would be as impossible as replanting the genuine wheat in a new, pure field. The final solution is a painful compromise: "Let them both grow until the harvest," when the evil tares will finally be expelled. If we may take this parable, especially with its allegorized interpretation, as having some bearing on the actual situation of Matthew's group, then it appears that the members of the Jesus faction were unable to expel the evil ones. Finding fission impossible, they remained in a state of acute tension with their neighbors, in disorderly conflict with their rivals for reform.

The type of interpersonal relation with God that the followers of Jesus could not construct and express in a rival synagogue went underground. These group members then prayed, fasted and gave alms "in secret" (6:3–4, 6, 17–18). They remained protected in the few "worthy" households where they could sustain their distinctive point of view and the behavior that followed from it (10:13). Interaction with their Pharisaic rivals remained unavoidably close and contentiousness stayed at an intense level. The group's boundaries continued to be precariously maintained by the identification of pollutants within the group and especially by witchcraft accusations against rivals outside the group. The expulsion of the Pharisees, which the Christian Jews earnestly desired, must grudgingly be put off "until the harvest," when God will separate them from the wheat.

1.5   Conclusion

We began by carefully noting that in the early segments of Matthew, not only do Pharisees accuse Jesus and his subsequent followers of being pos-sessed, but that Jesus and his followers likewise accuse Pharisees of demon possession. It is surely an understatement to describe this stratum of text in Matthew's gospel as a situation of intense and disorderly conflict. The proper identification of these charges lies in appreciating them from the perspective of cultural anthropology as accusations of witchcraft in first-century Mediter-ranean society. Drawing upon the works of Mary Douglas, we set up a model for describing the social system of a group that engaged in witchcraft accusa-tions. In particular, the model afforded a detailed and coherent look at the cosmology of the social group in which such accusations are made and at the function of these accusations. This produced an adequate scenario from a considerate reading of a foreign, ancient text.

Through the use of this anthropological model, our attention has been focussed not on black cats, broomsticks or sorcery, but on the social inter-action in typical witchcraft societies. Witchcraft accusations function there as a medium of control where intense contentiousness over leadership exists, and where procedures for settling claims of legitimacy are absent. Yet as enlightening as this type of investigation is, it raises important questions. For many non-Mediterraneans, it will not be particularly comforting to find in a sacred text the type of religious viewpoint or posture that is described in anthropological terms as a "witchcraft society." Nor will it be edifying to see how early Jewish followers of Jesus, our ancestors in faith and the primary witnesses of our faith, employed accusations of witchcraft as pointed polemic to denigrate their rivals, the Pharisees (see Matt 12:43–45). While this way of imagining behavior in the gospels often disturbs U.S. readers, it does have its value, for it presents us with a typical view of first-generation, Jewish followers of Jesus. Their perception and employment of witchcraft accusation, moreover, was not distinctive, for as we noted in the introduction to this chapter, similar accusations of demon possession are found also in John's gospel, Paul's letters and other early Christian documents as well. But the witchcraft model offers significant insights into the typical social dynamics of many early Christian communities, their view of the world and their patterns of conflict with those both inside and outside the group.

One final point, the use of an anthropological model coupled with historical and linguistic perspectives, identified one level of conflict in the history of Matthew's community. But the Jesus-movement group with which we associate this gospel evidently did not always remain in this situation, for it was later able to assimilate Mark's more liberal gospel. The final form of Matthew indicates that significant changes took place in the group's cosmology as a result of new experiences. The group became somewhat less dualistic in perspective, less perfection-oriented with the inclusion of Gentiles and other peoples (22:10). Concern for radical purity lessened and maintenance of impermeable boundaries diminished as Matthew's community became gradually more heterogeneous in membership. Thus, we are encouraged to assess the history of Matthew's community from a fresh perspective. We may not have fresh archaeological or historical data, but we can more clearly plot out the ways in which the later Matthean community differed from the earlier "witchcraft society," a term not applicable to the final editor's audience as intensely as to the early group. The use of this anthropological model, then, generates new ideas and fresh data for a continued critical reading of the text.

Remembering the focus of this study, Christology "from the side," this chapter has provided an initial set of Mediterranean scenarios that fit the social system realized in the language of some text-segments of the New Testament. Our task now is to move from an understanding of this Jewish group of followers of Jesus to their understanding and interpretation of Jesus. Just as their self-understanding and self-interpretation resulted from attack and counter-attack with a group of rivals, the same is true for their understanding and interpretation of Jesus, for New Testament Christology, too, was rooted in claim and counterclaim, in accusation and counteraccusation, of more or less equally situated groups in conflict. This is Christology "from the side." The death of Jesus indicates that certain accusations proved successful, yet early Christian groups not unlike those we have encountered in Matthew successfully turned around the stigma attached to his death. How did Jesus, the publicly proclaimed deviant, end up acclaimed as a globally significant prominent? This, of course, is the stuff of Christology, Christology from the side.

Jesus the Deviant

Labelling and Deviance Theory in Matthew 12

Understanding conflict in Matthew's gospel remains our focus. While concentrating once more on Matthew 12, we intend now to analyze the conflictual dynamics there in light of another social science model, labelling and deviance theory. This chapter will necessarily consist of two parts, an exposition of the social science model of labelling and deviance, and its application to Matthew 12. The reader's patience is requested in the first part, for deviance theory is somewhat complicated and an adequate exposition of it requires some nuancing. If biblical interpreters are to use social science models responsibly in their work, then they need to set out the models they employ with some sufficiency so as to avoid facile or slipshod appropriation and to allow for careful study and application.

2.1   Introduction: Labelling Theory

The synoptic tradition indicates that people were constantly being labelled, both positively and negatively (see Appendix, Table 2). Jesus labelled Simon of Capernaum "Rock," for his perception of something about Jesus that fitted the characteristics of the Jewish role designated "Messiah" (Matt 16:16); but he later called him "Satan," for rejecting another dimension of the role Jesus foresaw for himself (16:23). Jesus also designated his disciples as "mother" and "brothers" since they ostensibly did what pleased his Father in heaven (12:49–50), while he warned against certain enthusiastic persons whom he labelled "false prophets" (7:15, 21–23). Some of the groups with whom he interacted he likewise labelled negatively as "brood of vipers" (12:34; see 3:7) and "hypocrites" (23:13, 23, 25, 29). Jesus himself was positively labelled as "teacher" (12:38) and "prophet" (14:5), but negatively labelled as "demon-possessed" (12:24) and sarcastically as "king of the Jews" (27:39). Ostensibly, such labels are evidence of something significant in the tradition. Now what would such evidence mean? Conflict can be expressed and monitored in the ways people hurl harmful epithets, derogatory names and negative labels against outsiders, as well as in the ways they affix honorable titles, laudatory names and positive labels on acclaimed insiders. In the social sciences this sort of name-giving and name-calling is described as "labelling." And so *Calling Jesus Names* attends precisely to this process of name-giving and name-calling.

2.1a Labelling.   Labelling might be described as the successful identification of a person and his/her personhood with some trait or behavior. In U.S. sociology, explanations of the labelling process were developed in the sociol-

ogy of deviance to explain negative labels, called *stigmas*. But the same process
is equally involved in the other direction, that is, the process of honoring and
approving persons. In this regard we wish to explain positive labels, called
titles. In our study of how Jesus was assessed, we shall likewise follow historical precedent and deal first with the negative labels ascribed to Jesus in
Matthew.

Why labelling? Labelling people and things is an essential feature presumably
of every culture. In the previous chapter we noted at length that the meanings
that define people derive from socially drawn sets of lines that comprise the
purity arrangements of a society. Purity arrangements or boundary drawing
allow people to meet the fundamental need to know where they are and where
things around them fit in. Such sets of lines enable people in a given society to
interpret themselves, their groups, other groups, things in their environment
(both living and non-living), time, space and the like. Thus, lines, usually
imaginary and fictitious but quite real nonetheless, tell people how and where
they fit into a society that equally interprets everything else in the social
landscape as well. People and their things are expected to be where they
belong, to be "clean," to abide by the order of their society.

Given such expectations, every society must have a system of lines to tell
where things are in place, where they are clean. Things out of place would be in
disarray, in disorder. As a rule, "dirt" is matter out of place (Douglas 1966:35)
in some undesired way. Such matter falls outside its expected usual and customary place in the ongoing process of social interaction. This is negatively
assessed matter, matter perceived at least as being *not* where it ought to be.
Yet, things can obviously be "out of place" in a positive way too. At times
matter is found that goes beyond the boundaries in some surprising and non-
customary way. This out-of-place matter might be positively assessed, such as
rubbish that turns out to be "collectibles," such as diamonds and gold in a
mine full of dirt or a new design in art, clothing and architecture. Similarly,
persons "out of place" require evaluation and assessment. And just as things
"out of place" are labelled with special names that mark and interpret such
items as worthy of disgust, exhilaration or simply being ignored, so too with
people and their stigmas and titles.

2.1b Deviance.   Deviance refers to behavior or conditions that result in a
person's being out of normal place. Behavior is deviant when it violates lines;
conditions afflicting persons are likewise deviant when they leave people
permanently out of bounds in some negative way. For example, in the U.S.,
obesity, disfigurement and physical inability make a person deviant. Just as dirt
is matter "out of place" in some negative way, so too is a deviant.

Deviance is a socially shared interpretation of persons and their behavior.
Like Christology, deviance is "from the side." Of course, this interpretation is
rooted in the socially created and traditioned purity arrangements that enable
people to perceive deviant behavior. But unlike socially interpreted dirt, devi-

ance is often not a neutral matter. When violation of lines not merely puts a person out of place but results in the violator's being defined as a socially unfit person, we are dealing with *moral meanings*. This new definition of the violator of lines distinguishes an unclean person from a criminal or sinner. An "unclean" person would be a person simply "out of place," for example, in the U.S. a male who accidentally wanders into a women's restroom, or a person covered with paint or mud at a wedding. But a criminal or sinner is a person judged "out of place" and socially transposed to a new and negative place, often permanently. Thus, socially negative and unacceptable people are subject to public transformation of their personhood, the result of which is the creation of a special kind of person who cannot be trusted to live within the purity arrangements shared by the group. Such people do not live by the rules of society. The rule-breaker is thus an "outsider," qualitatively different from others in the group. This new definition of the deviant person and his or her outsider status takes place by means of a process called labelling.

To label a person or group negatively is a social act of retaliation for some alleged deviance. Under certain circumstances in most cultures, such labelling is (1) a serious challenge to honor or a means of satisfaction, (2) an unprovoked act of aggression or a preferred mode of retaliation, or (3) an act of assault or a means of defense. New Testament epithets such as "sinner," "unclean," "demon-possessed" and "brood of vipers," much like epithets in our society such as "whore," "ex-con," "Commie," "quack," "pervert" and the like, are not simply vaporous words. *They are social weapons.* In the hands of influential persons or powerful groups, they can inflict genuine injury, since they serve to define a person as out of social place, hence as permanently deviant. While putting a person down may be a joke or a serious challenge, it need not involve situating that person outside the accepted boundaries of society. But in a society built on grades of status, degrading terms that stick almost necessarily lead to collective avoidance, ostracism and isolation.

Negative labelling as well as positive name-calling can lead to serious social consequences, lethal in the negative instance, life-enhancing in the positive. As we all know, labels are used to tag deviant or prominent persons with consequent results for their social standing, social location and so on. In societies structured in hierarchical fashion (such as the U.S. military, the Vatican, the Communist Party in the USSR), such labelling is real and valuable, for to name is to know. In other types of societies, such as the U.S. mainstream, people bear numerous labels indicative of the social categories they occupy sequentially and/or simultaneously in the "teams" they join to score in the contentious game of life. We shall consider positive labels in chapter 4. Here we focus on negative labels and the deviance they highlight.

Negative labelling serves as a social distancing device, underscoring differences and thus dividing social categories into polarities such as the good and the wicked, heroes and villains, believers and infidels or the honorable and the shameful. Such labelling serves to underscore societal values by setting apart those who lack or flaunt them. They mark the existence of a sort of *decanonization* process by which a person becomes a non-saint, an instance of permanent uncleanness, impurity or lack of sacredness. When negative labels move from the level of gossip and challenge among equals to the level of officialdom, they may serve not only to express public recognition of deviance, but also to give increased salience to the deviant role itself. For example, Judas Iscariot, the one who betrayed Jesus, becomes Judas Iscariot, "The One Who Betrayed Him," a veritable last name. The same is true of the "thieves" or seditionists who died with Jesus; they become "The Thieves." Comparably, Matthew, who is negatively labelled as a tax collector, officially becomes Matthew "The Tax Collector" in the church list of the Twelve; likewise, Simon, the leper, became Simon "The Leper."

While positive labelling carries with it the force of celebrity standing, negative labelling bears the force of stigma. When carried out publicly or at times even secretly, such labelling can carry with it an institutional sanctioning of overwhelming proportions: positively by granting symbolic reward potential, negatively by granting symbolic devastation potential, both of deep and enduring quality.

2.1c Negotiation. In complex societies, people have effects on each other by plying each other with specific types of symbols (see Malina 1986a:68–97; see also Scheff 1968). For example, people are fully aware that money cannot be eaten for nutrition, worn, driven or used to build any stable building. On the other hand, money serves as a generalized symbolic medium of exchange. Not a few people live for this symbol, and perhaps a good number suffer and die for lack of it. There are four categories of symbols that work like money, and in fact money is a subset of one of them. These four categories are power, influence, inducement and commitment activation. Power is a generalized symbol that has effect because of a sanction known as force; and influence has effect because of its sanction, reasons for doing things. Inducement has effect because of its sanctions, goods and services, including money, while commitment activation (synonymous with solidarity, loyalty) has effect because of its sanction, embarrassment for the person who will not comply (for a full discussion, see Malina 1986a:68–97). The feature requiring explanation here is how negative labels come to stick. The reason for mentioning these generalized symbolic means of social interaction is that labelling is a consequence and outcome of the effective application of these symbols, notably the symbols of commitment activation, or loyalty, and of influence, either singly or in tandem, in a negotiation process.

For example, if a person is labelled a traitor, the force and impact of such labelling is not confined to the persons who intend labels to be effective. Other members of society are expected to recognize the traitor as traitor, while some who know the labelled person will deny the label as ridiculous. Those who labelled Jesus as an insurrectionist do not get the label to stick merely because they use it. Rather, labelling can and does provoke reaction. A person labelled due to another's influence or prestige can have recourse to his or her own influence or prestige, or to his or her own power or inducement ability.

In other situations, a generalized symbol of an equal or other sort may be hurled back as riposte to the challenge posed by the label (e.g., "It takes one to know one!"). This means, of course, that the generalized symbolic media in question are available to all social actors, with their choice and effectiveness dependent on grid and group situations. Persons labelled deviants are usually not without some social support, for example, kin, fictive kin, patrons, official "helpers" and the like. As a result, various forms of negotiation and bargaining are significant elements in labelling interactions, as in any other type of dispute resolution (Nader and Todd 1978:1–40). Negotiation, then, means that most people in most complex societies possess some power and/or loyalty (=activated commitment) for exchange in a labelling process.

2.1d Master status/role engulfment. Instead of further negotiation to get rid of a negative label, a person can be caught up in the deviant role indicated by the label and increasingly live out the demands of the new role at the expense of and in face of previous non-deviant labels and roles. Schur (1971: 70) notes:

> The concept of master status lies at the heart of role engulfment, for it is the increased salience or primacy of the deviant role for the individual that is the hallmark of such engulfment. And the deviant roles generally seem to have a kind of built-in primacy or master status, relative at least to certain other kinds of roles.

Labelling is intended to create a master status, a process often called "role engulfment." Schur notes that role engulfment does not take place all at once. Even formal degradation rituals do not mark a once-for-all attribution of a label, but can take place amid negotiation or even be reversed and undone. For example, the public humiliation and crucifixion of Jesus marked the high point of one such formal degradation ritual; yet motivated by their experience of his resurrection, his followers effectively reversed any permanent negative label, at least among a good number in his former faction. It would seem that the synoptic story-line itself bears out Schur's observation that labelling is a process, drawing its effect "within a context of continuous interaction, involving numerous relevant patterns of action and response and constantly shifting definitions of situation" (1971:71).

2.1e Deviant/prominent. As we describe the labelling process, we are ever aware that we are equally at work describing Christology "from the side." Our concern is not simply the clear exposition of a social science theory, but a better understanding of how and why Jesus had been labelled as deviant or prominent by the people of his culture. From the viewpoint of negative labellers, then, deviance refers to those behaviors and/or conditions perceived and assessed to jeopardize the interests and social standing of persons who negatively label the behaviors and/or conditions. On the other hand, prominence refers to those behaviors and/or conditions perceived and assessed to enhance positively the interests and social standing of persons who positively label the behaviors and/or conditions. (Etymologically, "prominence" refers to excellence in honor, ranking in precedence, while "eminence" refers to superiority in power, ranking in coercive ability). It depends, then, on one's point of view, on which side one happens or chooses to stand. Christology, then, can be done "from two sides."

A *deviant* is a person perceived to be out of place to such an extent or in such a way as to be redefined in a new, negative place—the redefinition, of course, deriving from the labellers. Labellers then view this being out of place and being in a new, negative place as a personality trait, a quality of personhood, rather than as a specific act of behavior or a happenstance condition. In Christology "from the side," outsiders viewed Jesus as a witch, a charlatan, a blasphemer—and this essentially and totally, since they judged that these features comprised his whole, essential personhood. He always was this, but it simply took time for the full dimensions of these features to be revealed. "Deviant" is thus a status assumed by persons identified as rule-breakers, that is, those who negatively step or stand out of place in some irrevocable way.

A *prominent* person is a person perceived to be out of place to such an extent or in such a way as to be redefined in a new, positive place—the redefinition, of course, deriving from the labellers. Labellers then view this being out of place and being in a new, positive place as a personality trait, a quality of personhood, rather than as a behavior or condition. Again, in Christology "from the side," insiders viewed Jesus as a prophet, a Messiah or even a Son of God—and this essentially and totally, since they judged that these features marked his whole essential personhood. He always was this, but it simply took time for the full dimensions of these features to be revealed. "Prominent," thus, is a status assumed by persons identified as positive limit-breakers, i.e., those who step or stand conspicuously above and beyond usual places in some irrevocable way (Malina 1986a:143–54).

The gospel of Matthew presents a retrospective interpretation of a person, Jesus of Nazareth, evaluated by those he called and/or helped as prominent, yet labelled by the gatekeepers of his society as deviant. The gatekeepers won in their assessment; witness the acclamation of the Jerusalem crowds at the trial scene. Thus, "Jesus the deviant" is duly shamed in public, symbolling the validity of elite judgment, elite interests and elite standing. Yet with his post-death appearances and even earlier, Jesus was perceived as prominent. Given the success of the Jerusalem elite in having Jesus labelled a deviant, it would be the task of those acclaiming his prominence to effect a transformation of the label. The labelling model allows the New Testament interpreter to articulate some of the major features in the gospel story and to discover the many implicit areas of interaction involved. Christology, we repeat, should be done "from two sides," a negative as well as a positive side.

The Cast of the Labelling Drama

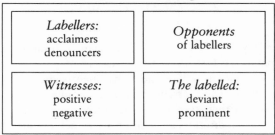

To begin with, labelling theory immediately shifts the focus of attention from the titles ascribed to Jesus in the New Testament to the labellers themselves, that is, to those who give and use those titles. Our question, then, is not the meaning of the titles and the functions they entail, but the interests and concerns of those employing the titles. For example, the persons who gave titles to Jesus were the moral entrepreneurs who, in one way or another, stood to benefit from having the titles stick. Thus, the cast of the labelling drama would include at least the following four classes of actors:

1. the *labellers* (positive and/or negative) and their interests;
2. the *opponents* of the labellers (who would reverse the titles) and their interests;
3. the *neutrals* or *observers* of the labelling contest, and their interests;
4. the *person labelled* as prominent or deviant.

Obviously, if the person labelled is alive and capable of directly interacting, he/she can be found in the ranks of (1) and (2) above; if not available to interact, those in (1) and (2) conflict over the assessment of the one labelled.

Consequently, if we take up the logical stages of the labelling process and apply them to Matthew's gospel, the steps would follow the sequence in Table 1, p. 43. How these stages occurred historically, for whom, in what contexts and the like form an interesting set of questions suggested by the model. It is not our task to unravel those questions here. Rather, we would focus on the logical steps. Thus, the first level would appear as a negative labelling process, on which we will focus in this chapter and the next. In the fourth chapter we shall attempt to define and illustrate the positive labelling process.

In other words, since witchcraft accusations are a form of negative labelling, it would seem useful to situate the accusations recorded in Matthew within some sort of systematic model so as to account both for the process of labelling and all the ways persons might react to social labelling. While developing the model, we will relate its elements to the logical steps in the process of naming Jesus, i.e., tracing the path from "Jesus the deviant" to "Jesus the prominent." These steps are schematically set forth in Table 1, p. 43.

2.2   The Model: Part One
Understanding Deviance

Step 1.   The Deviance Process: The Elite View of Jesus' Career

This stage marks the first phase of the career of Jesus. It is rooted in his actual, historical activity in Galilee and, subsequently and briefly, in Jerusalem. It is marked by normal Mediterranean agonism, conflict with those who were threatened by loss of their symbolic goods in proportion to Jesus' increased honor. The normal Mediterranean accusation in such circumstances is that of witchcraft, and the stories of Jesus' healings in Matthew bear adequate witness of behavior that might be labelled the work of witchcraft. The case in point in Matthew, however, is the accusation against Jesus by the Pharisees of his casting out of demons by the Prince of Demons. In the course of the gospel, Jesus puts out a rather large number of labels himself, as he attempts, rather successfully it seems, to evade the negative labels affixed to him by the Pharisees and other enemies. How are these dealt with by the labellers? What is the role of such labels in the gospel? We use the following model to help in answering such questions.

The deviance process is a process in which a group, community or society (1) interprets some behavior as deviant, (2) defines the person(s) who so behaves as deviant and (3) accords the treatment considered appropriate to such deviants. We can be more specific about various aspects of the deviance process, indicating who interprets, what steps go into the definition of a deviant and what this might look like.

2.2a *Agents of censure.* The agents of censure involved in the deviance process refer to those persons "from the side" who participate in the negative evaluation of someone. They might be called rule creators, rule enhancers, and deviance processor agents and agencies. We consider each in turn.

(1) Rule creators: Certain people can be identified as likely to initiate a deviance process and to mobilize the forces necessary to make it successful. Who are they? They tend to be people privy to the making and enforcing of societal rules. In a society, rule creating is the task of the moral entrepreneur, since rule creation is a moral enterprise. A moral enterprise is a process of constructing and applying meanings that define persons and their behaviors as morally adequate or not. The moral enterprise is thus an interpretation of a person. It requires both the making of rules, done by rule creators, as well as the application of rules to specific persons, done by rule enforcers. Rule creators form interest groups, i.e., coalitions focusing upon the shared and distinct interest of group members. In Matthew, the moral entrepreneurs who labelled Jesus as a witch are called Pharisees. Perhaps some aspects of behavior

Table 1. Steps in the Transformation Process

Step I
The Career of Jesus

The Deviance Process:
Jesus the Wizard, Seditionist

A. Censure-Worthy Behavior: Rule Creating, Rule Enhancement, Deviance Processing

   1. Rule Creating
   2. Rule Enhancement
   3. Activity of Deviance-Processing Agents

B. Retrospective Interpretation

   1. Responsibility Affirmed
   2. Injury Affirmed
   3. Victim(s) Affirmed
   4. Condemnation
   5. Appeal to Authority

C. Status-Degradation Rituals: Separation, Liminality, Reaggregation

D. Interrupting the Labelling Process

   1. Responsibility Denied
   2. Injury Denied
   3. Victim(s) Denied
   4. Condemners Condemned
   5. Higher Loyalties

Step II
From Sources to Jesus

The Transformation Process: from Deviant to Prominent

A. Neutralizers: Rule Ambiguity Rule Transformation, Transformation Processing

   1. Rule Ambiguity
   2. Rule Transformation
   3. Activity of Transformation-Processing Agents

B. Retrospective Interpretation I

   1. Aggrandizement Denied
   2. Claim of Benefit
   3. Beneficiary Affirmed
   4. Acclaimers Acclaimed
   5. Higher Loyalties

C. Status-Transformation Rituals: Separation

D. Reinterpreting the Labelling Process

Step III
From Matthew to Sources

The Prominence Process: Jesus as the Christ, the Son

A. Honor-Worthy Behavior: Rule Creating, Rule Enhancement, Prominence Processing

   1. Rule Creating
   2. Rule Enhancement
   3. Activity of Prominence-Processing Agents

B. Retrospective Interpretation

   1. Aggrandizement Denied
   2. Claim of Benefit
   3. Beneficiary Affirmed
   4. Acclaimers Acclaimed
   5. Higher Loyalties

C. Status-Elevation Rituals: Reaggregation

D. Reaffirming the Labelling Process

attributed to the Pharisees in Matthew better fit the time of the later Matthean community rather than the career of Jesus. Yet, the labelling is predictable enough for any healer. The symbolic goods at stake are power and loyalty, which accrue to the successful healer in various ways. Thus, the need of the Pharisees to allay any accumulation of power or loyalty by some unknown person was acutely felt by these gatekeepers of society (see Hollenbach 1981).

Using Douglas's group and grid indicators, weak group/high grid societies such as the U.S. find their moral entrepreneurs within interest groups whose members focus their activities upon common interests (pressure groups). Strong group/low grid societies, such as the first-century Mediterranean societies reflected in the New Testament documents, find their moral entrepreneurs within factions whose members focus their activities upon the central person who formed the faction to begin with. In whatever cultural script, interest groups assure a constant supply of deviance and deviants.

First-century Israelites were all publicly in favor of pleasing God by doing Torah, no less than contemporary persons in the U.S. are in favor of stamping out pornography for the sake of their children. All "right-minded" people will be expected to subscribe to these culturally specific and highly emotionally charged goals. And it is specifically these sorts of goals that the moral entrepreneur espouses. The moral entrepreneur, then, becomes socially unassailable, unless opponents can redefine the situation by neutralizing the constraint unassailability produces.

As rule creators, moral entrepreneurs and their followers wish to interpret some behavior as deviant for the purpose of obviating, preventing or correcting interferences *in their interests*. They wish to change, enforce or establish rules to these ends. They do so by defining both certain conditions and those who engage in those conditions as inimical to their values and interests—personal, group and societal. Through such social definition, a person or group attaches particular meaning to some objective person, thing or event. In other words, by means of such new interpretations, rule creators define a state of affairs by drawing or redrawing boundaries around something or someone of social significance, thus situating certain persons, things or events as "out of bounds." In this way, the definition marking a person "out of bounds" consists of a set of objective conditions seen as problem filled: negatively as posing a threat or danger (or positively as posing security or release). This step in the deviance process is usually called banning: interpreting some thing or event as bad, evil, wrong, immoral and imbuing it with negative judgment (guilt/fault). We might note in passing that in the prominence process, this first step would be called approval: interpreting some thing or event as good, right, moral and imbuing it with positive judgment (honor/merit).

When members of an interest group act to mobilize public opinion to ban someone, there are usually two main social aspects of this action, dissemination and broadening social respectability. Dissemination is a form of raising awareness in the target population. It involves giving a high degree of visibility to the meanings developed by the moral entrepreneur and his rule-creating coalition: e.g., public appearances, challenges, debates, opportunities to make views known. Broader respectability derives from linking the new interpretation or rule with some previously held positive values, while tying the opposed person's views to negative values. This attachment to currently held positive values is effected: (1) by "borrowing" respectability from existing persons and groups, such as persons on boards of directors, or by making alliances with better-known groups; (2) by seeking testimonials; (3) by finding endorsements from prominent figures.

Dissemination and respectability are further enhanced by raising awareness concerning the value of the new interpretation or rule itself. To this end, the rule creator has to pursue goals that people are reluctant to oppose publicly. Such awareness concerning the value of the new rule is developed and maintained by generating a sense of distress in the following ways: (1) demonstrating the lack of rules or inadequacy of existing rules; (2) demonstrating the lack of agencies to enforce existing rules; (3) in sum, highlighting the lack of means to allay and resolve the stress in question. The rule-creating group will then seek to resolve the distress either instrumentally (by getting a law passed or by directing law enforcement agencies toward the actions of others) or symbolically (by legitimating the interest group and its interests at the expense of others). How the foregoing applies to data in Matthew will be set forth in 2.4a below.

(2) Rule enhancers: Rule enhancers "convert" others to the interpretation or value being disseminated by the interest group. Such "conversion" notably occurs by altering other people's attitudes toward the newly defined deviance. Attitudes to deviance can be optimistic (It will pass, just a passing phase.), neutral (So what! What else is new?), normal (It is unusual, but within the range of the normal.), and pessimistic (It is an intolerable evil!). The moral entrepreneur must create a *pessimistic* attitude in as many people as possible. The opponents of Jesus, for example, were moral entrepreneurs out to interpret the Jesus movement pessimistically, while Jesus likewise attempte same against factions in conflict with him. Both the Jesus faction and the Pharisees, in turn, attempt broader respectability by relating their own groups with the one to which Jesus once belonged, the faction recruited by John the Baptist. On the other hand, both Baptist and Pharisee groups seem to have trouble understanding who Jesus was, what Jesus intended to do, what motivated him (see Matt 11:2–5//Luke 11:18–23). And the problem of labelling John the Baptist is equally in evidence in the gospel story (Matt 11:7–10, 18//Luke 7:24–27, 33).

Broader respectability can be achieved by converting others to one's point of view, that is, by development of a counter ideology. By "ideology" we mean that set of values, attitudes and beliefs that group members hold and that hold them, as it were, often unaware, to mark their group off from other contending groups and to bind group members together. For example, while most persons in the U.S. believe that they are tolerant and so espouse an ideology of tolerance, there are whole areas in which they feel themselves free to be

unashamedly intolerant. These other areas can be appealed to by moral entrepreneurs who would convert tolerant people to a counter ideology of intolerance. Parents can be converted to unashamed intolerance of a gay public-
school teacher, of a child with AIDS in the same school with his/her own
children, of a Communist on the school board, of a neighbor selling child-
pornography and the like. These areas of unashamed intolerance underscore
what people really believe in. The development of this counter-ideology is
essential if broader respectability is to be gained to label someone a deviant.

A counter-ideology points to some alternative values, attitudes and beliefs,
introduced to redirect a group's tolerance or intolerance. Such counter-ideol-
ogies can often be made to ride on the back of existing values. For example, if
in first-century Palestine before the destruction of Jerusalem, Galileans are
simply boorish dolts (see John 7:15; Acts 4:13), then a Galilean healer can be
made to appear as a harmful boorish dolt in the eyes of sophisticated Jerusalemites.

(3) Activity of deviance-processing agents: The anonymous heads of the
factions that actively opposed Jesus took steps from the outset first to keep
track of his activity and then actively to remove him from the scene. In Galilee
the opponents are seen as Pharisees and Herodians, while in Jerusalem the
threat of the Jesus movement comes directly to the sources of power: temple
priests, elites called elders and the Roman governor. What all these personages
seek to do is to place Jesus firmly in the deviance status.

Status can be considered either as actual position in a social system or as the
value of a position in that system. In a sense, the deviance status covers both
aspects. In general, status-as-position in a social system is assessed in terms of
what others perceive that position to be. Status, then, is a reciprocal reality.
Like a grant of honor, status depends on the perception and appraisal of
others. The appraisal of status may be based on ascribed characteristics and
achievements.

Ascribed characteristics include age, sex, birth, physical features and genealogy. This means that ascribed deviant status is based on some quality that
befalls a person by no effort of his/her own and that a person continually
possesses, i.e., some deeply discrediting feature or attribute (= stigma). Here
deviance are a matter of being, the very meaning of a person's being. For
example, to call a group of persons an "adulterous generation" means they are
all born out of wedlock, all bastards, all illegitimate for all those purposes
requiring legitimacy. Illegitimacy was an ascribed deviant status in first-century
Palestine.

Achievements include perceived acquisitions, marriage, occupation, feats
and the like. Thus, an achieved deviant status is based on a person's perfor-
mance of some publicly perceived overt action that is banned. Here deviance is
a matter of doing or saying. In first-century Palestine, any open violation of
Torah could earn one an achieved deviant status, should some moral entrepreneur find it in his interest to have the violator labelled a deviant.

Successful moral entrepreneurs are those who are effective in getting their potential deviants denounced. Such denunciation constitutes a first step in the process of labelling, for it marks a perpetrator as a potential deviant. How do such denouncers arrange for the successful denunciation of their perpetrators? Garfinkel (1956) developed a model of the denunciation rite. His model with its four variables might serve to raise a number of questions about the quality of early Christian groups: the denouncer, a perpetrator whose identity is to be transformed, some trait, behavior or event that serves as reason for the transformation of identity and witnesses who will denounce the perpetrator in his/her new identity. These variables are not unlike the cast of the labelling drama sketched previously, only here, *denunciation* leaves out opponents and instead highlights the trait, behavior or event that presumably provokes denunciation. Thus:

The Variables in a Denunciation Rite

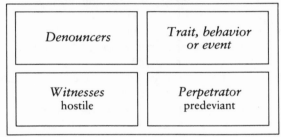

Denouncers	*Trait, behavior or event*
Witnesses hostile	*Perpetrator* predeviant

For the deviance-bestowing feature to be attributed to and effect transformation of the perpetrator, the following must occur:

(a) The perpetrator and the trait must be removed from the ordinary to the "out-of-the-ordinary" (thus, accusations of healing "through Beelzebub"; the "signless" prophet).

(b) The perpetrator and the trait must be rejected because

    (i)   the perpetrator and the trait are unique, lethal and typically symbolic of some negative feature of human existence (e.g., sedition, idolatry, blasphemy, etc.);

    (ii)   the symbolic quality of the perpetrator and the trait are seen by witnesses as stark opposites of the counter-symbolic figures available (e.g., the respected elites in the gospels, Pharisees, Sadducees, elders), so much so that it only makes sense to condemn the perpetrator. Not to condemn him or her is to reject the opposite.

(c) The denouncer must be so identified with the witnesses (the grantors of shame, individual or moral) that he is perceived as a publicly known person, not a private individual. Throughout the process the denouncer acts in his capacity as a public figure or head of a faction. In the gospel story, the denouncer is usually a group of nameless elites, speaking as one. Thus, the single spokesman is usually a faction bearing a general designation, e.g., Pharisees. Perhaps those handing on the stories no longer remembered the individual names of these central opposition figures or purposely left them unremembered. On the other hand, first-century stereotyping indicates that "Pharisee" or "High Priest" would be sufficient identification.

(d) The denouncer must underscore the core values of the group in question (here Israel) and deliver his denunciation in the name of those core values (thus: disobedience to God, flaunting Torah).

(e) The denouncer must be invested with the right to speak in the name of these core values (thus the importance of the stereotypical roles of Jesus' opponents and lack of need to specify them by name). In the strong group setting, only groups have the right to speak, not individuals (for a parallel structural case, see Beer 1984:100–28).

(f) The denouncer is seen as supporter of the core values of the group at large (i.e., binding and loosing in the community of Israel, official representatives of God-given authority, etc.).

(g) Both the denouncer and the witnesses must be made to experience distance from the perpetrator (e.g., Pharisees as attackers from the outside; the Jerusalem elite using intermediaries, etc.).

(h) Finally, the perpetrator must be made strange, i.e., beyond, above, behind the legitimate order, thus "outside" it.

(4) Deviance–processing agencies: The groups accusing and denouncing Jesus thus serve as channels to get him to the publicly approved deviance-processing agencies, that is, the Jerusalem elites and the local Roman government. These agencies register deviance by defining, classifying and labelling types of behavior or conditions deemed to be "out of bounds." On the basis of the stereotypes thus created, the agencies subject persons accused of deviance to a ritual of degradation, by means of which accused persons are depersonalized and successfully labelled. By this the accused are successfully placed within the category of "outsiders." The label now serves as a convenient stereotype for understanding and interacting with the newly labelled deviant. A person becomes what the label symbolizes; a person perceived to suffer from a certain condition is presumed to have the traits popularly associated with that condition.

To facilitate the work of these deviance-processing agencies, the person accused of deviance must be made *to be* an instance of what he or she is alleged to have done: from being afflicted with inability to see to being a blind person; from being afflicted with illness to being a mental case; from devious doer to deviant; from crime perpetrator to criminal. This process is called retrospective interpretation.

2.2b Retrospective interpretation.   As we shall see, the gossip reported by Jesus' Jerusalem opponents, along with the trial scene itself, provides a retrospective interpretation of Jesus' career in Galilee and subsequently in Jerusalem. Jesus is seen to be both witch and leader of sedition, hence deviant and worthy of death. Retrospective interpretation is a process by means of which the deviant actor is made into a typical case of the thing he or she is alleged to have done (Schur 1971:52–56). Behavior is fused with character, as the devious action and its actor become one in the deviant. This process entails the general categorizing of persons according to previously developed stereotypes (Schur 1971:38–50) and the subsequent placing of some specific person in the general stereotyped category by offering greater precision, more extensive documentation and evidence. This greater specificity seeks to provide some sense of consistency between the actor's behavior and character, as well as the treatment accorded him/her.

Retrospective interpretation seeks to transform publicly the doer of deviance into an outsider, specifically by labelling that person as such. While almost everyone breaks rules, often of a serious nature, without being caught or labelled, people persist in thinking only of the publicly identified rule breaker as qualitatively different from others. Labelling has as its purpose to cut off the rule-breaker from the rest of society by invoking the socially shared presumption that one thus labelled is essentially and qualitatively different from other members of society, an "outsider," "a special kind of person." The deviance is personified so that the person can be impersonalized.

Retrospective interpretation often takes place by subjecting alleged deviants to biographical scrutiny and character reconstruction. Such analysis begins with the present and looks back for information to clarify the present: some unrecognized character defect present in a person's biography or some events symbolic of a character consistent with the current deviant episode. Or, if nothing of the sort is forthcoming, then psycho-physiological examination, which looks for evidence of duress, brainwashing, evil spirits, etc., may take place. Retrospective interpretation then seeks new facts or the interpretation of old ones in an effort to establish consistency between the actor's deviant behavior and his or her character in order to explain the discreditable conduct and legitimate the label.

Official interpretation is the task carried out by imputational specialists, whose output is to be found in case records. Imputational specialists are found in those places where deviant actors are "served" or "treated": clinics and hospitals, jails and prisons, police stations, welfare agencies and so forth. In these places, imputational specialists are those functionaries who assemble information about selected aspects of a person's life and aid in assigning a person to the status of a deviant. Their task is to contribute to the unanimity of belief that the person in question is deviant by character, the type of person he or she is alleged to be.

> The importance of unanimity derives from the fact that its absence promotes conflict. In the absence of substantial agreement regarding the character of the actor, the legitimacy of regarding and responding to the person as deviant

is jeopardized, and the propriety of the labelling agency is called into question. Lacking the united front that unequivocal agreement provides, the alleged deviant may well claim to have been falsely accused and successfully avoid being labeled. Consensus among the labelers, on the other hand, serves to neutralize the accused's effort at resistance. By effecting consensus, then, the task of recasting achieves greater legitimacy and is more likely to succeed; that is, the actor will officially be certified as an "outsider" (Pfuhl 1980:178).

In compiling the "record," information is chosen selectively, specifically to validate the label, diagnosis or other attribution. Positive information is left open to doubt or ignored. Furthermore, data supportive of the label are expressed unequivocally. Consequently, little by way of professional neutrality can be expected. The collective accumulation and collation of such data bolstering judgments of deviance are a matter of partisanship, serving the interests and needs of organizations that process deviants.

As usual in bureaucracies, the individual person often takes on far less importance than the content of the case record. Furthermore, the use of such records serves to totally depersonalize the individuals to whom they refer. This establishes the distinction between the impersonal, non-credible, untrustworthy person and the personified, credible and trustworthy file. The file, of course, is filled with information created by various investigative bodies. If the investigative body consists of psychiatrists, for example, the file will contain the prevailing psychiatric interpretation of reality and the investigative body will find mental illness an appropriate label in this instance, because that is what it is trained to see. Similarly, if the investigative body consisted of purity experts, Torah experts or Roman governors, they will investigate in terms of a purity, Torah or Roman expert's interpretation of reality and will find uncleanness, infractions or insubordination because they have been trained to look for and find uncleanness, infractions and insubordination.

The outcome of retrospective interpretation inevitably entails the following elements:

(1) Responsibility affirmed: The deviant will be duly assigned responsibility for his deviant action. In the process, it will be noted that the deviant freely chose to act as he did, hence was fully in control, able to cease and desist when requested to, but freely refused to.

(2) Injury affirmed: It will be affirmed that injury or harm did indeed result from the deviant's actions; hence those actions were certainly deviant and immoral. It was not friendly antagonism, mischievousness or concern for Torah application, but downright viciousness that motivated the deviant's behavior.

(3) Victim(s) affirmed: Because of the damage done to so many (parents, friends, the ill, etc.) there is nothing about the deviant's case that might even remotely suggest forgiveness for rule-violating behavior. The victims are morally innocent, the deviant morally vicious.

(4) Condemnation: The deviant is condemned by all concerned: the populace at large, local officials, regional officials. This condemnation restores honor to the condemners and brands the one condemned as morally reprehensible. Thus, public attention is focused on the shame of the deviant.

(5) Appeal to authority: The condemnation and the deviant label will be justified by appeal to some higher-order norm: God's will, the good of the people, the honor of the nation and the like.

2.2c Status-degradation rituals. The activity of retrospective interpretation and the work of imputational specialists are said to culminate in status-degradation rituals (Garfinkel 1956:420–24). Status-degradation rituals are a process of publicly categorizing, recasting and assigning a moral character to deviant actors, resulting in a total change of their identity to that of a deviant. This new identity rests upon what the alleged deviant has done, as well as why he is supposed to have done it. Behavior moves into character and the two become one, a new "type of person" who would do what the actor is alleged to have done.

This transformation takes place in various social settings (trials, hearings, screenings) in which degradation rituals are expressive of moral indignation. Settings are denunciatory, the actor stigmatized. In the process of this denunciation, the actor's former identity is virtually destroyed and a totally new identity established. And so:

> The work of denunciation effects the recasting of the objective character of the perceived other: The other person becomes in the eyes of his condemners literally a different and new person. It is not that the attributes are added to the old "nucleus." He is not changed, he is reconstituted. The former identity, at best, receives the accent of mere appearance . . . the former identity stands as accidental; the new identity is the "basic reality." What is now is what, "after all," he was all along (Garfinkel 1956:421–22).

As we shall see, Jesus' arrest and trial served as a status-degradation ritual proper to his alleged career as a "deviant," culminating in his public humiliation and crucifixion. According to the classic definition of a ritual, Jesus is set apart for trial, judgment and castigation (separation), then crucified (liminality), then put in the tomb (reaggregation). The entombment marks the successful completion of the degradation ritual! Matt 27:62–66 informs us of those who wanted to insure the success of the process.

2.2d Interrupting the labelling process. In preparing for a status-degradation ritual, those officiating must be in control of the "clarity of moral meaning." This phrase refers to the point that right before labelling, an accused person's act must be perceived and assessed to be an *uncommon event* (particularly heinous, terrible, repulsive, etc.). In other words, the act must first be judged to be unconstrained (it might have been otherwise) and then be judged to have violated an important social rule. In this case, clear moral meaning is a requirement for the application of sanctions.

As the existence of the gospels themselves demonstrates, those opposing Jesus and his faction were not fully successful in maintaining clarity of moral meaning. Early on, some of Jesus' followers sought to obfuscate that clarity and provide an alternative retrospective interpretation. All the Synoptics offer information about traditions, hoping to reverse the labelling of Jesus as deviant (Cadbury 1937), while M provides some items of specific value in Jewish polemic (guards at the tomb: 27:62–66; 28:11–15). The whole tradition describes the usual neutralization ploys whereby Jesus escapes the negative labelling process.

How do persons simultaneously uphold institutional values in word and sentiment, yet violate them behaviorally? How do they overcome the unfathomable chasm between saying one thing and doing another? The technique is called *neutralization*. Using techniques that neutralize internalized constraints prior to engaging in deviant behavior enables one to deflect self-disapproval that results from internalized proscriptive norms. Pfuhl (1980:65–68) notes five possible techniques that are the obverse of the five elements of retrospective interpretation just discussed:

(1) Denial of responsibility: refers to the avowal that one has no control over one's actions, that one is driven by external forces to act (compassion, God's will, poverty, insanity, ignorance); thus one is essentially blameless because he or she is more acted upon than acting, e.g., God's will in the death of Jesus.

(2) Denial of injury: is rooted in the idea that the morality or deviance of one's behavior depends upon the injury or harm resulting from those acts. If unsettling activity caused no harm, it cannot be deviant. In Jesus' case the argument would run that his behavior caused no injury to anybody; as a matter of fact, it proved only helpful to those aided, as well as to Israel as a whole.

(3) Denial of the victim: refers to the procedure of redefining the status and role of the victim of deviant behavior in order to legitimate that behavior. The person whom the alleged deviant injured is not really a victim deserving of sympathy or recompense, but someone who deserved what happened to him, who had it coming to him. The victim is thus redefined as moral deviant, with the agent as legitimate moral avenger. Responsibility for rule-violating behavior is accepted and injury admitted, but both are presumed to be fully justified and warranted.

(4) Condemnation of condemners: refers to the rejected person's own moral condemnation of those who disapprove, reject or condemn the deviant. Jesus' behavior throughout his trial and execution was fully honorable. His condemners, on the other hand, proceeded quite shamefully and underhandedly. By condemning his condemners, it becomes an honor to have been rejected and condemned by such "morally reprehensible" people; the alleged immorality of one's condemners is taken to be far greater than anything done or likely to be done by one condemned. In this way, as in the actual gospel story line,

public attention is focused on the condemners rather than on the deviant, and the behavior of the condemners is seen as more reprehensible. This technique redirects the negative sanctions and condemnation from the deviant to the rule enforcers, which seems to be the prevalent technique underlying the Passion Narrative.

(5) Appeal to higher loyalties: refers to the justification of deviant behavior, which explains it as the outcome of a choice in a role conflict that is based upon some higher-level norm. In the gospel narrative, the use of the Hebrew Scriptures is crucial in this appeal (see Matt 26:56; 27:9). People often find themselves faced with conflicting demands as a consequence of inconsistency in the same role or in contending roles (see Malina 1986b). The choice of one set of values, demands or expectations entails the violation of another. The violated values, demands or expectations are then defined as being of lesser importance, while the ones followed are defined as being of greater importance for a host of reasons: time constraints, God's will, value to others, etc. Examples include avoidance of obligations to one's family in order to preach the gospel; association with known deviants (sinners and tax collectors) to facilitate their turning to God; recruitment of a large following due to healing activity yet denial of any intention to use the power potential of that following and the like.

Obviously, the only time people feel that they have to neutralize behavioral constraints is when they in some way share the values and norms of the prevailing social institutions. To neutralize is to explain in such a way that the accusations against one's behavior are no longer valid. Such neutralization, when carried on within the precincts of one's own conscience, is called rationalization or self-justification. In any case, the point is that the only time we feel the need to rationalize or justify behavior that others see as transgressing is when we view it as a transgression as well. Hence, one's conscience is activated only when one behaves against norms that one previously has accepted and adopted. To act against one's conscience requires neutralizing those norms that block action. Similarly, constraints keeping people from shoplifting need to be neutralized only when the potential shoplifter believes shoplifting to be forbidden and undesirable. Hence, the fact that early followers of Jesus sought to neutralize claims that Jesus was deviant indicates that most subscribed to the norms and views of the Pharisees and held the elites in great respect.

However, it is possible that the person accused of deviant behavior has previously rejected the prevailing conventions and advocated an alternative, even contrary perspective. To return to the example of the shoplifter, it is possible for the potential shoplifter to have previously rejected the notion that the goods in a given store actually belong to another person, or to have come to believe that all goods belong to all U.S. citizens or that taking those goods is restitution, not stealing. Thus, some rule-violating behavior would be intended to destroy the society's system of power, to change policy by means of violence and to remove those exercising power in the system forcibly. If countervailing structures are perceived to threaten the interests of dominant groups, they are necessarily deviant. In this case, Jesus' followers will not be perceived as peaceable, but as troublemakers worthy of sanctions. Our description of the early Matthean community indicates that this was indeed the case.

Furthermore, some rule-violating behavior eventually becomes morally indifferent, i.e., neither good nor bad in general estimation. For example, the Matthean group members eventually associated with non-Jews, a piece of behavior ostensibly favored by the Sadducee elites and their relationship with the Romans. Hence, Jesus' concern for the house of Israel and his avoidance of non-Jews goes by the boards. For non-Jewish members of the group, much of the typically Jewish interests witnessed in Matthean sources became truly irrelevant and often meaningless.

2.3. The Model: Part Two
Reactions to Deviance Labelling

Step 2. The Transformation Process: From Deviant to Prominent

Not all attempts at deviance labelling succeed. For, while labellers are working to label someone a deviant, it frequently happens that the one they attempt to label has some power, influence or loyalty that might be activated to avoid the deviant label. In this second part of the model we will examine reactions to deviance labelling depicted in Matthew, either from Jesus himself or from the faction(s) loyal to him. Not only are reactions to deviance labelling important for a full understanding of the labelling process, these reactions are of considerable interest in the description of Christology "from the side." Such reactions often set the groundwork in which we may begin to discern the outlines of a prominence process, the successful transformation of an attempt at deviance labelling into an occasion for prominence labelling (see Table 1, p. 43).

Obviously, the retrospective interpretation of the career of Jesus presented in Matthew derives from a group that believed in the prominence of Jesus. Given what the traditions about Jesus report, it is clear that between the time of the acknowledged condemnation and labelling of Jesus as public deviant and the writing of the retrospective interpretation of his career, a faction or set of factions transformed his status from deviant to prominent. It would be in this earliest phase that the hypothetical sources and/or documents used by the Synoptics belong: Q, M, even Mark as a source of Matthew (or Luke). All these collections presume an ongoing retrospective interpretation of Jesus toward the extremely positive end of the spectrum. From a social science perspective we have adopted here, we now ask what typical or necessary actions would have to be taken by the Jesus factions if they were to react successfully to the deviance labelling of their founder.

2.3a Neutralizers. The primary task at this early stage was to neutralize any dissonance within the initial group of Jesus' followers after word of his degradation began to spread among those who knew him. This neutralizing process is a mirror image of the deviance process. If in creating a deviant, one needs rule creators, rule enforcers and deviance processors and the like, a successful reaction to this process would require comparable figures: those who proclaimed the ambiguity of the rules, who transformed the rules and who acted as the transformation-processing agency. Neutralizers are needed to counter the deviance process.

(1) Rule ambiguity: The initial neutralizers of the labels attached to Jesus were moral entrepreneurs within a specific faction opposed to and in conflict with those who branded Jesus as deviant. It was in their interest to demonstrate the ambiguity of the behavior assessed as deviant by Jesus' accusers: his practice of witchcraft, his sedition against Rome, his misleading of Israel and his recalcitrant relationship to his own family.

(2) Rule transformation: Moral entrepreneurs who espoused the cause and person of Jesus needed to transform what was assessed as ambiguous about "Jesus the deviant" into something positive, thus neutralizing previous negative labels. Those who would have concurred with this neutralized interpretation of Jesus' behavior formed the initial group of Israelites who accepted the interpretation of the core faction. Rule transformation marked the first stage of persons adhering to the Jesus-movement group in response to the activity of central disciple makers and acclaimers of Jesus.

(3) Neutralization processors: This looks to the agents and agencies responsible for neutralizing the accusations against Jesus. Undoubtedly it was some persons among the first followers of Jesus who effected the initial neutralization of those accusations. And as these first followers recruited their own abiding factions, these groups would serve as enduring agencies both of secondary neutralization and of primary prominence processing.

2.3b Retrospective interpretation. If these neutralizers were to be truly successful, they would have to evaluate Jesus positively, focusing their retrospective interpretation of Jesus apologetically so as to replace the negative interpretation elaborated by his detractors. The gospel of Matthew as we have it is surely the best evidence of a concerted retrospective interpretation of Jesus. But prior to that final redaction there were earlier collections of material that functioned in the same way. Perhaps this is where the Q traditions and pre-Markan blocks (e.g., Mark 2:1–3:6; 12 and the basic Passion story) fitted in. These are the extant remainders of the first successful retrospective interpretations of what Jesus' activity was thought to mean, including the acceptance of Jesus as normative interpreter of Torah, at least for a core group. It is with these articulations and the moral entrepreneurs of this stage that a successful status-elevation ritual was effected and acknowledged by the core group and its subsequent followers.

2.3c Status-transformation rituals. Like all rituals, a status-transformation ritual would have three phases to it: separation, a liminal phase and reaggregation. What is involved is the usual social line-crossing process, only here the result is the transformation of the status and/or being of a person. The first phase is separation: the one to be transformed is set apart and prepared for the process. Then the person is placed in the liminal or transitional phase, neither here nor there, unbounded by anything but sheer existence. Finally the person passes over and through the transitional phase and is reaggregated on the other side, as it were, now fully transformed and treated accordingly (see Turner 1969). Minimally, what had to take place at the opening stages of the regrouping of Jesus movement followers after his execution and appearance was some assessment of Jesus as separate, as set apart by God, from all that was generally available in Israelite experience up until then. This perception of separation would have to be coupled with some initial appreciation of his liminal situation with God on behalf of his group, of Israel and eventually of "all nations." Of course, this appraisal developed with the help of the neutralization procedures sketched out above. Yet, even when fully neutralized, the objections against Jesus required final resolution with the confirmed acclamation of Jesus as truly prominent. Some display of Jesus as Messiah with power was required to demonstrate final, successful reaggregation. Clearly, the lack of this sort of reaggregation, usually called the delay of the Parousia, remained the lurking problem.

2.3d Reinterpreting the labelling process. Among Jesus' followers there was some general acceptance that Jesus indeed had successfully completed a ritual of status transformation, soon to be demonstrated with his assumption of power as God's Messiah. The initial results of this general acceptance were the first notable reinterpretations of Jesus that might put him into the "outsider" category in such a way that one might in fact be warranted to say that perhaps there was nothing commonly human, usually human or normally human about him at all. With these first attempts at relabelling, we find ourselves on the path to Jesus' acclamation as prominent.

We have seen, then, the social science models that are needed to understand labelling and deviance, as well as the model for understanding typical and successful reactions to this process. We turn now to Matthew 12 to examine that text-segment once more in the light of these models.

2.4   The Model Applied

The labelling approach to deviance provides a useful model for understanding Matt 12:24–32 and in fact 12:22–45. In Matthew's account, it is apparent that in 12:24 the Pharisees negatively labelled Jesus as "demon-possessed." They "say a word against the Son of man," implying that he did not have God's Holy Spirit, but an unclean spirit (12:30–31). Since the attempt to affix a negative label to Jesus belongs to the same tradition studied in the previous chapter, we are reminded that Jesus is described in a highly conflictual situation, as the holy agent of God proclaiming a radical perfection in keeping God's law and as God's prophet who detected and exposed evil, especially evil disguised as good. This context, then, is one of intense conflict, rivalry and contentiousness. It portrays an attempt by Jesus' rivals and enemies to label him a deviant.

The negative label defining Jesus as demon-possessed was an act of social retaliation against Jesus. It was aimed at decanonizing him, that is, proving that he was assuredly and permanently a non-saint or a minion of God's enemy, the Devil. If such labelling were successful, Jesus would have become in fact what he was called. For all concerned he would have become a permanent "outsider," rightly ostracized from the synagogue and from Jewish society. He and his teaching would necessarily be avoided. He would become a "deviant."

2.4a Interest groups. Jesus' healing of a "blind and dumb demoniac" (12:22) became the occasion for the Pharisees to label him as "demon-possessed." His dealing with that demoniac was perceived by them as completely unwarranted trafficking with demons. For them, it sufficiently underscored and uncovered a typical and abiding characteristic of Jesus' personhood. In the eyes of his opponents, this healing/exorcism became a symbol of all that was wrong with Jesus. He associated with deviants (the blind, the dumb); he broke rules, and this sufficiently indicated to them his permanent disregard for purity concerns (for example, 12:1-8, 9-13); he had contact with demons. Matt 12:22, then, indicated to the Pharisees that Jesus was a voluntary and incorrigible rule breaker.

As we noted in the exposition of the model, deviance theory pays particular attention to the labellers themselves: how and why they label another is rooted in their own interests, as well as in the interests of the group that creates rules and would have them enforced, and how and why they react to alleged deviance is the result of their being threatened or fearful of the deviant.

Although the triple tradition narrates an incident in the gospel story at which challenging moral entrepreneurs mobilize against Jesus, the specifics about that incident differ from gospel to gospel. Thus:

Matt 12:14: But the Pharisees went out and took counsel against him, how to destroy him. Jesus, aware of this, withdrew from there. And many followed him.

Mark 3:6: The Pharisees went out, and immediately held counsel with the Herodians against him, how to destroy him. Jesus withdrew with his disciples to the sea, and a great multitude from Galilee followed, also from Judea and Jerusalem and Idumea and from beyond the Jordan and from about Tyre and Sidon a great multitude hearing all that he did, came to him.

Luke 6:11: But they (the scribes and the Pharisees) were filled with fury and discussed with one another what they might do to Jesus.

Consequently, it is in the segment in which accusations of demon possession are alleged against Jesus that Matthew portrayed the Pharisees as moral entrepreneurs representing an interest group in opposition to what Jesus stood for.

On behalf of this group, they instigated a deviance process against Jesus. This is in itself a compositional change in the narrative, inasmuch as the original Q tradition in which this episode was embedded apparently did not identify the labellers. In point of fact, Matthew has made this identification quite specific. First he stitched together the Markan report of the Sabbath controversy (Matt 12:1–14//Mark 2:22–3:6) with the Q accusation of demon-possession (Matt 12:22–45//Luke 11:14–26). Inheriting from Mark the identification of those critical of Jesus' Sabbath observance as "Pharisees" (Mark 2:24; 3:6), Matthew simply edited all of chapter 12 to clarify that those who contested Jesus' Sabbath observance were the same people who attempted to label him negatively. In short, Matthew has concentrated the conflicts of Jesus into this single, extended narrative.

Sabbath Conflict

Matthew	*Mark*
The Pharisees saw it and said (12:2)	The Pharisees said (2:24)
But the Pharisees went out and took counsel against him to destroy him (12:14)	The Pharisees went out and immediately held counsel with the Herodians against him (3:6)

Demon Accusation

Matthew	*Luke*
But when the Pharisees heard it, they said "It is only by Beelzebul . . ." (12:24)	But some of them said "He casts out demons . . ." (11:15)
Then some of the Scribes and Pharisees said to him (12:38)	When the crowds were increasing, he began to say (11:29)

Matthew, moreover, has prepared us for this major conflict scene in chapter 12. He already questioned the righteousness of the Pharisees, first when this "brood of vipers" came to John for repentance (3:7), and then when Jesus demanded that the righteousness of his followers exceed that of the Scribes and Pharisees (5:20). And he narrated in 9:34 that on a previous occasion the Pharisees took offense at Jesus' healing of a "dumb demoniac" and tried to label him "demon-possessed" even then. It was that episode that conditioned the reader for the conflictual narrative in 12:24.

Matt 9:32–34	*Matt 12:22–24*
1. a dumb demoniac healed	a blind and dumb demoniac healed
2. positive crowd reaction: "Never was anything like this seen in Israel"	positive crowd reaction: "Can this be the Son of David?"

Matt 9:32–34	*Matt 12:22–24*
3. negative labelling by Pharisees: "He casts out demons by the prince of demons"	negative labelling by Pharisees: "It is only by Beelzebul, the prince of demons, that this man casts out demons"

Yet the narrative in chapters 8–9 provides scant evidence of Jesus' conflict with the Pharisees, and it does not allow for a negative judgment on Jesus in virtue of the healing miracles. The brief mention of conflict in 9:32–34 would seem to function as a literary foreshadowing of the debate that will rage in chapter 12. That mention seems intended to prepare the reader for a future conflict, much as the Infancy Narrative suggested certain themes that would be developed later in the narrative (Brown, R. 1977; Nolan 1979).

But why were the Pharisees identified as the interest group that engaged in the deviance labelling of Jesus? Although it is difficult to know much about the first-century Pharisees, their emergence as the rule creators and moral entrepreneurs of village and synagogue life is not at all implausible. The writings of Jacob Neusner are of considerable help in understanding the Pharisees and their concerns, as the following summary of his remarks will indicate:

1. The Pharisees were a collection of factions consisting of Torah-concerned laymen, who even though not priests, nevertheless sought to extend into the lives of ordinary Jews the concerns of ritual purity usually associated with priests and Temple.
2. Pharisees were especially known for their ritual-purity rules that organized and classified things, times, persons, etc. It was integral to their sense of "separateness" (or holiness) to be able to know and determine what was permissible or proscribed, clean or unclean.
3. Pharisaic purity concerns were especially focused on agricultural rules, which specified not only what might be eaten, but out of which dish or vessel and with whom one might eat. Included here is Pharisaic concern over tithing of foodstuffs, for this indicated what foods might be eaten in ritual cleanness.
4. Pharisees developed traditions that either clarified and specified the Scriptural laws or amplified the Law's principles, making them applicable to new situations. Their tradition extended a hedge around the Law (Neusner 1973b).

Neusner's data include two passages from Matthew that illustrate this summary description. Matthew repeated the Markan reports of the controversies between Jesus and the Pharisees:

(a) Jesus ate with tax collectors and sinners (Matt 9:11//Mark 2:15–17).
(b) Jesus did not keep a strict Sabbath observance, especially in regard to agriculture and eating (Matt 12:1–8//Mark 2:23–28).

Jesus, then, might be perceived by the Pharisees as not keeping the customary purity rules of his society (Neyrey 1986:107–9), a point noted by these rule enforcers. The Pharisees, moreover, may be called rule creators as well, for it was part of their strategy to build a hedge around the law so as to protect it; this was the purpose of their "traditions":

> (c)   Jesus did not keep the washing rites, "the tradition of the elders" (Matt 15:2//Mark 7:2, 5).

It would seem to have been part of the strategy of being a Pharisee to be zealous for the Law, both in the building of a hedge around it and in guarding that hedge against transgressions. It would hardly seem accidental, then, that the Pharisees would be portrayed as the moral entrepreneurs of Israel's purity system, as the rule creators of a tradition that protected this system and as the rule enforcers who stepped in to blow the whistle on those who would violate it.

Rule creators and moral entrepreneurs are not assured of success in a given society. In a typical village, the synagogue would be peopled with Jews holding a variety of opinions on how to live as a Jew (Simon 1967), the Pharisees being but one party in the synagogue. And they need not have been particularly numerous or powerful. Yet they staked a claim to be the teachers of Torah. They formed interest groups of moral entrepreneurs who aspired to leadership roles, for they claimed the authority to specify just what constituted purity and pollution. These interest groups, moreover, found themselves more threatened by Jesus than by the usual Mediterranean agonism that characterized social interaction within their own groups, for Jesus was also a teacher and leader, yet he proclaimed a Torah different from that of the Pharisees. Conflicting claims, then, were the background of the labelling in Matthew 12. The crowds that observed Jesus' actions were "amazed," and, we are told, they began to label Jesus positively as a legitimate leader: "Can this be the Son of David?" (12:23). This, of course, represented a clear threat to the Pharisees. No wonder they appeared to be fearful of Jesus! According to the flow of the narrative, this fear mobilized them to label Jesus negatively as "demon-possessed" (12:24).

The Pharisees proceeded to define Jesus' dealings with the "blind and dumb demoniac" as inimical to their own interests. As "the Separated Ones," they avoided all uncleanness and especially contact with the blind, the dumb and sinners. They saw this rule as essential to being a righteous Jew, for the avoidance of all uncleanness implied that one was in a state of purity such as that maintained in the Temple, where God was encountered. Because of Jesus' contact with physically deviant people (the blind) and by his dealings with moral deviants (sinners, the possessed), according to 12:22 the Pharisees banned his action as something bad, evil and wrong.

They did not keep this displeasure to themselves (as in 12:14). Although they openly criticized Jesus for his Sabbath violations (12:2, 10) and privately "took counsel against Jesus how to destroy him" (12:14), it was pivotal to their strategy to publicize their negative labelling of Jesus before "all the people." As good moral entrepreneurs, they strove to marshall public opinion in favor of their interpretation of Jesus' action. They explained the healing incident in such a way that their remarks might be perceived as another extension of their guardianship of Israel's purity—a positive value shared in varying degrees by all Jews. Their interpretation of Jesus, moreover, attempted to link his dealing with the blind and dumb demoniac (12:22) to other violations by Jesus of Israel's purity rules (for example, violation of Sabbath observance in 12:1–13). In the process they positioned themselves not only as the ones knowledgeable about purity concerns but as the unique guardians and champions of those concerns. Comparably, they attempted to show how this one action of Jesus was characteristic of Jesus' complete disregard for Israel's purity rules. Stereotypes were created on both sides; polarities were drawn up between the good and the bad.

In this, the Pharisees are depicted as engaged in the process of rule enhancement, that is, "converting" others to the values of their interest group. We noted above that in varying degrees, all Jews espoused "purity" as a value. The Pharisees' own particular ideology (that is, set of values, attitudes and beliefs, which a group holds to mark itself off from other contending groups and which binds its members together) was enhanced by this appeal to "purity." Consider the ideology developed by the Pharisees opposed to Jesus:

1. Society (fellow Jews) is in grave and immediate danger as a result of Jesus and his group.
2. Jesus is dangerous because his behavior is degenerate (he is a sinner, an associate of sinners and the like).
3. He is unable to control himself because he is controlled by some larger, evil force (Satan, demons).
4. This condition makes him identifiable as a potential threat to Israel's peace and security.
5. Hence, he should be banned, exiled, punished and never be free to inflict harm on others.
6. Or else his freedom (and readmittance to society) must be dependent upon his being truly exorcised and duly repentant.
7. The care and treatment of people such as Jesus should be the concern of professional social managers, such as scribes, priests and Pharisees, who are best equipped to deal with him.

At this point in the narrative, however, the Pharisees seem to stand alone as Jesus' enemies and rivals. Although they tried to disseminate their interpretation of Jesus' behavior as deviant, they seem unable at this point to make the labels stick or to persuade the crowds that Jesus constituted a major threat to Jewish life. There seem to be no groups with which they might form alliances against Jesus, and no prominent people whom they might enlist on their side. The situation at Jesus' trial will be quite different, as coalitions will be formed against Jesus and broadening social respectability gained by enlisting testimony against Jesus. But in chapter 12, the strength of the interest group appears to be much too weak to create and enforce a rule against Jesus.

2.4b *Deviant status.* As the Pharisees engaged in the labelling drama, they would understand Jesus' deviant status as due to his own choices. It was *achieved* deviance. Thus, Jesus' alleged deviance was not an ascribed characteristic or quality, such as blindness, illegitimacy, gender or age, but his own achievement based on his public, overt action, which was or should have been banned.

The specific deviant label that the Pharisees attempted to affix to Jesus is "demon-possessed healer": "It is by Beelzebul, the prince of demons, that this man casts out demons" (12:24). To be a "demon-possessed healer" was to be deviant, since such a healer performed his task by virtue of the power of the Evil One who dwelt within him. Such a healer was clearly co-opted by the forces of evil and situated within the realm of the prince of demons. Jesus, then, was alleged to be "out of place" as regards Jewish values and practice to such an extent that he was not simply a one-time rule breaker but a type of person who always had been and would irrevocably continue to be an enemy of God according to the canons of Jewish righteousness. A master status was being created for Jesus as that of "Evil Deceiver," who was in league with God's enemy, the Devil. While things might appear otherwise, the fact was that nothing he did in healing was good; all was evil. Hence, even the apparent good he did was but a masking of seductive evil.

2.4c *Retrospective interpretation.* As the Pharisees engaged in the process of labelling Jesus as a deviant, they might be said to be developing a retrospective interpretation of Jesus. The present incident (12:22) allowed them to consider Jesus according to the stereotype of an "out-of-bounds" person. Jesus' past public actions and his character were scrutinized and past instances of his deviance were noted (12:2, 10): he broke the Sabbath; he ate with sinners and tax collectors (11:19//Luke 7:34). Through selective instances, they would describe Jesus as a person who always and purposely disregarded purity rules (see 15:1, 12). This official interpretation of Jesus was created by the local imputational specialists, the Pharisees, whose place in the synagogue was that of those who know what constituted purity and pollution.

2.4d *Status-degradation rituals.* The Pharisees clearly were engaged in a status degradation ritual. This was not a formal courtroom trial, such as Jesus would endure later in the Passion Narrative, but it was a trial nonetheless. In public forum before "all the people" (12:23–24), the Pharisees charged Jesus with and labelled him as being "demon-possessed." Status-degradation rituals are intended to shame or publicly dishonor an alleged deviant. Some accuser calls upon all those present to witness that the deviant "is not as he appears but is otherwise and *in essence* of a lower species" (Garfinkel 1956:421). A new and negative identity is given to the deviant. He or she is reconstituted as new person. He is now what, "after all," he was all along—a "deviant."

And this is what occurs in Matthew's narrative. The Pharisees clearly sought to dishonor Jesus in public by their deviance label. They wished to point out that this person, who claimed to speak for God and to deal with sin and sinners, was not what he appeared to be, but was of the opposite camp, the realm of the Devil. He claimed to speak for God but in fact acted as the servant of the Devil: "It is by Beelzebul, the prince of demons, that this man casts out demons" (12:24). Through the deviance-labelling process, Jesus would be reconstituted as having been demon-possessed all along, even from the beginning of his career. At least such would be the case if the status-degradation ritual were successful.

2.4e Reactions to deviance labelling. A person accused of being a deviant can engage in many strategies (we follow the strategies listed by Rogers and Buffalo 1974:101–18). Jesus, of course, did not acquiesce in the label of "demon-possessed," nor did he flee the village or synagogue to start afresh where he was not known. To acquiesce in a deviant label or to flee and begin anew elsewhere are two of the strategies available to a negatively labelled person. Among other alternatives, we find Matthew describing Jesus' response as including repudiation, evasion and redefinition.

(1) Repudiation: Jesus' first strategy toward the deviant label was an immediate repudiation of being "demon-possessed." Assuming that allies do not wage war against each other, Jesus put forth an analogous argument to prove that he and Satan were not allies but mortal enemies (Neyrey 1986a:110–11). Every kingdom divided against itself is laid waste; no city or house divided against itself will stand; if Satan casts out Satan, he is divided against himself. How then will his kingdom stand? (12:25–26). No! Jesus was not demon-possessed, but the enemy of Satan. The deviant label was false!

(2) Evasion: Then Jesus is described as engaging in evasion strategy. This strategy consists of using techniques of neutralization to produce justification for one's reputedly deviant behavior (see Sykes and Matza 1957 and Pfuhl 1980). We have previously noted how those in the early Jesus-movement groups sought to neutralize the accusations of deviance levelled against Jesus, their faction founder. Here we note how according to the story line, Jesus himself was said to have neutralized accusations by denying responsibility, by denying injury to others, by denying that any one has been a victim, by condemning his condemners and by appealing to higher loyalties. Consider each of these in turn:

(a) Denial of responsibility: The accused might insist that he was not responsible for his deviant behavior. For example, deviant behavior might be due to forces outside the individual and beyond his control, such as parents, companions, neighborhood influences and the like. The gospel rightly recalls at this point Jesus' commissioning by God, whereby God's Holy Spirit came upon him and impelled him to certain behavior: "Behold my servant whom I have chosen, my beloved with whom my soul is well pleased. I will put my Spirit upon him and he will proclaim justice to the Gentiles" (12:18). This reminds

Matthew's readers/hearers of Jesus' baptismal commissioning by God: "This is my beloved Son, with whom I am well pleased" (3:17). At that programmatic event, "The Spirit of God descended on him like a dove" (3:16). Jesus was then "led by the Spirit into the wilderness to be tempted by the devil" (4:1). Responsibility for Jesus' dealing with the Devil or with those possessed by demons, then, rested with God and God's Spirit, not with Jesus. In fact, Jesus asserted that to speak against this Holy Spirit, which he claimed motivated him, was a verbal insult that can find no forgiveness: ". . . blasphemy against the Spirit will not be forgiven . . . whoever speaks against the Holy Spirit will not be forgiven, either in this age or in the age to come" (12:31–32).

(b) Denial of injury: Jesus has harmed no one by his exorcism of the blind and dumb demoniac (12:22). He himself has not been harmed, nor has society. On the contrary, he positively healed someone, surely a good thing (Neyrey 1986a:111–12).

(c) Denial of a victim: The only person harmed in the encounter is Satan himself, for Jesus bound the "strong man" (Satan) and "plundered his house" (12:29). Yet Satan could hardly with any sympathy be called a "victim." He was the mortal enemy of God and humankind who ought to be bound, defeated and plundered. He deserved this!

(d) Condemning the condemners: With this strategic move, the focus of attention is shifted from the behavior of the alleged deviant actor to the motives and behavior of those who disapprove of his or her violations. The condemners, it can be claimed, are themselves hypocrites and deviants in disguise; they are impelled by personal spite (Sykes and Matza 1957:668). In Matthew, this seemed to have been Jesus' strategy. We note the following:

(i)   Jesus argued that his accusers were themselves "sinners" who blasphemed against the Holy Spirit of God (12:31–32) and so they were hypocrites in their charge that Jesus was "demon-possessed" or evil.

(ii)   Jesus condemned their labelling, charging that on the day of judgment they would account for every careless word; for "by your words you will be justified, and by your words you will be condemned" (12:36–37).

(iii)   He then condemned them for not being able to read the signs of the times correctly. His casting out of a demon must logically be construed as a sign that "the kingdom of God has come among you" (12:28//Luke 11:20). Having given the sign of exorcism, Jesus became irate when the Pharisees subsequently "wished to see a sign" from him (12:38//Luke 11:29). He condemned their culpable blindness to his many signs (12:22, 28), which should have proved that he was "greater than Jonah . . . greater than Solomon" (12:40–42//Luke 11:30–31).

(iv)   Finally, he resorted to his own deviance labelling of his condemners. They were like a person dispossessed of an unclean spirit, who, when discovered to be "empty," was repossessed by the original demon and "seven other spirits worse than itself" (12:45//Luke 11:26). In context, the Pharisees are the ones like the dispossessed person in question. They were the "Separate Ones" who were originally purified of evil. But they were "empty" and so were recaptured by an evil infinitely worse than what had possessed them at first. Their attempt to label Jesus negatively was now interpreted as deviance on their part, proof that they were religious hypocrites (23:13, 16, 23), that they were deviants in disguise (23:25–27).

(e) Appeal to higher loyalties: Jesus admitted the behavior that had caused this controversy. He did expel the demon, but he did so in loyalty to God, who sent him to proclaim the kingdom: "If it is by the Spirit of God that I cast out demons, then the kingdom of God has come upon you" (12:28//Luke 11:20).

(3) Redefinition: Jesus sought to redefine the situation. He adamantly rejected the negative label and continued the behavior (see the exorcisms in 15:22 and 17:18). What was previously labelled "deviant" came to be called "normative" for Jesus. The characteristic behavior of Jesus, then, remained the same, but society had altered its view and redefined the deviant behavior in positive terms of approval.

The model of labelling and deviance, then, offers a fresh, insightful and coherent scenario for understanding the attempts of the Pharisees to dishonor and ban Jesus. This model, moreover, demonstrates what Christology "from the side" looks like, both in terms of the attempts of the labellers to evaluate Jesus in a negative way and in terms of the transformation process whereby Jesus and/or his followers neutralized the alleged deviant label.

2.5   The Models Compared

The same datum of accusation of demon possession has been considered according to two different models, witchcraft and labelling/deviance theory. At this point it may be helpful to compare the results of the use of these two models. There is clearly a high degree of agreement in the profile of the situation in Matthew according to both these models.

In the first place, the same accusation of demon-possession can be called either a witchcraft accusation or a deviance labelling. Second, in both cases, the charge was said to have been made by a group that perceived itself threatened and attacked by the alleged witch or deviant. Third, in either case, the accused needed to be processed by a specialist: (a) the "witch" needed to be discerned by a figure who could read the truth behind the surface and spot the attacking witch, and (b) the deviant needed to be labelled and processed by a special moral entrepreneur. Fourth, the purpose of the witchcraft accusation or deviant label was roughly the same: to maintain the status quo and its values and institutions by the expulsion or ostracizing of the alleged witch or deviant. Fifth, in both cases, the accusers or labellers may be said to act out of self-interest or the rivalry of conflicting self-interest. Finally, in both models, a similar defensive strategy was described whereby the accused or labelled person might resort to a comparable charge or negative label against the very accusers, condemning the condemners.

The two models, then, offer complementary and confirming assessments of the same conflictual dynamics. The models differ, however, in significant ways. The witchcraft model derives from cultural anthropology, which is ever sensitive to cross-cultural and comparative differences. It both indicates how the label is a typical stereotype and also offers a plausible explanation of why the most damaging accusation or label in Mediterranean societies is precisely that of "demon-possession." Labelling theory cannot adequately assess these features, largely because the theory belongs to sociology, that is, the study of U.S. society by Americans. It has no built-in, cross-cultural concerns to offer an adequate scenario of Mediterranean culture. Apart from thriller films and esoteric groups, U.S. sociologists, as well as most mainstream Americans in general, have no particular interest in Satan, demons or demon-possession as such. Furthermore, witchcraft modeling attunes us to the important cultural perception of pervasive deception that exists in groups rife with contentiousness and rivalry. Things are not what they seem: evil masquerades as good and "Satan is disguised as an angel of light" (2 Cor 11:13). This makes salient the need in this type of society for persons who can read hearts, unmask hypocrisy and discern the inner truth. Similarly, witchcraft models offer a window into the systematic aspects of the charge of demon-possession, as it describes the cosmology of the social system that employs such accusations with predictable frequency. This systematic overview offers a plausible and successful scenario that enlightens many diverse aspects of the text and relates them in a coherent way. Its coherence and comprehensiveness are a welcome guide to clues for reconstructing the social experience of the group that engaged in such accusations.

The deviance model, on the other hand, invites us to investigate more carefully the role of the labellers, their position in society, their motivation and the procedure they follow in labelling a deviant. The deviance model also outlines the strategies available to those negatively labelled. Whereas the witchcraft model offers a comprehensive and coherent view of the social system, deviance theory serves as a more refined tool for unpacking the specific factors and elements in the conflictual process recorded in a text such as Matt 12:22–32. In short, we see the two models as fundamentally complementary and confirming. Together they offer a precise, detailed and culturally specific way of examining the dynamics of conflict in biblical texts. Given the specifics of the culture of the time and place, such dynamics involved Jesus as well as Paul and other early Christians well into the time of Constantine.

What image of the early Matthean community do these two models suggest? A minority, but a threatened group, the Pharisees acted in rivalry and out of self-interest to attack Jesus and his followers. Jesus' faction was a contender of theirs in the process of trying to reform Israel's ideology in the chaotic second-temple period. Some Pharisee group selected a specific instance of Jesus' behavior and interpreted it as a typical character trait of his, as an indicator of what he really was: demon-possessed. In this, they resorted to the dualistic stereotypes of observant/non-observant Jews. Posing as the legitimate guardians of Israel's purity, as the figures who were competent to deal with threats to that purity, they accused and labelled Jesus so as to ostracize him and remove him from leadership contention.

The attack on Jesus seems to have failed, and both models point to reasons for the failure. According to the witchcraft model, since authority is weak in witchcraft societies, and since definitive solutions to conflict are rare, the nature of the contentious dynamics in such reciprocal accusations and rebuttals predictably emerges in stalemate. Thus, given the unchanging cultural script followed in the Roman-controlled, Eastern Mediterranean of the first century, without recourse to and intervention by elites, the Pharisee-Christian challenge and riposte would inevitably result in stalemate. On the other hand, according to deviance theory, non-elite labellers were unable to label Jesus successfully, both because they proved incapable of persuading the public that Jesus' exorcism was an evil thing and because Jesus enjoyed considerable resources (honor from the crowds, influence) so as to resist the label. The results from both models suggest a continuing conflict in which mutual accusations and labels continued to be hurled back and forth. Jesus was never successfully canonized by the populace, nor did the Pharisees successfully ban him. The record of Jesus' success in honor-shame contests with his rivals suggests that the accusations and labelling continued, but without definitive success. Jesus continued to be attacked, harrassed and challenged, and so it remained until he ran afoul of Jerusalem's elites. This interaction is described at length in the reinterpreted degradation ritual called the Passion Narrative, which is the concern of the next chapter.

Jesus on Trial

Labelling and Deviance Theory in Matthew 26–27

3.1 Introduction

Given the agonistic quality of Mediterranean society, past and present, we believe it is safe to say that in public Jesus was continually engaged in conflict. This conflict came to a climax with his arrest, trial and execution in the section of the gospel story usually called the Passion Narrative. This segment of the gospel text has always attracted special attention; some have even described the gospel itself as a Passion Narrative with an introduction (Kähler 1964:80). The dominant questions with which scholars have addressed this part of the gospel have tended to be of a literary and historical nature. These approaches, however, will be of little use now, since we will consider this part of the gospel story within the perspective developed in the last chapter, namely labelling and deviance theory.

We have occasionally alluded to this section of the gospel in our development of the model of deviance. While they may at first seem alien to Jesus' suffering and death, labelling and deviance offer the prospect of a coherent view of the conflictual dynamics of the episodes recorded. For example, although the Passion Narrative is composed of individual episodes, each with its individual history and redaction, deviance theory suggests how the whole in fact coheres. This is important for several reasons. Perhaps the fundamental one has to do with the nature of the Passion Narrative as a piece of language. Literary forms or literary genera are not part of language. They cannot be studied in terms of linguistic categories. The reason for this is that literary forms and genera derive from social systems, not from linguistic systems. Hence, to understand and interpret a literary form or genus, one must necessarily understand the social system realized by means of language in a literary piece.

In order to see how the Passion Narrative coheres, we need a scenario deriving from social behavior, and it is deviance theory that enables us to produce such a scenario. Its models provide a vantage point for an overall view of Passion Narrative episodes, along with fresh insights into the various strategies of the antagonists and protagonists. The models allow for a scenario that provides fresh appreciation of the emotional importance of the dishonoring of Jesus in the trials and the mocking. This type of approach, then, offers insights into typical patterns of conflict and the strategies necessary to achieve or thwart them, and so offers an adequate scenario for interpreting this vital series of events in the New Testament story.

71

As the evangelists tell the story, toward the end of Jesus' career he went on pilgrimage up to Jerusalem for the festival of the Passover. This journey represents not only a shift in geography (from Galilee to Judea) but a shift in the focus of Jesus' activity and a shift in the personages who form the cast of the drama told in the story. Jewish life in Galilee centered around the synagogue with its contending assortment of would-be leaders and factions, including Jesus' group, Pharisees and others. None of the persons encountered in the Galilean period of Jesus' life belonged to the elite of the Jewish nation, much less to the elite of Roman imperial society. Local elites were one thing, and Jesus engaged in conflict with these elites with impunity.

The national and international elites, however, were quite another category to trifle with. Furthermore, the issues of conflict in Galilee dealt with general practices of Jewish life: Sabbath observance, purity rituals and the like. These largely symbolized commitment to God and solidarity with one's fellows. They were the practices that underscored common elements in the shared meaning of everyday life. But Jerusalem, the scene of Jesus' arrest, trial and execution, was the home of Israel's temple, its major shrine. It symbolized many things: God's power, Israel's sacred ethnic and cosmic center and the way of life of God's holy people. The temple was staffed and administered by a clearly defined, elite social group, the priestly aristocrats, who were people of pre-eminent, inherited honor, hence people of wealth, learning, influence and power. Jesus' advent into Jerusalem and its temple meant his coming to the very symbolic center of Israel's life. As center, Jerusalem in general and the temple specifically served as the national touchstone, the norm for all dimensions of life in God's land. Thus, Jesus' arrival became the occasion for a new and remarkably different set of conflicts with the legitimate guardians and administrators of the temple, hence of national norms.

We must remember that Matthew's account of Jesus' suffering and death is just that—his account of those events, which was acceptable and approved by his community. There is surely a wealth of history contained in this account, but it remains a "version" of the events, ostensibly from a faction whose remote founder lost in his encounter with national and international elites. With this in mind, we now turn to sketch Matthew's Passion Narrative from the perspective of deviance and labelling theory.

3.2   Interest Groups

As we noted in the previous chapter, the conflict that issues in the process of deviance labelling is managed by representatives of some specific interest group. An interest group consists of people whose interests are threatened by the behavior of some person whom they consider deviant. Interest-group members are the active or supporting moral gatekeepers of the values and structures being offended. From their ranks often derive individuals who serve as pre-eminent moral entrepreneurs. In turn, interest-group members frequently function as rule creators for the society at large. And these rule creators likewise command rule enforcers.

Jesus' arrival in Jerusalem was marked simultaneously by his coming into immediate conflict with a full range of interest groups. Gradually, the chief priests (and elders) took the initiative and became the controlling group in the developing set of interactions. In the process of taking control, they quickly moved to label Jesus as a deviant. In general, the narrative describes Jesus' stay in Jerusalem in chapters 21–24 as a period of continuous and intense conflict with all the major political factions of his day.

That these "religious" groups are more accurately described as "political" derives from the fact that in the social system of that day, religion was embedded in politics and kinship (Malina 1986d). In Jerusalem among Israel's elite, it was religion as embedded in politics that held sway. The criticism of religion was essentially and automatically political criticism, just as it is in Iran today. To criticize Judaism was to criticize Israel and its political center in Judea. Priests in charge of God's temple were directly or indirectly in charge of God's land, supported by divinely willed taxes paid by God's people. The significant feature of Jesus' stay in Jerusalem is that now one of the political factions that Jesus attacked would finally emerge as the interest group that succeeded in having Jesus labelled a deviant, to the satisfaction and conviction of the city's populace.

Matthew describes Jesus' initial interaction among the city's inhabitants in terms of questions and answers. To a Mediterranean audience, these questions and answers are in fact veritable verbal challenges and ripostes. Specifically what do these episodes mean? Some time ago, David Daube (1973:158–69) pointed to a passage in the Babylonian Talmud (*b. Nid.* 69b–70a) which, from a form-critical perspective, seems to have considerable bearing on the traditional synoptic account of Jesus' conflict in Jerusalem. The passage reads:

> Our Rabbis taught: Twelve questions did the Alexandrians address to R. Joshua b. Hananiah. Three were of a scientific nature, three were matters of *aggada*, three were nonsense and three were matters of conduct.

The four types of questions need to be more adequately explained as:

(a) questions of a "scientific nature": halachic questions about the application of the law to specific situations;

(b) questions of "aggada": supposed contradictions in the non-halachic portions of Scripture;

(c) "nonsense" questions: attempts to ridicule a scholar and his interpretations;

(d) "matters of conduct": questions that deal with theoretical principles of behavior in the Torah, issues larger than halachic questions of specific practices.

Jesus' conflicts in Matthew 21–22, then, may be schematized according to this pattern of four types of questions:

(a) A "scientific question" is asked of Jesus by the Pharisees: "Is it lawful to pay taxes to Caesar or not?" (22:15–22).
(b) A "nonsense" question is put to him by the Sadducees on the hopelessly complicated nature of levirate marriage, which is intended to ridicule Jesus' teaching on the resurrection (22:23–33).
(c) A question about "principles of behavior" comes from a lawyer who asks what is the great commandment in the Law (22:34–40).
(d) The "aggadic" question, however, is not asked of Jesus by any group, but rather Jesus queries the assembled Pharisees about the contradiction in the Scripture, whereby the Christ is said to be both "Son of David" and yet David's "Lord" (22:41–46).

According to the literary arrangement of Matthew 22, Jesus intentionally engages and bests each of the major political groups in Jerusalem on every type of question. The successful outcome proves that he is superior to all of them. The scope of the conflict, then, is sweeping in terms of the types of questions asked and comprehensive in terms of the groups engaging Jesus. Yet these are not yet the central elitist groups that rise up to arrest, try and execute Jesus.

Matthew received an account of Jesus' last days in which Jesus is described as coming into conflict for the first time and quite immediately with the Jerusalemite chief priests and the scribes. It is they who will ultimately emerge as the interest group that prosecutes Jesus. His first action upon entering the holy city is the "purifying of the temple" (Mark 11:15–19//Matt 21:12–13), an attempt at rearranging matters in a sacred place. This act necessarily led to a confrontation with the temple guardians (Mark 11:27–33//Matt 21:23–27), who were themselves quite sure about the temple arrangements required by God. As far as the rest of the gospel story is concerned, this act sets the tone and meaning for what follows. As Matthew reworked the narrative of Jesus' Jerusalem conflicts which he received from Mark, he gave increasingly more attention to the emergence of the chief priests and elders as Jesus' new and most dangerous opponents. This is clear from the following points:

(1) Matt 21:14–17: Whereas Mark 11:15–19 merely told of Jesus' "temple purifying," Matthew records an addition to the story in which "the blind and the lame came to him in the temple, and he healed them" (21:14–16). According to Lev 21:17–18, the blind and lame are cultically unclean people; because impure, they must *not* come into the holy temple (Malina 1981:137). Criticism of Jesus' welcome of these unclean people and his curing of them in the holy temple is raised by the appropriate interest group: "The chief priests and the scribes . . . were indignant" (21:15). They object, moreover, to the positive labelling of Jesus by the crowds: "Hosanna to the Son of David" (21:15). At this point the antagonists here are simply not able to act against Jesus in the face of this massive public approval of him as an honorable figure. But the lines of conflict are clearly drawn; the central interest group simply waits for an

appropriate time to act. Matthew has highlighted Jesus' apparent disregard of the existing temple arrangements and what they stood for in the popular mind. Thereby he promoted these inaugural events in Jerusalem as programmatic statements of the conflict that will surely follow.

(2) Matt 21:23–27: Matthew's version of Jesus' second day in Jerusalem begins with a confrontation between Jesus and the chief priests and elders in the temple. In this Matthew has followed his Markan source, but his tight editing of the episode draws our attention to several points. It is characteristic of Matthew to telescope the details and narrative events of stories about Jesus. Whereas Mark has Jesus enter Jerusalem, then walk about the temple where the priests curiously confront him, Matthew focuses the story quickly and to the point.

Matt 21:23	*Mark 11:27*
And when he entered the temple,	And they came again to Jerusalem, and as he was walking in the temple,
the chief priests and the elders of the people came up to him as he was teaching.	the chief priests and the scribes and the elders came to him.

Matthew's version dramatically sharpens the conflict: the place is the temple, where Jesus is teaching, and where the temple authorities demand to know his authority.

The essence of this confrontation consists in a factual, political question about Jesus' authority, not an academic or theoretical question about Torah. The question itself is a hostile challenge to Jesus to justify his maverick behavior: "By what authority are you doing these things; and who gave you this authority?" (21:23b). Although the setting is the temple on Jesus' second day in Jerusalem, the narrator intends his audience to relate this demand for credentials to Jesus' "cleansing of the temple" on the previous day (21:12–17). The location is the same, the temple; and the antagonists likewise are the same, the chief priests. In 21:15 the chief priests objected to the "marvels which he worked," whereas in 21:23b they demanded to know by what authority "you work these works." In other words, the previous conflict was not allowed to pass. Ambivalent and maverick actions in regard to the temple, especially at a time of pilgrimage and festival, could not be permitted to go unchallenged, if only because they threatened the values and status of the Jerusalemite elites.

As the story progresses, Jesus answered the chief priests' question about his authority with a counterquestion, a typical defensive move in an honor-shame interaction (Malina 1981:32–34).

A   *Question of the chief priests to Jesus:*
"By what authority are you doing these things, and who gave you this authority?"

B   *Counterquestion of Jesus to them:*
      "I will ask you a question; and if you give me an answer, then I will tell
      you by what authority I do these things."
C   *Challenge:*
      "The baptism of John, whence was it?
      From heaven or from men?"
C′   *Challenge unanswered:*
      They argued among themselves:
      "If we say 'From heaven,' he will say to us, 'Why then did you not believe
      him?' If we say 'From men,' we are afraid of the multitude, for they hold
      that John was a prophet."
B′   *Unanswered counterquestion:*
      So they answered: "We do not know."
A′   *Unanswered question:*
      And Jesus said to them: "Neither will I tell you
      by what authority I do these things."

The story is a classic example of a public loss of face, for it describes how one
answers a question with a question and so puts the original challenger/ques-
tioner on the defensive. The result is a grant of honor for the victor, and shame
for the vanquished, who was the original challenger. Yet such public shaming
requires satisfaction for injury done, and Matthew's Mediterranean audience
would expect to hear about that shortly in the narrative.

Even apart from this, the story forces the audience to reach back and to
stretch forward. The answer about Jesus' authorization takes the audience
back to Jesus' baptism (3:17–18) and transfiguration (17:5) where, the author
told us, he was commissioned as God's authorized Son. The answer looks
forward to Jesus' trial before these same priests when they will again question
him under oath about this authority as God's "Christ" and "Son." This episode
functions as a major incident in the growing conflict between Jesus and the
Jerusalemite priestly elite who will emerge as the major interest group in having
Jesus labelled a deviant. At present Jesus clearly has the upper hand in the
conflict, yet he is playing a most dangerous game with deadly opponents on
their home turf.

(3) Matt 21:28–46: Confrontation with the chief priests continues unabated
in Matthew's narrative through a series of parables told about these central
authorities. Mark 12:1–12 records a parable by Jesus about the failure of
tenants to tender fruit to the owner of the vineyard. At the conclusion of the
parable, Mark 12:12 merely records "*they* tried to arrest him," which probably
indicates that 12:1–12 was addressed to the same group that had just engaged
Jesus in conflict, "the chief priests, the scribes and the elders" (11:27). Matthew, however, tells three parables in succession, all of which in virtue of their
content and proximity have to do more explicitly with Jesus' own public
criticism of this very group of Jerusalemite elites. Consider the initial vineyard
parables.

The first of Matthew's vineyard parables, Matt 21:28–32, contrasts obedient
and disobedient sons. The parable works in a dialectical manner, contrasting a

son who said he would go to work but did not with a son who initially said no but finally did go and work. Matthew records Jesus' addressing this parable to the group who had just challenged his authority to tamper with temple arrangements, namely the chief priests and the elders. The interpretation of the parable that follows in 21:31–32 likens the chief priests and elders to the first son, and the tax collectors and harlots with the second son. Aside from being insulting, this interpretation reverses the popular perception of who is observant and who is not. While Matthew seems not to have composed this parable himself, he locates it here in combination with the vineyard parable in 21:33–46 to reinforce the polemic against Jesus' opponents in Jerusalem. Jesus' conflict with the chief priests, then, is a matter of prime concern to the narrator.

Second, in Matt 21:33–46, we find that Matthew basically repeats Mark's version of the vineyard parable. But by joining it with the previous vineyard parable in 21:28–32, Matthew sharpens its bite. He heightens the drama of the story as well:

(a)   According to Matthew, more servants are sent and these are even more shamefully treated, according to his version.

(b)   The justice meted out to the murderers of "the Son" is quite emphatically narrated by Matthew. According to him, Jesus engaged in a question-and-answer session with his hearers in which he caustically asks the very people with whom he is in conflict what justice these murderers deserve. And they respond, "He will put those wretches to a miserable death and let out the vineyard to tenants who will give him the fruits in their season" (21:41), ironically passing judgment on themselves. Such narrative embellishment serves only to heighten the conflict between Jesus and the chief priests.

(c)   The power of this account lies in the way Matthew has Jesus' opponents pass judgment on themselves. For in another Matthean addition, Jesus repeats their own words back to them as a prophetic judgment:

Their Judgment (21:41b)	*Jesus' Judgment (21:43)*
"He will let out the vineyard to other tenants who will give him the fruits in their season."	"The kingdom of God will be taken away from you and given to a nation producing the fruits of it."

(d)   Whereas Mark 12:12 only implied that this second vineyard parable was addressed to "the chief priests, scribes and elders," Matthew makes it quite explicit, with the addition of v. 45, "When the chief priests and the Pharisees heard his parables, they perceived that he was speaking about them."

(e)   As in Mark 12:12, Matthew narrates that they "tried to arrest him"; but he also notes that their mobilization of action against Jesus is blocked by the honor granted Jesus by the multitudes acclaiming him a "prophet" (21:46b).

Matthew's narrative, then, has carefully indicated that Jesus' conflict in Jerusalem begins and remains at an extremely intense level with all of his significant rivals. Yet first and foremost among Jesus' antagonists are the chief priests and elders, who immediately become and remain Jesus' premier opponents. According to the labelling theory previously sketched out, we should expect a particular group to emerge from among Jesus' many opponents, who would become *the* major interest group. This group would initiate the deviance process against Jesus, although other interest groups might be equally concerned. And in the story, it is the Jerusalemite chief priests and elders who come forward as this central interest group, with concerned groups not too far in the background (22:15–16: Pharisees and Herodians).

After a period of intense conflict, the group that first attempts in 21:45–46 to arrest Jesus is described as finally mobilizing its resources for a more concerted effort: "The chief priests and the elders of the people gathered in the palace of the high priest, who was Caiaphas, and took counsel together in order to arrest Jesus . . . and kill him" (26:3–4). Their plan receives a boost from the offer by Judas to betray Jesus to them (26:14–16). The chief priests, then, who had been Jesus' major critics in Jerusalem, emerge from a pack of Jesus' enemies as his chief antagonists who would arrest him (26:47), have him tried (26:57–58) and executed (27:1–2). Consequently, for the Matthean community, they were the major interest group. But why should this group emerge in this role? Why not the Pharisees, as in chapter 12? Is this simply a random fact of history? A bias on the part of the Matthean community? Or are there sufficient data in the narrative that might suggest, when processed through the deviance model, why this group quite obviously must have taken the initiative in Jesus' destruction?

Interest groups serve both as rule creators and ultimately, as rule enforcers, for even if interest group members do not directly enforce rules, they surely control those who do enforce them. Interest group members function as moral entrepreneurs who indicate to their society that certain actions by some alleged miscreant are deviant in a system to which all are committed. The deeds of the disturber of the peace are of such a magnitude that they threaten the system and those most directly benefiting from the system. Hence, the deviant actor must be curtailed. What did the central Jewish authorities find objectionable in Jesus? It is surely a tautology to state that the chief priests have to do with Jerusalem's temple. Theirs was the task or role of administering and guarding the system centered in the temple and symbolized in its farthest implicit reaches by the temple. If the U.S. flag stands for liberty, freedom and the American way, then the temple stood for what pleased God at the center of God's creation at the center of God's own land, which was meant for God's own people. Yet the narrative emphatically describes Jesus as acting unconventionally and even antagonistically toward the temple. A full explanation of how "temple" functioned as the primary symbol of Jewish life in first-century Palestinian Judaism would detour us from the present task (Neusner 1973a,

1978). But even a brief explanation would greatly facilitate an understanding of how and why the chief priests became the major interest group in the affair with Jesus. To this end, we sketch a few of the main elements that might clarify the importance of the temple in Palestinian Jewish life at the time of Jesus.

The temple was more than a building. It symbolized a system or encoded a set of values that found structural expression there. Most basically, the temple expressed the presence of the God of Israel in terms of that primary relational value so emphasized in the Scriptures, namely God's holiness: "Be ye holy as I am holy" (Lev 11:44–45). "Holiness" in this case meant morally sanctioned order and classification (Douglas 1966:41–57). Even ordinary Jews would understand that God's first act and therefore God's programmatic action was creation, and that creation purely and simply entailed an act of ordering and classification. Such ordering and classification resulted in a purity system, a system of lines marking off a place for everything. Given the fact, however, that it was God who marked off, defined, set the limits of the purity system, this system was not simply one among many systems. It was an exclusive system, exclusive to the God of creation, the God of Israel. Just as there is but one God, so there can be only one act of creation and one purity system. This system, consequently, was the exclusive system created and chosen by God. Now purity plus exclusivity results in the sacred, in holiness. Thus, in that act of creation, the exclusive God expressed his "holiness" by creating a series of specific and exclusive maps for the proper location and identification of all things in the world. The result, of course, is the sacred order willed by God:

(a) *maps of persons:* Adam was created bodily whole and set apart from the rest of creation, and so pure and holy; he is then the ideal, prototypical person;

(b) *maps of things:* Earth and sea creatures were created in full and perfect form; no hybrids were created, such as are prohibited by Leviticus; each creature was assigned its own proper food, the first dietary rules;

(c) *maps of time:* Six days were assigned for work, with a seventh day for rest and festival; and so the principle of a calendar is established;

(d) *maps of places:* Each creature was assigned its proper sphere; sea creatures should stay in water and not come on land; sky creatures should stay in their proper sphere and not hop about on the earth (Soler 1979).

The priestly account of creation in Genesis 1 reflects the basic pattern of God's holiness-as-order. It is the official program that should serve as a basis for correct living as members of God's covenant (Lightstone 1984:7–10).

This sacred order of God, moreover, is replicated in the temple as its most concrete expression and symbol. Like creation, the temple is carefully mapped out, but mapped out precisely according to the system encoded in the account of creation:

(a) *maps of persons:* Only physically whole people may enter the temple (Lev 21:18–21); the priests must be bodily whole, as well as have pure bloodlines for full priestly pedigree;

(b) *maps of things:* Only unblemished offerings may be made, and offerings only of clean animals, which by definition are those which fully correspond to the perfect species made at creation;

(c) *maps of places:* There is clearly a hierarchy of space in the temple, as the following text indicates:

1.   The Land of Israel is holier than any other land . . .
2.   The walled cities (of Israel) are still more holy . . .
3.   Within the walls (of Jerusalem) is still more holy . . .
4.   The temple Mount is still more holy . . .
5.   The Rampart is still more holy . . .
6.   The Court of the Women is still more holy . . .
7.   The Court of the Israelites is still more holy . . .
8.   The Court of the Priests is still more holy . . .
9.   Between the Porch and the Altar is still more holy . . .
10. The Sanctuary is still more holy . . .
     The Holy of Holies is still more holy . . .

(m. Kelim 1.6–9)

Corresponding to this graded sense of progressively holy space is an indication of what persons may stand in what space:

1.   Gentiles: outer parts of temple
2.   Women: closer within temple
3.   Male Israelites: still closer
4.   Priests: sanctuary of temple
5.   High Priests: Holy of Holies.

And so the map of places indicates a series of concentric circles whose movement is from the exterior to the interior and that indicates a progressively holier space in proportion to proximity to the Holy of Holies in the temple. Like the map of places, people are mapped in terms of grades of holiness, which corresponds to the degree of proximity to the holiest part of the temple.

(d) *map of times:* The temple's calendar is a map of what feasts are celebrated when, what offerings are to be made according to the calendar, when Israelites should make a pilgrimage to the temple, etc.

In conclusion, the premier purity value of Judaism, God's exclusivity-in-order, is found first in Israel's Scriptures, where the Genesis account of creation expresses this order. Then it is found in its temple, where God's perfect order, hence holiness, is replicated once more. All of this serves to explain the importance of the temple in Israelite ideology. It also explains the significance of the role of the chief priests as rule creators and rule enforcers of things pertaining to the major symbol system of the traditional faith of Israel. Their role, then, is that of moral entrepreneur, safeguarding the fundamental cultural cues of perception that are symbolically encoded in the Jerusalem temple (compare Barton 1986).

If the chief priests are the guardians and administrators of the major symbol system, how has the text of Matthew described them vis-à-vis Jesus and his actions in the temple? It is hardly accidental that the sole charge against Jesus in his Jewish trial is hostility to the temple: "This fellow said, 'I am able to destroy the temple of God . . .'" (26:60–61). When questioned about this charge, Jesus remained silent. Such silence was equivalent to pleading guilty to the charge, for then as now, silence means consent. Recall that the interest group in Matthew 26–27 consists of chief priests and landed aristocrats (elders) whose role it was to tend the major symbols of Israel's life and culture. Obviously, these major symbols supported their standing in the community, the order undergirded by law and custom. Consequently, they were expected to enforce known rules relating to the temple and to serve as entrepreneurs of the values and structures encoded in it (Cassidy 1983:148–62).

3.3 The Labelling Process

As we saw in the last chapter, the process of labelling someone a deviant might be broken into four phases: (a) the labelling and banning of the deviant, (b) the dissemination of the label through the seeking of broader support, hence respectability, (c) the actual processing of the deviant by the creation of a retrospective interpretation of the deviant's life and (d) a status-degradation ritual, such as a trial with negative outcome.

3.3a Negative labelling. The text of Matthew clearly indicates that the chief priests (and elders) attempted to brand Jesus as a deviant. More specifically, they charged him with being a non–observer of the temple system (26:61), a blasphemer against all that Israel held holy (26:65) and a deceiving charlatan (27:63–64). Of course, "Israel" here means the Jerusalem aristocrats. On the other hand, we do not find in this Passion Narrative any precise negative label attached to Jesus such as "thief," "assassin," "insurrectionist" or the like. The closest we get to such labelling is the priests' ironic gibes at Jesus with titles and identity tags that even they considered utterly false and pretentious. For example, they ask Jesus under oath to declare if he were "the Christ, the Son of God" (26:63), clearly signalling their conviction that he could not be such in virtue of his hostility to God's temple. In reaction to his oath, they mock him with the label of "prophet" (26:68). And as he hangs on the cross, they ironically taunt him again for his claim to be God's holy, anointed one: "He is the King of Israel . . . he said, 'I am the Son of God'" (27:42–43).

While no definite negative label is attached to Jesus in this process, the whole degrading interaction underscores that fact that he was a thoroughgoing deviant worthy of utter contempt. Thus, the major features of labelling Jesus as deviant are found in the priests' ironic and ostensibly preposterous labels: "Christ," "prophet," "King of Israel" and "Son of God." From their perspective, no one who claims to be God's favorite (27:43) could either attack God's temple or come to such an ignominious end. Labels of honor are ironically used to dishonor Jesus as a presumptuous, insolent non-conformist. These labels function in the Passion Narrative much as sarcastic labels we might use, for example, "Mr. Know-it-all" or "Ms. High-and-mighty" or "Mrs. Holier-than-thou."

Although the deviant labels applied to Jesus are used in irony and sarcasm, the text gives us a clear sense of a search for an overarching master label for Jesus, such as "sinner" or "blasphemer." In the search for an appropriate negative label, "the chief priests and the whole council sought false testimony against Jesus" (26:59). In other words, they search for the appropriate charge against Jesus to label him a deviant. The search initially proves fruitless (26:60). But finally, two witnesses come forward and claim: "This fellow said, 'I am able to destroy the temple of God, and to build it in three days'" (26:62). Matthew's version of this process differs from his Markan source on several small points, a consideration of which can help us to grasp the importance of the charge in 26:62.

Matt 26:60–63	*Mark 14:57–61*
1. Witnesses: "At last two came forward and said" (26:60)	"False" Witnesses: "Some stood up and bore false witness against him" (14:57)
2. Jesus' claim: "I am able to destroy the temple of God and in three days to build it" (26:61)	Jesus' claim: "I will destroy this temple made with human hands, and in three days I will build another not made with human hands" (14:58)
3. Status of Testimony:	Status of Testimony: "Yet not even so did their testimony agree" (14:59)
4. Question by the high priest and Jesus' silence: "Have you no answer to make? What is it that these men testify against you?" But Jesus was silent (26:62–63)	Question by the high priest and Jesus' silence: "Have you no answer to make? What is it that these men testify against you?" But he was silent and made no answer (14:60–61)

Matthew's characteristic telescoping of narratives (Vanhoye 1967:9) only serves to heighten whatever compositional changes he might make in the narrative. First, unlike Mark, Matthew does not brand these witnesses as "false witnesses," nor does he indicate that their testimony "did not agree." It is implied, then, that the charge should be taken as an accurate account of Jesus' position. Whereas in Mark, Jesus is alleged to contrast the present temple with a future, even messianic temple (Juel 1977:143–57), Matthew notes only that Jesus was accused of speaking against "the temple of God," a Matthean turn of phrase found also in 21:12 and implied in 23:19–22. There is no attack on the temple as a mere physical building, as in Mark; it was "the temple *of God*" that Jesus would destroy, and so the affront was all the stronger. Matthew's audience would then realize that Jesus' claim "to destroy" the temple would have been heard as a claim to profane the place where God dwells, a most serious charge indeed (see 24:15). Jesus' silence, however interpreted, would be seen from the perspective of the chief priests to be an admission of the charge. And it would seem to be the case as well for Matthew (see 22:12b).

Prophets of old spoke against the temple, but then they were prophets, figures with legitimate authority, at least in the eyes of subsequent generations. But by virtue of what did Jesus speak against the central shrine? The next logical question becomes the issue of Jesus' identity and authority, and in this sequence the present episode parallels an earlier incident involving Jesus and the temple.

Matt 21:12–16, 23–27	*Matt 26:60–64*
1. anti-temple activity: "cleansing" of the temple (vss 12–16);	anti-temple speech: pronouncement of ruin of the temple (vss 60–61)
2. authority to do this: "By what authority are you doing these things, and who gave this authority?" (vs 23).	request for authority: "Tell us if you are the Christ, the Son of God" (vs 63).

Following the charge of anti-temple activity, Jesus is questioned under oath by the high priest. Mark made no mention of an oath, while the oath has become a solemn feature of the Matthean account. Previously in the narrative Jesus once declared that good Israelites should not swear oaths in business at all (5:33–37; see Lieberman 1965: 113–41). In this antithesis of the Sermon on the Mount, he is described as alluding to the popular debate over gradations of oaths. These were perceived to be the more solemn and binding in business in proportion to the way they were sworn by what is more sacred in the temple (5:33–37). Subsequently, Jesus then criticized this progression of oaths by indicating that when one swears in whatever context by anything sacred in the temple, one swears by God:

> For which is greater, the gift or the altar that makes the gift sacred? So he who swears by the altar, swears by it and by everything on it; and he who swears by the temple, swears by it and by him who dwells in it; and he who swears by heaven, swears by the throne of God and by him who sits upon it (23:19–22).

Jesus contested the current attempt to calibrate the seriousness of oaths in proportion to the object by which they are sworn. All oaths, then, are solemn oaths of the highest degree because they all ultimately summon God as witness. Jesus' oath in 26:63 is just such a solemn oath, "sworn by the living God." He is asked under oath to tell the truth: "Tell us if you are the Christ, the Son of God," and he responds affirmatively. Jesus' affirmative answer corresponds to the answer requested of him in 21:23, "By what authority are you doing these things?" According to Jesus' answer within the general tenor of the narrative, the insight experiences described initially at the Baptism (3:16–17) and again at the Transfiguration (17:5) indicate that God gave him authority and consti- tuted him his anointed Son. Yet in the eyes of the high priest, Jesus' remark suggests that he is an enemy of the temple's sacred authorities. Therefore, he simply could not be "anointed" or "the Son of God." And so Jesus' oath itself is labelled insulting to God's honor, outrageous: "He has uttered blasphemy" (26:56). With this an official deviant label surfaces that seems to sum up the case against Jesus. This is a label that stuck. "You have heard his blasphemy. What is your judgment?" (26:65–66); the court agrees to the label: "He deserves death" (26:66).

Jesus' anti-temple posturing would have been bad enough, but he is per- ceived as making the extravagant claim to legitimation as God's anointed Son. Together, these preposterous avowals would be interpreted not simply as occasional rule-breaking but as the usurpation of status. Such behavior would clearly indicate the type of person Jesus really was: a sinner (anti-temple) who claims to hold exclusive, God-given rank ("christ"), an impossible mixture. The Jerusalem elites then pass judgment on Jesus, crediting him with a deviant master status, that of blasphemer and self-deluded charlatan. In the jargon of labelling theory, this would be an achieved deviance, not ascribed deviance such as blindness from birth. In the eyes of these moral entrepreneurs, he is an evil person masquerading as a sincere figure concerned about God's honor. His claim to be God's anointed is quite obviously blotted out by his engaging in behavior that disregarded God's will and plan, which in fact publicly dis- honored God.

3.3b Dissemination.   The process of labelling Jesus as a deviant and ban- ning him from Israel's life appears in Matthew to be a difficult one. First, although Jesus had many opponents in Matthew 21–23, the opponents could not readily be expected to agree upon very much, since they were fierce contenders, some defending the system and others speaking as voices of reform (Theissen 1977:52–58, 80–87). Their fundamental concern through- out, of course, would not be substantive matters that might alter the status quo, but rather the question of who would benefit by having Jesus condemned. Second, although Mark notes that Jesus was so honorably acclaimed by the populace in Jerusalem that no public move could be successfully made against him (Matt 21:46//Mark 12:12; Matt 26:4–5//Mark 14:2), Matthew adds to this other items of the same stripe. For example, when Jesus enters Jerusalem, "All the city was stirred, saying 'Who is this?' And the crowds said, 'This is the prophet Jesus from Nazareth of Galilee'" (21:11). After Jesus performs healings in the temple and "cleansed" it, children sing praises in his honor (21:15–16), in words seen as the fulfillment of Ps 8:2. Finally, in the course of the Jerusalem challenge-riposte episode in which Jesus parries a set of questions that make do for sword thrusts, Matthew notes that "the crowd heard it . . . astonished at his teaching" (22:33). Even as Jesus' enemies are carefully noted, so are his numerous supporters. It is the approval of those supporters that blocks rapid dissemination and approval of any labelling of Jesus as deviant.

The attentive reader would have noted that the enemies of Jesus are themselves mutual rivals, and that Jesus gains an honorable reputation that would have served to insulate him from any immediate, effective negative labelling. The result is a dramatic stand-off. And yet the outcome is not a total loss for the Jerusalem elites either, for the narrative indicates that the chief priests do launch a moderately successful process of disseminating their deviant labelling of Jesus among Jerusalemite elites. Further, in this process they are able eventually to enlist the support of rival groups and even of the crowds.

3.3c Borrowing respectability. The chief priests are the paramount moral entrepreneurs in the city. Now it is evident from the narrative that these members of the elite themselves actively begin to take steps to denigrate Jesus (26:3–4). After Jesus' arrest, they are instrumental in gathering "the whole council" together (26:59). This would include scribes as well as priests (26:57). The high priest Caiaphas then orchestrates this body's collective labelling of Jesus as a blasphemer (26:66–68).

3.3d Endorsements from prominent figures. The chief priests and elders then successfully disseminate the deviant label among the Romans by bringing Jesus into the governor's custody (27:2) and by accusing him (27:12–13). Moreover, the process of seeking broad support for the labelling of Jesus takes one more step when this elite interest group enlists the Jerusalemite crowds against him. As the following juxtaposed passages indicate, Matthew's version seems to highlight this process of disseminating the deviant label.

Matt 27:20	*Mark 15:11*
Now the chief priests	But the chief priests
and the elders	
persuaded the people	stirred up the crowds
to ask for Barabbas	to have him release
and to destroy Jesus.	for them Barabbas instead.

Matthew remarks that the chief priests and elders "persuaded" the people. Now this suggests a more studied, formal and less mob-like process than Mark's note that they "stirred up the crowds." Matthew also narrates that the chief priests not only seek for Barabbas' release but for Jesus' destruction as well. While this point might be implied in Mark's account, it is not formally noted. Like Mark, Matthew records how this dissemination appears to have succeeded in mobilizing the people of Jerusalem to share in the labelling of Jesus as deviant. Twice they cry out "Let him be crucified!" (27:22–23). This portion of the process climaxes in Matthew's special note about the assumption of responsibility by "the people" : "*All the people* answered, 'His blood be on us and on our children'" (27:25). In one final incident, Matthew especially calls attention to the group that the chief priests gathered at the foot of Jesus' cross.

Matt 27:41	*Mark 15:31*
So also the chief priests	So also the chief priests
with the scribes and	mocked him to one another
elders mocked him.	with the scribes.

In Matthew, they mock Jesus more intensely, laughing at his alleged righteousness or relationship with God: "He trusts in God; let God deliver him now, if he desires him; for he said, 'I am the Son of God'" (27:43). Matthew notes, moreover, how this became the very taunt of those political agitators crucified with him:

Matt 27:44	*Mark 15:32*
And the insurrectionists	Those
who were crucified	who were crucified
with him	with him
also reviled him	also reviled him.
in the same way.	

The chief priests and elders, then, are ultimately successful in disseminating their deviant label of Jesus, not only among the scribes and the whole council, but among the Romans, among "all the people," and finally among those crucified with Jesus. Their achievement in deviance labelling would seem to have been successful precisely in proportion to their ability to borrow respectability and find endorsements in winning various parties and even the Jerusalemite crowd to their point of view.

3.4   Retrospective Interpretation

In the course of establishing a deviant label that might serve to redefine a person, either the interest group or some official agency inevitably will construct a "biography" of the alleged deviant to show that the offensive behavior is not just a single instance of deviant activity but that it represents a total identity, a long-standing pattern or an uncontrovertible indicator of a totally perverse character. A retrospective interpretation of the alleged deviant is made, which selects and highlights data that support the allegation that the deviant always was such, constantly did such or continually was drifting to such activity.

We recall that the charges against Jesus, which form the basis for his being labelled a deviant, are his anti-temple behavior and his pretension to be God's prophet, Son or Messiah. The narrative indicates how in the construction of Jesus' retrospective biography, the moral entrepreneurs in question call up previous incidents in Jesus' career and use them to confirm this long-standing presence of deviance in these two areas. A total retrospective biography, however, cannot be found because we have no records from the chief priests. Yet it is interesting to assume their viewpoint and then to survey the narrative as it stands to see what data they might point to as part of Jesus' being a type of person dedicated throughout his life to anti-temple activity.

To begin with, Jesus appears to have come to Jerusalem with a long-harbored intention to bring down the temple and thus attack all it stood for as the center of Israelite life and culture. After entering the city in triumph, he went to the temple to disrupt its activities, driving out "all who bought and sold," overturning the tables of those who changed currencies for temple services and stopping the sale of pigeons for sacrifice (21:12). He took it upon himself to claim that the temple should be a "house of prayer," not a place of cultic sacrifice (21:13), a point that he had made several times earlier in his career.

The fact is that his anti-temple activity did not begin the very day he entered Jerusalem. For he did indeed employ the words of Hosea, "I desire mercy, not sacrifice" (6:6), both when he attacked established religious customs (12:7) and when he legitimated unusual behavior that flaunted purity concerns dear to the temple (9:13). And he mocked the custom of vowing objects to God, while challenging the reputation of those who would defend this behavior (15:5–6). His motto all along had been ". . . not sacrifice!" Of course, his insistence upon denying such crucially symbolic behavior could mean only "not traditional values or customs!"

Jesus' disregard for the holiness of the temple can be further illustrated by his welcoming of "the blind and the lame" in that holy area (21:14). These are the unclean and unwhole people, who according to Torah are prohibited by God's Scriptural word from the temple (Lev 21:18). When this is pointed out to him by the legitimate authorities (21:15), he scoffs at them, further showing conscious antagonism to the temple and all it stood for (21:16).

The allegation in 26:61 that he invoked the temple's destruction is not false testimony at all according to Matthew, for on one occasion Jesus told his disciples, "Truly I say to you, there shall not be left here one stone upon another, that will not be thrown down" (24:2). And he went so far as to speak of the profanation of the holy temple, alluding to the "desolating sacrilege" of Dan 9:27 that he said would reappear in the temple. No, the charge in 26:61 appears to be quite an accurate summary of his persistent, explicit attitude and behavior toward the temple of God. He always was antagonistic to the holiness of Israel's temple, always egregious in regard to the central symbol of Israel's faith, always hostile to the God-given, Scripture-based values and structures encoded in the temple.

Jesus, however, would justify his maverick stance toward the temple by claiming some legitimation as a prophet or specially anointed agent of God. Even if he did not personally claim this role for himself, he basked in the honor heaped upon him by the ignorant crowds when they acclaimed him such. First, under oath he affirmed the aptness of the titles of "the Christ, the Son of God" (26:64) in his own regard. But he was always accepting such pretentious honors. At his entry into the holy city, he accepted the mob's acclamation of him as "Son of David" (21:9). This behavior was repeated in the temple itself (21:15). He thus basked in the popular, yet unwarranted acclaim that he was a prophet: "This is the prophet Jesus from Nazareth of Galilee" (21:11; see 22:33). He then shrewdly utilized this acclamation to legitimate his criticism of the temple, as he repeatedly used words from the classical prophets in criticism of Israel's central shrine (21:13//Isa 56:7; Jer 7:11).

The chief priests ask him for clarification of his authority to engage in anti-temple activity: "By what authority are you doing these things?" (21:23). Instead of replying with respect, he challenges his God-appointed betters with a riposte, answering their legitimate question with a dishonoring question (21:24, 27). He thus scorns their divinely legitimated authority and unwar-rantedly assumed the popular label of a prophet. And so, he is eventually caught in his pretensions and reproached for being a (false) prophet (26:68) and arraigned for being a (false) King of the Jews (27:11) and a (false) Christ (27:17). He is finally unmasked as an evil person masquerading as an authorized and righteous figure approved by the God of Israel. Jesus' answer under oath in 26:64 is but the latest example of his presumptuous acceptance of honors and titles. He has always been behaving in this way, to the initial irritation and shock of this Galilean opponents and now to the chagrin of legitimate author-ity, to the deception of the crowds and to the profanation of the temple of God. The inquiry in 26:57–68 establishes that Jesus is a type of pretender, a type of deviant. The specific charges made in the trial are not isolated incidents, for he has always behaved in deviant fashion. Jesus' master status, then, is that of a deviant, a blaspheming temple-profaner and a presumptuous fraud.

3.5   Status-Degradation Rituals

After a deviant label has been affixed to someone and after imputational specialists have finished their retrospective interpretation of a deviant's bio-graphy, there still remains the process of publicly categorizing and recasting that person. The intended outcome is the assignment of an abiding negative moral character to a deviant actor. The whole process generally effects a social transformation and total change of identity of the alleged deviant. This trans-formation process, which is a form of status degradation, takes place by means of rituals performed in various social settings. Such status-degradation rituals include trials, hearings, public punishments and the like. The Passion Narrative contains numerous degradation rituals that climax with Jesus' shameful public execution.

The first of these degradation rituals occurs in Jesus' trial before the whole council of Israel (26:57–68). Shameful as it is to be arrested (26:50), that shame is compounded by charges made against Jesus (26:61), to which Jesus appears to acquiesce by his silence. His own solemn testimony under oath is rejected as preposterous and ridiculed (26:65–66). This leads to his dishonorable treatment by the council: "Then they spat in his face and struck him; and some slapped him, saying, 'Prophesy to us, you Christ! Who was it who struck you?'" (26:67–68). This trial of Jesus by his fellow Israelites leads not only to the fixing of the deviant label on Jesus but to a concomittant loss of standing and honor in the eyes of council members. Dishonor is characteristically shown by actions which affront the symbolically honorable parts of a person, the head and face. In this case, it is the striking of Jesus' face and the spitting upon him that underscore dishonor. Spittle, like any bodily excretion such as urine, menstrual blood or faeces, conveyed uncleanness upon contact with another person; Jesus is rendered unclean by the spittle spat in his face. Far from being God's "anointed," Jesus was rendered unclean, a replication of his deviant status outside the realm of decent human beings. The title of honor, "prophet," is now used in a sarcastic manner to ridicule Jesus, accentuating his reversal of status in the eyes of legitimate Israelite authorities in Jerusalem. The trial of Jesus by the council, then, becomes a ritual of status degradation as Jesus is transformed into a properly dishonored, humiliated deviant.

A second trial ensues. And by virtue of its very occurrence this trial serves as another degradation of Jesus. His own fellow Israelites disown him and hand him over to their common captor, the Romans (27:2). The chief priests and elders continue to accuse Jesus of deviance in a new forum. Jesus again remains silent at these accusations (27:12–13), and this further serves to brand him as a complete outsider to Israel. The high point of the Roman trial occurs in the formal rejection of Jesus by his Jerusalemite fellow nationals and in their expression of the corresponding wish to have a "notorious prisoner," Barabbas, released instead (27:15–21). The Roman magistrate allows the Jewish crowd to decide which prisoner would be released "according to custom": "Whom do you want me to release to you, Barabbas or Jesus who is called Christ?" (27:17). Jesus' own fellow Israelites reject him. Thus, they shamefully dishonor him before the Romans, denying him status as one of their own (27:21). Not only do they choose Barabbas, but they twice call for Jesus' shameful death in the Roman manner of execution, "Let him be crucified!" (27:22, 23). The public grant of honor given Jesus by the Jerusalemite crowds upon his entrance into Jerusalem (21:11) is now formally revoked, and instead of acclaiming Jesus' status as that of a revered prophet, the crowds heap reproach and dishonor on him. To be rejected and cut off by one's own, whether family or clan or ethnic group, is surely a total loss of respect and honor. This second trial of Jesus, a public spectacle witnessed by Romans and Jews alike, ends with Jesus' complete loss of any claim to honor and his degradation to the level of disowned, public criminal who is condemned to a shameful death.

In a third instance, the narrative describes in great detail a particularly degrading ritual in the mock investiture of Jesus as "King of Israel." The account of the incident is carefully crafted in typical chiastic form, which serves to highlight the humiliation of Jesus in its central panel:

A   The soldiers took Jesus into the praetorium
B   and they stripped him;
     (and put a scarlet robe upon him;
     (and plaiting a crown of thorns . . .
C   (and put a reed in his right hand . . .
     (and kneeling before him, they mocked him . . .
     (saying, "Hail, King of the Jews!"
B′   they stripped him of the robe
     and put on him his own clothes
A′   and led him away to crucify him.

As the pattern indicates, the importance of the episode has little to do with Jesus' physical pain, a point which came to be emphasized only in Christian medieval piety. Rather, the ironic dishonoring of Jesus as "King of the Jews" becomes the focal incident itself in a parody of royal investiture:

(a) an emperor's robe is put on Jesus (Senior 1975:265–66);
(b) he is crowned with a wreath of thorns;
(c) a reed scepter is put in his hand;
(d) royal soldiers acclaim him sovereign;
(e) they bend the knee before him who is their inferior.

This parody serves as a classic instance of a status-degradation ritual, as the action and intentions of the actors deny Jesus his former status as God's Christ and Son of David. Again, Jesus' head and face are the locus of dishonor, as his head is crowned with thorns and struck with the mock scepter. It may be presumed that the reference to the soldiers' spitting on him implies that his face was the target. The narrative, moreover, insists on the formal character of these actions as degrading; twice it is noted that "they mocked him" (27:29) and "when they had mocked him" (27:31).

The climax of Jesus' status degradation is his public execution by crucifixion in the company of two insurrectionists (27:38). That shameful event is heightened in the narrative by the public disowning of Jesus by all present. First, passersby "derided him": "You who would destroy the temple and build it in three days, save yourself! If you are the Son of God, come down from the cross" (27:40). The deviant labels of temple antagonist and pseudo Son of God, which were established at Jesus' trial, are seen to stick as he is reproached with them by a new group that did not consist of members of the council. Second, the interest group of chief priests with the scribes and elders "mocked him" by calling attention to his alleged devotedness to the God of Israel ("He trusts in God") and God's evident disregard of him by letting him be rejected (27:43). Finally, the political agitators crucified with him "reviled him in the same way" (27:44). Disowned, dishonored and degraded, Jesus dies as the false King of the Jews, the false Son of God. He is proved impotent in face of the legitimate powers of the day. No one comes to his rescue, neither God nor Elijah.

3.6   Conclusion

The labelling model seems to offer many advantages for studying Jesus'
Passion Narrative. Because social science models deal with the recurring typical features in human interaction, as a rule they cannot deal with strictly and
specifically time-bound, historical or factual issues. Yet such models do offer a
coherent framework for producing an overview of the typical dynamics of
conflict that are all too common then and now, i.e., arrest, trial and execution.
The labelling model serves to develop a rather full scenario of what was
reported to have happened in the arrest, trial and execution of Jesus. It results
in such a scenario because the model requires us to highlight aspects of the
narrative that might tend to be ignored or be thought insignificant, but which
are characteristic of typical deviance processes. The model cannot reconstruct
the history of Jesus' arrest, trial and execution; that is neither its purpose nor a
legitimate use of it. But it does offer a sense of the way such conflict tends to
occur and to be perceived, if only to indicate how typical of such conflictual
situations the Matthean account is. The model would at least offer an accurate
scenario of the viewpoint of this one gospel.

And when fleshed out, the model offers plausibility for the account of Jesus'
arrest on several levels: (1) the grounds there were for Jesus' being perceived as
a deviant, a devil in disguise and (2) the reasons why of all Jesus' opponents, the
chief priests might rise up against him and engineer his execution. Further, the
model gives proper emotional weight to the various degradation rituals narrated, indicating how they functioned to reverse Jesus' status from that of
honorable, revered prophet to that of discredited, rejected charlatan.

We have not dealt with the strategy whereby the deviant label affixed to
Jesus might be neutralized, manipulated or obliterated. That is a project worth
much closer investigation, a task to be taken up in the next chapter. There we
will present a model of prominence to illustrate how Jesus was transformed
from a deviant who was executed as dangerous charlatan to a prominent who
was enthroned as Lord of all.

Jesus Proclaimed

Prominence Modelling in Matthew 26–27

This chapter relates closely to chapters 2 and 3, for it continues the work begun in them. We indicated in the initial exposition of labelling and deviance in chapter 2 that just as someone may be denounced as a "deviant," so that same person may be proclaimed as a "prominent." Social scientists do not seem to have developed formal prominence models as they have for deviance. It is, however, our hypothesis that the same basic processes at work in deviance labelling operate as well in prominence labelling. In this chapter, we develop a model of prominence that closely parallels the deviance model presented and applied previously. In terms of modelling, then, chapters 2 and 4 have much in common.

Furthermore, this chapter focuses basically on the same text-segment studied in chapter 3, the Matthean Passion Narrative. But this time we shall search for clues as to how the account of Jesus' ostensibly shameful death as a deviant has been retrospectively interpreted by the Jesus-movement group to serve as an argument for his prominence. Thus chapters 3 and 4, then, have much in common, for they both address Christology "from the side," but from opposite points of view.

The procedure we follow here will be the same as it has been in each of the preceding chapters. When social science models are used for biblical interpretation, we believe it is imperative that the model be explicitly presented before it is applied to any specific instance, in this case, the Passion Narrative. And so the chapter will have two parts: (a) a model of prominence and (b) its application to the Matthean Passion Narrative.

4.1   What Is Prominence?

As we saw in chapter 2, a person who is labelled a "deviant" is never helpless in the process, because the alleged deviant or some group of supporters might employ a variety of strategies to offset the labelling process. For example, one might acquiesce in the label, manipulate it or even obliterate it. It may happen that the very process of attempting to label someone a deviant might be deflected and redirected by the person being labelled, so that he or she is not proclaimed a deviant at all but instead emerges as a prominent person. The gospel versions of Jesus' arrest, trial and execution are in fact retrospective interpretations of the close of Jesus' career and thus interpretations of the person of Jesus in terms of conflicting labels. These versions eventually served as the record of the attempts by members of the Jesus-movement group to deal with the deviance rooted in behavior associated with death on a cross (Deut 21:23//Gal 3:13), a death that was "a stumbling block to Jews and folly to Greeks" (1 Cor 1:23). Yet in the perspective of not a few of his former followers, Jesus was far from being a deviant! Rather, in and because of his death on a cross, Jesus attained a significant rank among the prominent of God's people, Israel. *Prominent*, however, is not simply the deflection of a deviance label.

On one level, prominence would appear to be the antithesis of deviance, and the process of labelling someone a prominent would be a mirror image of the deviance process. For as we noted in section 2.1e above, deviance refers to those behaviors and/or conditions perceived and assessed to jeopardize the interests and social standing of persons who negatively label them. Deviant refers to a person perceived as out of place to such an extent or in such a way as to be defined in a new, negative place—the definition, of course, deriving from the labellers. Alternately, prominence refers to those behaviors and/or conditions perceived and assessed to enhance positively the interests and social standing of persons who positively label them. Prominent refers to a person "out of place" to such an extent and in such a way as to be redefined in a new, positive place—the definition, likewise of course, derives from the labellers. Deviance and prominence, then, tell us much about the labellers. This is why a consideration of prominence belongs in this study of Christology "from the side." Prominence, like deviance, describes the attitudes and behavior of the group that acclaimed Jesus a prominent person.

When labelling is successfully carried through, deviance and prominence are viewed as personality traits and as qualities of personhood, rather than merely as incidences of behavior or as transient conditions. Deviance or prominence defines the status as well as the very being of the persons being identified either as rule breakers or rule transcenders. A person who is convicted of one instance of shoplifting, lasting ten seconds, becomes "the shoplifter" for life. Similarly, a person acclaimed for an act of heroism lasting ten seconds becomes "the hero" for life.

What, then, is the prominence process? As we noted at the beginning of this book, deviance and prominence bear some resemblance in that both deal with purity lines. The labelling of persons and things as prominent and outside the realm of the ordinary likewise derives from the human need to know where one is. By drawing imaginary but real lines around persons, groups, things, time, place and the All, humans set up their systems of meaning, their purity systems. Prominence looks to those experiences that are perceived to go beyond the usual limits or definitions in some positive way. Thus, prominence looks to transcendence.

Persons "out of place" can be assessed either negatively or positively. A person negatively "out of place" is a deviant. Such a person is perceived as one "out of place," who does not live up to societal limits or tampers with the minimums of those limits. On the other hand, a person positively "out of place" is a prominent person, who goes beyond or stands above or encompasses the limits that usually define members of a given society. We use expressions such as "She is in another league!" or "He stands heads and shoulders above his peers!" or "They broke the mold when they made him!" Prominence, then, refers to behavior or conditions that result in a person's being out of normal place in some positive way. A person's being in a condition of prominence is rooted in the perception of that person's being permanently out of bounds, for example, heroes, saints, founding ancestors and the like. Thus, the prominent person is viewed as an extraordinary being, just as treasure is extraordinary matter because it exists uncommonly and is out of the ordinary.

It follows, then, that prominence is a social creation, just as the lines that produce it. When the transcending of lines not only puts a person "out of place," but results in the transcender's being defined as a socially new type of person, we are dealing again with *moral meanings*. Socially positive and heroic persons are subject to public transformation of their personhood—a special kind of person who can be trusted to live by and beyond the rules that make life in the group meaningful. The rule transcender is thus an "outsider," qualitatively different from others in the group, yet seen positively to epitomize all that the group stands for. This new definition and its outsider status also takes place by means of a labelling process.

Again, few if any persons engage in rule-transcending behavior at every moment. Acknowledged heroes do not behave heroically during every waking moment of their lives. A single, often extremely brief action often suffices to make a lifelong hero. Similarly, a messianic claimant in first-century, Israelite sections of Palestine did not go around continually doing messianic things; a single act would suffice to win recognition (Malina 1986b:51–52). In other words, as a rule people are not committed to either prominent or non-prominent values and behavior. Usually people embrace both, since prominence and non-prominence are not mutually exclusive, but fall along a continuum. As a rule, transcendence of social norms is occasional, situation-specific, short-lived behavior, and is not generalizable, much like a heroic feat of short duration. Consequently, a prominent label makes the specific, episodic and sporadic into the general, permanent and continual. The prominence process, then, is the process by means of which a prominent label is successfully affixed to some person.

4.2 The Model: Understanding Prominence

It is our aim to develop a model of prominence that will indicate the how and why of Jesus' being acclaimed a prominent, which is another form of Christology "from the side" (see Table 1, p. 43).

4.2a Agents of approval. The first steps in the prominence process entail understanding the agents who promote someone's prominence, i.e., rule creators, rule enhancers, and prominence-processing agents within the interest group itself.

(1) Rule creators: Matthew's gospel is itself a retrospective interpretation of Jesus. Hence the very document is a significant datum in the process of labelling Jesus a prominent. It and its earlier editions indicate that there was an ongoing interest group that engaged in maneuvres typical of processes whereby someone is created a prominent. And where there is an interest group, there are moral entrepreneurs concerned with rule creating and rule enhancing.

Rule creating here refers to the formulation of norms for assessing prominence. Such rule creating is the task of some moral entrepreneur and his or her following. What did Jesus do that was worthy of an assessment of prominence? This sort of rule creation is a moral enterprise—a process of constructing and applying meanings that define persons and their behaviors as morally adequate or morally inadequate. The moral enterprise requires both the formulation of norms (rule creators), as well as the application of those norms to specific persons (rule enforcers). Rule creators, then, are interest groups. Usually, interest groups are coalitions focusing upon the shared and distinct interest of group members. In the U.S., we are familiar with pressure groups, that is, interest groups attempting to make their interests into public law. In Jesus' Palestine, interest groups concerned with Jesus' prominence would be the faction(s) Jesus founded.

What rules are being created? As it now stands in its final form, the gospel of Matthew prominently presents Jesus as "the Son" or the "Son of God," a title found in the triple tradition: Q, M and Matthew. It is important to underscore the Mediterranean character of the father-son relationship. Sons stay with their father until the latter's death; it makes little sense for a male to have sons if they eventually leave the paternal household without affording the permanent bond of support "till death do them part," which was the primary meaning of "Honor your father and mother." As a prominent Son, Jesus was and is the one who was uniquely obedient to the God of Israel, the only God. For this he is rewarded by his Father with maximum prominence:

(a) being raised from the dead,
(b) endowed with "all power,"
(c) being made the Messiah-to-come,
(d) becoming the faction founder and patron, who wishes to have disciples and clients in the here and now.

These disciples, moreover, are the persons who report to us of Jesus' obedience to his Father and the Father's elevation of the Son as a uniquely loyal Son and as a supremely prominent figure. It is not so much a question, then, of creating a new rule on behalf of Jesus' prominence, but of making it salient in his case.

(2) Rule Enhancers: Interest-group members seek to enhance their chosen position by having others support their assessment of some person as promi-

nent. These members look to the recruitment of others to join the factional interest group clustered about and including the moral entrepreneurs at the focus of Matthew's community. The making of disciples and their obedience to God in terms of all that Jesus taught guarantees the group's cohesion against outsiders.

Not all recruited, however, are allowed entrance into the core of the interest group. A series of concentric rings marking off different levels of solidarity with the values of the central group often marks the pattern of the expanding group. Again, in any study of Christology "from the side," the question is, What interests of the peripheral or marginal group members does faith in Jesus serve? What do such members expect to gain by attempting to live according to Jesus' directives and by believing in Jesus as Messiah? What of their enemies, of their family? The gospel narrative attempts to offer answers to all such questions, for in promoting Jesus' prominence, his promoters expect to participate in that prominence, and so achieve a courtesy prominence (see Matt 19:27–30). Benefit is spread all around, to Jesus as well as his promoters.

(3) Activity of prominence-processing agents: Those first persons who succeeded in having some positive label(s) stick to Jesus would count as prominence-processing agents here, since they were the ones who won recognition for Jesus as a person situated outside and beyond the ordinary level of human experience. Of course, this process might have already been under way during Jesus' Galilean activity, but its most strenuous period must have been the time after Jesus' successful degradation by the Jerusalemite elites, viz., his death on the cross. In Matthew, these prominence-processing agents would include Peter and the faction about him, figures perhaps from Jesus' Galilean career, but certainly active after Jesus' execution.

4.2b Retrospective interpretation. As previously noted, the gospel of Matthew itself is a retrospective interpretation of the career and person of Jesus of Nazareth: a one-time disciple of John the Baptist, healer, teacher, wonder worker, critic of the political situation of Israel in general and one who hoped to see God's rule over Israel come soon. As the next stages indicate (and the story line recalls), Jesus was by all accounts initially accused of witchcraft by opponents, but in fact he always was what he turned out to be, Son of God, with all power in heaven and on earth. Yet how could respectable people such as the Jerusalemite elite utterly misjudge him? On the other hand, in the face of his insignificant social status as a deviant artisan from an insignificant settlement in Galilee, how could anyone assume to rank him so significantly (see John 7:15, 52; Acts 4:13). His retrospective interpretation, then, will have to deal with neutralizing such objections. We have seen how some of these neutralizations took place in the Passion Narrative, where the main technique was reinterpretation; prominence was shown to lie hidden in supposed deviance.

On the other hand, prominence requires a type of neutralization of its own. While deviant neutralization aims to show that the presumed deviant person was really quite normal, prominent neutralization has to explain why the prominent person is not really a usurper. Mediterranean people have always been prey to opportunistic appropriators of community goodwill and limited resources.

Furthermore, willingness to participate in limit-transcending behavior is very often obstructed by contravening norms and values to which a preprominent is committed. In other words, before somebody such as John the Baptist or Jesus could engage in public activity and attempt to transcend the limitations and definitions of the gatekeepers of their society, they would have to come to grips with the values and norms to which they were committed and which would have kept them from acting. Among these, for example, would be respect for the temple and its priesthood, awe in the face of the behavior and significance of Pharisee groups in their environment, proper peasant behavior toward aristocratic betters and the like. What contravening norms and values kept Jesus from being a public person sooner? Did he have to learn from John the Baptist how to lock horns with Pharisaic opponents? Did he put off the inevitable trip to Jerusalem in order to heal and teach in Galilee? And in his healing and teaching, were his actions in line with the usual norms of behavior in Israel or did they contravene these norms? How do persons simultaneously uphold institutional values in word and sentiment (e.g., not to stand out in/of the group; not to do better than others), yet transcend them behaviorally? How do they overcome the unfathomable chasm between saying one thing ("I respect tradition") and doing another (". . . new wine in new skins")? Again, the technique is called neutralization.

Using techniques that neutralize internalized constraints prior to engaging in prominent behavior enables the deflection of self-disapproval that results from internalized proscriptive norms. These techniques are moral-bind release mechanisms. For persons in the process of becoming prominents, there are five such release mechanisms (adapted for prominence from Pfuhl 1980:65–68; see sections 2.2b and 2.2d above):

(1) Denial of aggrandizement: The prominent person avows that he or she has no control over his or her actions; he or she is driven to prominence by others, by the needs of others or by external forces. A hero at a fire or in a battle claims to have done what anyone else would have done. He or she just happened to be in the right place at the right time. Thus, one is not to be envied for being prominent because one feels or felt more acted upon than acting. Slogan: "It could have happened to anyone; I'm just lucky."

(2) Claim of benefit: The prominent person might lay claim to the perspective that the morality/merit of one's behavior depends upon the benefit or gain resulting from those acts, e.g., how much good happened to/or for so many. Slogan: "I only did it to help others."

(3) Affirmation of the beneficiary: This feature refers to the procedure available to a prominent person to redefine the status and role of the beneficiary of

prominent behavior in order to legitimate that behavior. Here the prominent person tells all the people he or she has helped how great and deserving they are, as in the case of an entertainer telling an audience that they are wonderful. The beneficiary is thus redefined as moral prominent, with the agent as legitimate moral benefactor. Responsibility for rule-transcending behavior is accepted, benefits are acclaimed and both are presumed to be fully justified and warranted. Slogan: "You are wonderful people; you deserve all the good that happens to you."

(4) Acclamation of acclaimers: The prominent person might likewise acclaim as prominent those who have acclaimed him to be prominent. Thus, the elevated person morally approves of those who have approved of him or her as a prominent on the basis of his or her actions, just as a politician on election night will acclaim those who nominated and voted for him or her. In the acclamation of one's acclaimers, it becomes an honor to have been elevated and acclaimed by such "morally irreproachable" people. The alleged morality of one's acclaimers is taken to be far greater than anything done or likely to be done by ordinary people. In this way, public attention is focussed on the acclaimers rather than on the prominent, and the behavior of the acclaimers is seen as more irreproachable. Slogan: "If it were not for you, my enlightened and noble supporters, I would be nowhere."

(5) Appeal to higher loyalties: Prominent behavior may be justified and explained as the outcome of a choice based upon some higher-level norm. People often find themselves faced with conflicting demands as a consequence of inconsistency in the same role (Merton's "sociological ambivalence"; see Malina 1986b) or in conflicting roles. For example, in the U.S. a teacher is to be totally dedicated to students and totally dedicated to study and totally dedicated to family. Or a physician is to be totally dedicated to patients, as well as to research, to family and to public service. The same ambivalence holds for nearly all professional roles in our society. The choice of one set of values, demands or expectations often in fact entails the neglect of others. The violated values, demands or expectations are then defined as being of lesser importance, while the ones followed are defined as being of greater importance for a host of reasons. Slogan: "For God and country and family and the children, and so forth."

A prominent person might use the foregoing neutralization techniques to offset the threat that his or her prominence poses to persons who are often well placed in existing social arrangements. These would include elites, aristocrats, power wielders and other authorities.

4.2c Interrupting the labelling process. The story of Jesus is not simply one of prominence, for Jesus was once quite successfully accused of deviance within certain circles, both during his career and after. A close reading of the career of Jesus in Matthew indicates the constant need to deal with those who would attempt to maintain the negative labelling of him. The old and original labels of witchcraft and sedition had to be dealt with, and so must those persons within the geographical area of the Matthean faction who continued to affix these labels to Jesus. To this end, there is a set of neutralization techniques that are in fact the flip-side of those we have just noted.

As we noted, one aspect of the prominence process entails a retrospective interpretation of the alleged prominent and his behavior in which the person and his career are positively presented (for details from Matthew, see 4.3d below). However, should that person have been previously (or subsequently) subject to deviance labelling, supporters would have to resort to some defensive strategy of evasion to neutralize any possible surfacing of deviance labels (Sykes and Matza 1957:667–69; Pfuhl 1980:65–68; for details from Matthew, see 4.3e below). The same generic steps of neutralization, then, may function positively or defensively, depending on the situation.

Positive Affirmation	*Defensive Strategy of Evasion*
1. Denial of Aggrandizement	Denial of Responsibility
2. Claim of Benefit	Denial of Injury
3. Affirmation of Beneficiary	Denial of Victim
4. Acclamation of Acclaimers	Condemnation of Condemners
5. Appeal to Higher Loyalty	Appeal to Higher Loyalty

In response to attempts by others to label someone negatively, the alleged deviant may employ one or more of the following defensive strategies:

(1) Denial of responsibility: The alleged deviant (or supporters) might claim that his or her behavior was unintentional or that his or her acts were due to forces outside his control (e.g., insanity, drunkenness or the "Twinkie" defense of the killer of Harvey Milk). Slogan: "I did not mean it! I could not help it!"

(2) Denial of injury: The alleged deviant might claim that his or her behavior, although counter to the law, did not cause any great harm. Auto theft, for example, might be viewed as temporary borrowing of a car, if done for fun. Slogan: "I did not really hurt any one!"

(3) Denial of the victim: The alleged deviant might claim that the injured party had no right to claim victimization, if it could be shown that he or she acted as an avenger of wrong done and as one who balanced the scales of justice. Slogan: "They had it coming to them!"

(4) Condemnation of the condemners: The alleged deviant might shift the focus from his or her own deviant acts to the motives and behavior of those who disapproved of him, claiming that they were hypocrites, deviants in disguise or wicked people impelled by personal spite. Slogan: "They were out to get me!"

(5) Appeal to higher loyalties: External social controls might be neutralized by insisting that the demands of a smaller social group to which the alleged deviant belonged (family, friends, town, region, religious group) had to take precedence over the demands of the larger society. The alleged deviant did not

act out of anomie or anarchy, then, but in principle on behalf of God or kith or kin. Slogan: "I did not do it for myself!"

So it follows that as the controversial person or his or her interest group positively interpret his or her behavior, thus neutralizing stigma, the person and his or her group engage in their own negative labelling of the accusers.

4.2d Status-elevation rituals. Any communicative interaction between people whereby the public identity of some person is irreversibly transformed into something considered as higher in the local scene of social types will be called a status-elevation ritual. The identity referred to must be a total identity, that is, a master status, based on who a person is, which is based on the reasons why the person acts the way he or she does.

(1) Moral elation: From the perspective of social psychology, elevation rituals fall within the study of the social dimensions of moral elation. Moral elation is a social affect. Roughly speaking, it belongs to those types of feelings people experience when they are honored by others or when they feel good at a job well done, since it fits norms set by others and the like. As a social feeling, moral elation requires the evaluation and recognition of others who in some way come together to evaluate and give recognition. In other words, feeling elated because of the positive recognition of others is rooted in the more or less organized ways that human beings develop as they live out their lives in one another's company.

Any affect has its behavioral paradigm, its concrete symbolization. That of honor, for example, is found in the adornment of that portion of the body that socially defines one's public appearance—in our society, the head. The paradigm of honor is found in the phrases that denote furtherance of the self in public view, i.e., remarks such as "He stood head and shoulders above them," "I felt as if I were walking on air," "I thought I was on top of the world." The paradigm of moral elation is public acclamation. We publicly deliver the blessing, "I call upon all people to bear witness that so-and-so is not as he appears but is otherwise, and is *in essence* of a higher species." Moral elation serves to effect the ritual reconstruction and transformation of the person acclaimed.

It is important to note that being honored and experiencing moral elation do not have the same social outcome, for unlike honor, which does not bind people together but focuses on the honoree, moral elation often reinforces group solidarity. In the market and in politics, a status-elevation ritual must be counted as a non-religious form of communion. Structurally, an elevation ritual bears close resemblance to rituals of investiture and degradation. We shall see how such a ritual may bind persons to some wider group when we take up the conditions of a successful acclamation.

When we say that moral elation brings about the ritual reconstruction of the person being acclaimed, reconstruction is intended literally. The work of acclamation effects the recasting of the objective character of the perceived other. In the eyes of his acclaimers, the other person literally becomes a different and *new* person. It is not that the new attributes are added to the old "nucleus." He is not simply changed, he is re-interpreted, re-constituted and thus re-constructed. If there is any "social construction of reality," it is the reality of social personality that is thus constructed and reconstructed. The former identity of the elevated person at best receives the accent of mere appearance. The new identity is the "basic reality." What he is now is what, "after all," he was all along.

(2) Acclamation rite: How can one make a good acclamation? How do successful acclaimers arrange for an acclamation for their honorees? Following and adapting Garfinkel's (1956) model for degradation, we think the following model might serve to raise a number of questions about the quality of early Christian groups and their assessment of Jesus. The model has four variables: (1) the acclaimer, (2) an honoree, that is the party who is to be acclaimed and whose identity is to be transformed, (3) some trait, behavior or event that serves as reason or motive for the transformation of identity and (4) witnesses and their shared values who will acclaim the honoree in his or her new identity. Thus, the cast of the drama of prominence processing would include:

The Variables in an Acclamation Rite

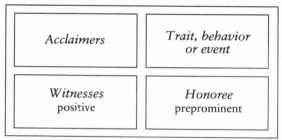

Acclaimers	Trait, behavior or event
Witnesses positive	Honoree preprominent

Who are the acclaimers of Jesus' prominence? It is not apparent that Jesus promoted himself, and this feature seems fully in accord with Mediterranean culture (see the acclamation of Jesus by others at Caesarea Philippi in Matt 16:13–16). The author of Matthew and the Jesus-movement group that he represented would appear to have been the most evident acclaimers of Jesus. Yet Matthew's text clearly indicates that for his group Peter emerged as premier spokesman for Jesus' prominence. Although we will show how Matthew enlarges Peter's role as a primary acclaimer of Jesus, he is building on traditional reminiscences of Peter's special place among Jesus' original followers (Brown, R. 1973:75–107). In a more abstract way, however, let us see how the gospel text orchestrates the four variables of an acclamation rite.

In any status elevation ritual, the acclaimer, the witnesses and the honoree must all effect some reordering of their respective interpretations of the situation, as the following list indicates:

(1) The honoree and the trait must be removed from the ordinary to the "out of the ordinary." In the gospel narrative, it is Jesus' increasing honor, his "fame" (4:24) or "report" (9:26), deriving from his successful behavior that points in this direction.

(2) The honoree and the trait must be preferred because (a) the honoree and the trait are unique, superior and typically symbolic of some feature of human existence; (b) the symbolic quality of honoree and the trait are seen by witnesses as stark opposites of the counter symbolic figures available (e.g. Jesus' enemies in the gospels, Pharisees, Sadducees, elders), so much so that it only makes sense—objectively, morally, obligatorily—to choose the honoree. Note: to choose the honoree is to reject the opposite (Matt 12:30//Luke 11:23).

(3) The acclaimer (e.g., Simon Peter in 16:13–20) must be so identified with or by the witnesses (the grantors of honor) that he is perceived as a publicly known person, not a private person. Significantly, throughout the gospel account Simon Peter acts in the capacity of a public figure and spokesman for Jesus' faction, although in the gospel story line this too may be retrospective interpretation. We shall return to Peter's role in the story further on.

(4) The acclaimer must underscore the core values of the group in question (here Israel) and deliver his acclamation in the name of those core values (thus, obedience to God).

(5) The acclaimer must be invested with the right to speak in the name of these core values; thus, the importance of Jesus' giving Simon his nickname and the insistence that he speaks because of a divine revelation (16:17).

(6) The acclaimer is seen as supporter of the core values of the group at large (i.e., binding and loosing for Heaven as in Israel).

(7) Both the acclaimer and the witnesses must be made to experience closeness to the honoree (e.g., Simon Peter, as the first one called; disciples, as follower of God's Son).

(8) Finally, the honoree must be made strange, i.e., beyond, above, behind the legitimate order, thus outside it. It is the final feature that is realized most sharply in the Passion Narrative and prepared for by the titles given to Jesus, for Jesus ends up standing beyond the human pale, giving an edict for all time as a veritable king of humankind (28:16–20).

While we have occasionally illustrated the foregoing model with bits of information from Matthew, at this point we should like to take up this task of formally interpreting the gospel from the perspective of prominence modeling in a more focused way. Hence, we move on to a detailed application of the model.

4.3 The Model Applied

How did a person such as Jesus become prominent? As previously noted, the defensive strategies available to one being labelled a deviant may be so success-

ful that the alleged deviant may be able to convince others successfully that he
or she is not a deviant at all, but is in fact "a prominent." One mode of the
prominence process, then, may lie in the successful redefinition of the deviance-labelling process itself. But that indicates only a particular situation in
which the process itself may occur. But what constitutes a prominence process? As we have previously noted, we work with the hypothesis that a prominence process consists of the same elements as a deviance process, but in the
opposite direction. In fact, it would appear to be a mirror image of that process
in which:

(a)   an interest group
(b)   labels someone a prominent,
(c)   and disseminates this and wins broad respectability for it;
(d)   it creates a retrospective biography of the one being labelled, illustrating
      genuine prominence,
(e)   and engages in status elevation rituals.

The process applied to Matthew suggests the following observations.

4.3a Interest groups.   The labelling model described previously suggests
that the interpreter look first of all to those who might benefit from affixing a
given label. That there were such persons among the followers of Jesus is
evidenced by the existence of the gospel tradition itself. However, the character, motives and strategy of the original interest group (that is, Jesus' immediate disciples and followers) lie hidden in the earliest years after Jesus' resurrection, a period quite inaccessible to us from the document under consideration. And yet the gospel of Matthew is itself evidence that some groups
shared in the ongoing labelling of the crucified Jesus as a prominent person.
What was scandal to some and foolishness to others was wisdom and power to
them. This gospel, moreover, represents at least the ideology and self-understanding of several generations of Christians who continually saw in Jesus'
death a claim to his prominence.

(1) The disciples: Attempts have occasionally been made from a non-scien-
tific point of view to treat this earliest group of Jesus' disciples in terms of their
initial strategy for dealing with the deviant status implied by Jesus' shameful
death. For example, Wrede's study of the "Messianic Secret" suggested that
Jesus concealed his messiahship (1971:215), since it was an idea that the
disciples were incapable of comprehending. It was revealed to them only after
the resurrection and read back into the career of Jesus (228–29). "Jesus," then,
"did not actually give himself out as Messiah" (230). Rather, comparing the
post-resurrection revelation of Jesus' messiahship with parallels in gnostic
literature, Wrede noted that "speeches of the Risen One were . . . invented in
plenty in the first century of the church" (247).

Whatever else Wrede did, he called attention to the fact that there must
have been some process whereby Jesus' earliest disciples acted as an interest
group in having him declared him a prominent. Wrede was primarily interested

in historical questions, such as the status of Mark as the original and unbiased report of Jesus and his career. In the present investigation of Matthew's Passion Narrative, however, we are interested in a different set of questions and a different procedure. We intend to describe the elements necessary to have a person socially assessed as prominent, and so we proceed according to a model of prominence. Our focus rests on the typical steps whereby someone, Jesus or any other person, becomes labelled a prominent by supporters. Again, this is Christology "from the side." At this point we do not intend to investigate the original events themselves, whether actual or invented. Rather, we hope to discover the interpretation of Jesus and his dishonorable death given by a later generation and in particular by the "evangelist" Matthew.

(2) Peter: Once again, the topic of interest groups necessarily raises the question of moral entrepreneurs in this gospel. We would do well to notice that in Matthew's telling of the story, Simon Peter proves to be the moral entrepreneur par excellence, for in the story line Peter figures quite prominently as the explicitly named person in charge, and this in a culture that favors stereotypes:

4:18	He is the first called to follow Jesus.
8:14	Jesus stays in his house.
10:2	He is ranked "first."
14:28–29	He walks on the water.
15:15	He can presume to seek explanation from Jesus.
16:16	He reports for the group.
16:18	His name is a parable (nickname) given by Jesus.
16:22	After the new name, he presumes to advise Jesus.
16:23	The advice is rejected with a new name given him, "Satan."
17:1–9	He views the Transfiguration of Jesus and comments on it.
17:24	Jesus magically provides tax payment for him.
18:21	He can presume to ask direct questions of Jesus.
19:27	He can presume to ask Jesus about reward.
26:33–35	His deviant disloyalty is foretold (and denied).
26:37	He is chosen to await arrest with Jesus.
26:40	He is personally berated by Jesus for sleeping at the time of his arrest.
26:58, 69	He follows Jesus from afar after his arrest.
26:73–75	He denies being in Jesus' faction at all.

Given the way he is featured in the story, it seems certain that in the tradition of Matthew's group, Simon Peter was considered the focal moral entrepreneur of the Jesus faction represented by this gospel.

Matthew's portrayal of Peter enlarges the figure of this special disciple in ways that further enhance his traditional stature as the premier moral entrepreneur. For example, to the Markan portrait of Peter, Matthew added items that indicated that Peter received special revelations (16:17; 17:24) and performed miraculous feats (14:28–29). Thus, Peter came to have not only ascribed status because of Jesus' call and appointment, but also achieved status by virtue of his own special abilities and activities. In this Matthew is fully in line with developing Christian tradition about "Peter," in which he is the special recipient of revelations, theophanies and the like (Neyrey 1980:509–10).

(3) The evangelist: What we are able to study in the text of Matthew as it presently exists is a somewhat later stage of a process in which Jesus is proclaimed a prominent. Of course, the process is still ongoing among Christians, but by studying Matthew we obtain an appreciation of those first-century followers of Jesus who received and further developed a prominent interpretation of Jesus that is rich in many respects. Labelling theory would have us realize that at times the document says more about these followers of Jesus than it does about Jesus himself. And, even though we may not be able to use the prominence model for historical reconstruction of Jesus' life or the earliest preaching about him, it does have considerable utility in analyzing in hindsight the maintenance of the Jesus-movement group as this is narrated by Matthew. The model, furthermore, suggests that we think of the evangelist's task in writing this gospel in terms of (a) his entrepreneurial activity in promoting the labelling of Jesus as a prominent, (b) his endeavor to shape societal rules and enforce them (at least for Christians) and (c) his capacity to disseminate this label of Jesus and to build a broader consensus of respectability for him. Granted that the gospel of Matthew contains information about various interest groups, the question eventually must be asked: What interests of the moral entrepreneurs does faith in Jesus serve? What do they expect to receive by forming this faction focused on Jesus' prominence? What is to happen to their opposition? To contending Christian faction members?

4.3b Defensive strategy. Ostensibly, much of the prominence processing in Matthew took place in the context of his community group's dealing with the negative labelling of Jesus. Before we examine the Passion Narrative to see how Jesus is prominently labelled, we would like to recall that when persons are labelled as deviants, there are several characteristic strategies available to them and their supporters for responding to the imputation of a deviant label. These strategies have a direct bearing on our understanding of the perspective from which the Passion Narrative is told.

Jesus did not acquiesce in the deviant labels that defined him as an unholy person, a lawbreaker and a pretender, nor did he repudiate the charges that he was critical of the temple, or that he might legitimately be called a prophet, Messiah and Son of God. He neither fled from the process (see 26:46, 51–56) nor channeled the deviant label as a positive and constructive outlet. And he did not modify the deviant label by obliterating its negative qualities. Rather, according to Matthew's version of the Passion Narrative, Jesus' reactions to the deviant label might be characterized as the strategy of reinterpretation.

(1) Reinterpretation: In his trial, Jesus is described as manipulating the occasion to obliterate the negative connotations of his actions and to turn the incident into an occasion for proclaiming his prominence. The very process

that Jesus' enemies used to have him labelled a deviant is used by the evangelist to reinterpret him; for he argues that Jesus was not a sinner but a saint, not a deviant but a prominent. After all, trials may serve to exonerate as well as to condemn, and, in the honor and shame society of the Mediterranean, public trials are notorious venues for parading the crimes and foibles of higher-status accusers who cannot be challenged because of their unequal status. That Jesus' higher-status accusers would bring him to public trial was a risk they believed they could take (see Malina 1981:39), at least so the tradition tells us.

(2) Opportunities for testimony: Concerning the potential of trials as occasions of reinterpretation, the narrative has already schooled the audience to expect that when followers of Jesus were put on trial for their faith, it would be an occasion "for testimony." This is a specific defensive strategy for dealing with the imputation of deviance.

In an early speech, Jesus predicted a series of future tribulations that would come upon his followers, one of which was the public dishonor of arrest and trial: "Beware of men; for they will deliver you up to councils and flog you in their synagogues, and you will be dragged before governors and kings for my sake, *to bear testimony* before them and the Gentiles" (10:17–19). Matthew's treatment of this traditional passage has considerable bearing on his version of Jesus' behavior during the Passion Narrative, and so it deserves our closer attention.

Although the passage comes to Matthew from Mark 13, he made a number of important changes in it. First, he relocated it from a discourse about the exceptional events of rather grandiose dimensions (Mark 13:9) into a more domestic setting. His is a discourse on the trials of those sent out to effect changes in line with Jesus' program and the tribulations of those who might adopt those changes (Matthew 10). Thus, it is a discourse about common, even typical events that would regularly befall Jesus' followers.

Second, Matthew added a number of items to the passage that have the cumulative effect of bringing the predicted fate of Jesus' followers closer in line with Jesus' own experience in his trial and execution:

(a) "they will hand you over" (10:17): this technical term refers to Jesus' betrayal (26:15–16, 21–25, 45–46; 27:3–4) and arrest (26:2; 27:2, 18, 26);

(b) ". . . to councils" ($\sigma\nu\nu\acute{\epsilon}\delta\rho\iota\alpha$) (10:17): Jesus was himself brought before "the whole council," the Sanhedrin (26:59);

(c) "they will flog you": in a prediction of his own shameful treatment, Jesus announced that he, too, would be flogged (20:19);

(d) "you will be hailed before governors" (10:18): only Matthew names Pilate as $\acute{\eta}\gamma\epsilon\mu\acute{\omega}\nu$, governor (27:2, 11, 14–15);

(e) "to bear testimony before them and the Gentiles" (10:18): only Matthew makes a point of this dual testimony before "them" (i.e., Israel) and "Gentiles" (presumably Romans), a point that corresponds to Jesus' trial testimony to the Judaean council (26:64) and the Roman governor (27:11).

Matthew would seem to be drawing parallels between the process to which Jesus' followers and the master himself would be subjected (Hare 1967:19–62). This suggests why the rule-creating moral entrepreneurs in the Matthean faction would be motivated to label Jesus unequivocally as prominent, for if Jesus' followers have to deal with the same deviant status as Jesus did, should Jesus in fact be proved to be prominent all along, so too his followers. This is a form of courtesy prominence. It is only a prominent Jesus who could become a model of behavior and strategy for persons on trial for deviance (see 11:29 and 20:28). Such situations call for a vigorous defensive strategy whereby "testimony" is to be given, testimony that refers to the positive acclamation of Jesus. In the technical terminology of this chapter such testimony is prominence labelling.

While publicly labelling Jesus as prominent, those of his followers on trial themselves reinterpret their own situation away from deviance to that of prominence as well. Trials and forensic proceedings, which are intended by rule enforcers to be inherently status-degradation rituals, can be manipulated to become the occasion for prominence processing. Matt 10:17–19, then, has direct bearing on the presentation of Jesus in 26:59–68. "Trials" call for positive "testimony."

This "testimony," moreover, will not be the disciples' own clever apology (see 1 Cor 1:17; 2:1–5), but a type of divinely induced speech on Jesus' behalf. First, no preparation will be necessary or warranted: "Do not be anxious, how you are to speak or what you are to say" (10:19b). Second, the Christian witnesses will be given a statement from God to communicate: "What you are to say will be given you" (10:19c), and so the witnesses become legitimate agents of God. Third, the witnesses should truly be called "prophets" because they will be inspired by the "Spirit of your Father" (10:20). Just as Jesus himself was authorized by the "Spirit of God" to speak and act (3:16; 12:18), so Christian witnesses will likewise be legitimated by the "Spirit of God" and their trial testimony will be authorized, heavenly speech on behalf of God's Christ, that is, prominence labelling. Divinely induced or bold speech became a hallmark of Christian testimony for Jesus when on trial, both in Matthew and elsewhere in the New Testament (see παρρησία in Acts 4:13).

Turning to the trials of Jesus, according to the defensive strategy outlined in 10:17–20, Jesus' remarks at his own trials should be construed as examples of "testimony" or prominence labelling for God's Christ and Son. The trials before the Sanhedrin and Pilate have a similar structure:

Jewish Trial: (a) charges (26:59–63a) =*SILENCE;*
          (b) questioning under oath about God's Christ and Son (26:63b–65) =*TESTIMONY;*
Roman Trial: (b) questioning about Israel's legitimate king (27:11) =*TESTIMONY;*
          (a) charges (27:12–14) =*SILENCE.*

A pattern unmistakably emerges: no speech in response to charges, but speech when questioned on a topic that we would identify as a question about Jesus as a prominent.

The silence is somewhat perplexing, but not hopelessly so. There would seem to be no remote allusion to the silent lamb of Isa 53:7 which, when led to the slaughter, "opened not his mouth." This is a forensic situation in which silence might mean several things: consent to the charges (*silence means consent*) or disdain for the judges and their questions (as seems to be the case in John 19:9–11). It is difficult to sort this out in Matt 26:29–63 and 27:12–14. Our explanation in large measure rests on the perception that the evangelist is not ignoring the charges, but rather presumes a defense of Jesus that he favorably reported earlier. For example, in regard to one of the most serious charges, we suggest that an adequate apology for Jesus' attitude toward the temple has already been made earlier in the narrative, a defense that the evangelist would expect to be remembered. The evangelist, then, seems not to ignore the charges at the trials, but to focus on the defensive strategy of having Jesus give testimony as to his prominence at the very time when he is being processed as a deviant. But this calls attention to a feature of the gospel that is important to an understanding of how Jesus is proclaimed a prominent. Not all of the defense can take place in the Passion Narrative; much of it is done earlier.

A pattern has already been established in the gospel that conditioned the audience about how to interpret various accusations that Jesus is a maverick relative to the system and a flagrant rule breaker. For example, Jesus did not observe the traditional strict Sabbath practice, a distinguishing mark of an authentic Israelite (Smallwood 1976:123). A full, formal defense was offered on that occasion when Jesus cited as precedent for his behavior the action of David, who "entered the house of God and ate the Bread of the Presence, which it was not lawful for him to eat nor for those with him, but only for the priests" (12:4). David, of course, was *not* a priest, but rather, according to Matthew, a symbol of a type of covenant relationship with God different from the Mosaic covenant that undergirded the temple system (Clements 1967; Weinfeld 1976). He was not acting irreverently, then, but sought only to realize fundamental Israelite values by means of a different institutional arrangement.

On that occasion Jesus cited a second precedent for his actions, namely the fact that priests themselves profaned the Law by "working" on the Sabbath, but were guiltless (12:5). These two precedents have bearing on the issue at hand because

(a)   "something greater than the temple is here" (12:7);
(b)   the Scripture explicitly states that "I (God) desire mercy, not sacrifice" (12:7a/Hos 6:6); and
(c)   "the Son of Man is Lord of the Sabbath" (12:7b).

The claim to be "greater than the temple" should be seen alongside claims to be "greater than Jonah" and "greater than Solomon" (12:41, 42). Being "greater" than the temple implied that Jesus represented and inaugurated a new and better sort of social arrangement for Israel, namely a superior type of covenant relationship between God and his people, different from that encoded in the temple, strict Sabbath observance and the Mosaic covenant. Jesus counterbalanced the negative interpretation of his behavior by appealing to equally traditional covenant behavior apparent in David's action and in Hosea's prophetic statement. Being "greater than Jonah and Solomon" would imply as well that Jesus' status was more prominent than that of a classic prophet and of David's mightiest son. It is as the (rejected) Son of Man that Jesus claimed legitimation to pronounce about Sabbath observance. Again, he did not act in ignorance of custom or as a lawbreaker, but according to social arrangements that were different from the culturally prevailing ones, yet nonetheless in line with traditional values and principles. They were, therefore, legitimate.

According to the narrative, this incident occurred in the Galilean ministry of Jesus, but it is seen by the evangelist as of a piece with Jesus' activity in Jerusalem and in particular with his actions and attitudes toward the major symbol of Israel's culture and faith, the temple. All along, Matthew has been arguing two points: that Jesus fulfilled the covenant type represented by David and Abraham and that Jesus was the legitimate heir of David, and so the leader of Israel. His being a prophet (16:13–14), in fact being greater than a prophet (12:41; 16:16), laid the groundwork for Jesus' Jerusalem activity as prophet (21:11; 22:33). His being greater than David's mightiest son (12:42) and heir of David's throne (1:1; 2:2, 4–6) legitimated the acclamation of Jesus in Jerusalem as "Son of David" (21:9, 15). Being greater than the temple (12:6) validated Jesus' radical criticism of the Jerusalem temple. Matthew's gospel narrative has prepared attentive readers in such a way that in Jesus' trial they are expected to recall incidents such as Jesus' strategy in 12:1–14.

Jesus' silence before his accusers was not acquiescence in their negative labels. The gospel has conditioned its audience as to how to assess those deviant labels that would attempt to situate Jesus sinfully against God's temple and have him pretentiously take honors to himself. The negative impact of these charges was clearly deflected by the gospel narrative, for Jesus was representative of a different type of covenant. He espoused a different set of social arrangements, embodying a different set of structural relationships. He was not *against* the system so much as he was the spokesman of another system. Jesus did not need to speak in his defense in 26:63a and 27:12–14, for this defense had already been set forth adequately earlier. Response to charges, moreover, could find no place in the directions for proper trial behavior as mandated by Jesus in 10:17–20. Silence, then, was not anomalous or scandalous, as it was in 22:12b.

When Jesus did speak, his remarks had to do with positive testimony on behalf of the one whom God has authorized as "Christ," "Son of God" and

"King of the Jews." Speech was appropriate here, even mandated by Jesus' earlier directives. His remarks, then, both to the chief priest and to Pilate should be construed as prominence "testimony," God-induced speech inspired by the "Spirit of God." Jesus should speak out affirming the prominence of the figure whom God has sent as absolute leader of the covenant community. In conclusion, then, trials were occasions for manipulating what normally would be a dishonoring process and turning it into a prominence process. The key is the "testimony," or prominence labelling, and the social outcome should be the recruitment of others.

4.3c Prominence labels. The positive labels affixed to Jesus offer the clearest clues to the interests of early Christian factions. For example, the titles and tags of identity and legitimation in the Passion Narrative that the chief priests and others found so offensive were not repudiated by Jesus or his followers according to Matthew's gospel. Indeed, they could not be if Jesus was to be accepted as a prominent rather than a deviant person. In fact, the Passion Narrative contains all the major prominence titles of Jesus in the gospel and dwells on them more intently than the rest of the narrative:

Christ:	26:63; 27:17, 22
Son of God:	26:63; 27:40, 43, 54
King of the Jews:	27:11, 29, 37, 42
Prophet:	26:67–68
Son of Man:	26:64

If the chief priests considered these titles pretentious and preposterous while Jesus' followers valued them, how was the audience expected to judge? Was it only the *a priori* matter of being a believer that allowed one to consider Jesus a prominent figure? Or did the narrative provide an interpretative principle that conditioned its first hearers to acquire clues for a "correct" perception of what was going on? Such a "correct" perception would make it not seem dissonant or contradictory that the rejected, dishonored and executed Jesus was really God's Anointed because of *the very process of rejection.* We submit that the narrative does in fact contain a hermeneutical perspective that not only allows but even requires that prominence be predicated of the one rejected by Israel.

(1) Son of Man: The precise technique of turning rejection into prominence had already been carefully worked out by some earlier moral entrepreneurs in interest groups of the pre-Matthean traditions, especially as regards the content and significance of the label "Son of Man." At first, "Son of Man" appears to have been merely a derogatory statement by Jesus' rivals and opponents about him, a label that denoted rejection and disdain: "The Son of Man came eating and drinking and they say, 'Behold a glutton and a drunkard, a friend of tax collectors and sinners'" (11:19). In time, and through a process that appears to be part of the retrospective biography of Jesus, the label "Son of Man" came to be reinterpreted in light of a figure in the late Jewish writing called the book

of Daniel. There, one like a Son of Man was rejected, even martyred on earth by men but vindicated in heaven and given dominion by God (Dan 7:14).

The reader who has been prepared for this process of vindication-in-rejection can then appreciate the special use of the "Son of Man" label in Jesus' trial. It is hardly accidental that in the very course of Jesus' trial, when he is formally rejected as God's "Christ, Son of God," he refers to himself as "Son of Man," both as the one who is being rejected by men on earth, but especially as the one whom God will vindicate and enthrone in heaven: "Hereafter you will see the Son of Man seated at the right hand of the Power and coming on the clouds of heaven" (26:64). According to a biblical pattern such as Daniel 7, it so happens that God's chosen one must be handed over on earth, but then vindicated in heaven (16:21; 17:22–23; 20:18–19). The sequence set in Daniel 7, therefore, came to be the preferred example of how rejection and dishonor are reinterpreted as warrant for the affirmation of the essential prominence of this agent of God.

The final validation of this pattern occurs in 28:16–20, the concluding appearance of Jesus. Here the vindicated Lord of All, who was once dishonored and crucified, has now been granted power and authority by God, just as he predicted would be the case. The rejected "Son of Man" has become the vindicated Lord of all. Among others, Hubbard (1974:7–8, 80–82) pointed out how the description of Jesus in 28:16–20 draws directly on the text of Dan 7:14:

Dan 7:14	*Matt 28:18–19*
"and given to him	"Given to me
is authority	is all authority
and all the nations	in heaven and on earth
and all glory	
(that) they worship him"	going, make disciples
	of all nations"

By the conclusion of the story, then, the "Son of Man," who was rejected and dishonored especially during the Passion Narrative, has been vindicated and made a most prominent person. Here is a clear instance of a process that we argue is operative also in regard to other prominent labels of Jesus.

(2) Prophet: Matthew constantly reminds his audience that prophets were rejected by Jerusalemites, the elite of their own people. Jesus labelled his own disciples "blessed" when men "persecute you and utter all kinds of evil against you . . . for so men persecuted the prophets who were before you" (5:11–12). It was a characteristic trait of genuine prophets to be rejected! John the Baptizer, for example, was but the most recent example of this (11:7–10, 18; 14:5); he followed in the tradition of "prophets, scribes and wise men, some of whom you will kill and crucify and some you scourge in your synagogues and persecute from town to town" (23:34). In fact, as typical as it was of prophets to suffer and be rejected, it was likewise characteristic of "Jerusalem" to be the agent of their rejection (23:37).

Jesus himself came to be labelled a prophet, not just a miracle-working prophet like Moses, Elijah or Elisha, but also a rejected and martyred prophet like Jeremiah (16:14). Consequently, when Jesus was acclaimed a prophet in Jerusalem (21:9; 21:46), Matthew's hearers would hold their breath in expectation of the rejection of the prophet Jesus, which finally occurs at his trial before the council (26:67–68). Like "Son of Man," the label "prophet" bore in its very denotation the feature of rejection as touchstone of its authenticity.

(3) King of the Jews: Jesus' kingship is likewise presented in an ironic mode. He is indeed God's anointed, Son of David and King of Israel. But at the first proclamation of his kingship in the Infancy Narrative, that honor is ambivalently treated: the chief priests and the scribes indeed knew according to Micah 5:2 where Israel's king was to be born, but they did not act on the knowledge. Herod also knew, but tried to kill the new king (2:7–8, 16–18). The new king was thus initially treated with shame and dishonor. Yet, although his own rejected him, the non-Jewish Magi came to Jesus and "fell down and worshiped him" (2:11). Two programmatic notes are signalled by this initial narrative: (a) his own reject his kingship while non-Jews accept him and (b) kingship labelling occurs in the context of threat to life and deep dishonor.

Matthew repeated aspects of this pattern in Jesus' entry into Jerusalem. Crowds acclaimed him "Son of David" (21:9), while the chief priests and elders rejected this (21:15)—honor is balanced with dishonor. Finally, in the Passion Narrative the full pattern of Jesus' kingship labelling recurs:

(a)   his own reject him as king (27:42),
(b)   he is acclaimed king (27:11, 29) in the context of his execution (27:37).

While according to God "king" would be an accurate label for Jesus, the title does not occur in honorable situations where power and status are symbolled, but in contexts of dishonor (2:1–18; 27:11, 29, 37) and demeaned status (21:5, 9). Still, Jesus is finally worshipped as king (28:17) and in fact performs a truly royal task by issuing the edict with which the gospel of Matthew ends (28:18–20). This final royal edict, moreover, parallels the final royal edict with which the Jewish bible ended in the time of Jesus (2 Chron 36:23): "Since in the time of Jesus . . . Chronicles seems always to have been the last book of the Hagiographa (the close of the Hebrew bible), and it is doubtful whether at that time more than two different orders for the canonical books were known" (Beckwith 1985:211). Thus, Matthew begins with allusions to the book of Genesis (the gospel's first words are: βιβλος γενέσεως) and comes full circle by concluding with allusions to the end of the Bible, a new normative revelation for Israel (see Malina 1971).

This feature simply underscores those recent studies of the Infancy Narratives (Brown, R. 1977:47–49; Nolan 1979:104–7) that have argued for a close connection between the events and themes of chapters 1–2 with those in chapters 26–28. This material has a direct bearing on the present argument.

The numerous and noteworthy parallels between the beginning of the gospel and its end may be quickly grasped in the following synopsis:

Infancy Narrative	*Passion Narrative*
1. Jesus=King of the Jews (2:2)	Jesus=King of the Jews (27:11, 29, 37)
2. Jesus=Son of God (2:15)	Jesus=Son of God (27:40, 43)
3. Negative reaction: "all Jerusalem troubled" along with chief priests and scribes (2:3–4)	Negative reaction: chief priests (26:65) and all Jerusalem reject him (27:25)
4. God's providential care of Jesus, his escape (2:13–14, 20)	God's vindication of Jesus in his resurrection (26:64; 28:1–10, 16–20)
5. Dreams on Jesus' behalf (2:13, 19)	Dream of Jesus' innocence (27:19)
6. Events fulfil Scripture (2:6, 15, 18, 23)	Events fulfil Scripture (26:24, 56)

This parallelism suggests that the same Christological message that had long been found in the Passion Narrative was consciously introduced into the Infancy Narrative. The result would be a coherent story whose rhetorically significant places, beginning and end, correspond identically. But the treatment of the Christology in the Infancy Narrative is highly significant, since, as we have shown, Jesus is rejected as "King of the Jews" and is the "Son of God" in exile and hiding. The evangelist would seem to be conditioning his audience to understand that the major labels of Jesus, while true, honorable and prominent, occur in contexts that are dishonorable.

(4) Interpretative principle: The patterns of perception that we have observed in regard to "Son of Man," "prophet" and "King of the Jews" are embedded in the narrative itself. But in several places Jesus articulates a formal principle by which we are expected to discern the main value encoded in these titles. For example, Zebedee's wife pleads with Jesus for honor and status for her sons, "that these two sons of mine may sit, one at your right hand and one at your left, in your kingdom" (20:22). Jesus instead offers the sons a share of his cup, presumably a cup of rejection and suffering (see 26:39). In formal explanation to the assembled Twelve, Jesus articulates the principle of ironic reversal that applies to him and his followers:

> "Whoever would be great among you must be your servant;
> whoever would be first among you must be your slave" (20:27).

"For," Jesus continued, "the 'Son of Man' (who, of course, is the Christ, Son of God and Son of David) came not to be served but to serve" (20:28). And so, according to the perspectives developed in the course of the gospel, honor and status are not symbolled in structures of power, prestige and pomp, but in their opposite, in situations of lack of power, low rank and social insignificance, hence even in dishonor. After all, those who wear soft garments are in kings' houses (11:18). So it came to pass that Jesus, Son of David, entered the royal city "humble, and mounted on an ass" (21:5/Zech 9:9) instead of on that symbol of power, the horse. This logic might be extended to the sayings of Jesus, where the audience is repeatedly told that the last are first and the first are last (19:30; 20:8, 16); those who would save their lives must lose them (16:25).

Recall the observation made in the first chapter that one of the characteristics of the cosmology of Matthew's gospel is its sense that things are not what they seem. There is a lack of consistency between external appearances and inner reality, and evil may be disguised as good for purposes of deception. We spelled this out in the context of "witches" and their disguise. In the context of concealed prominence, however, the converse may also be true of genuinely good, honorable people. Honor may lie hidden in dishonor, beatitude in distress, holiness in seeming alienation from God. The fact that a "king" is disgraced and crucified is no argument against the truth that so-and-so is truly a king. In this world, there is necessarily a hiddenness about persons, places and things (11:25), a hiddenness that is due to God's own actions and that needs to be revealed. Just as evil and deviance must needs be unmasked (10:26), so prominence must be revealed, not to the wise, however, but to babes (11:26–27; 16:17).

In summary, the gospel conditions its hearers and readers to view Jesus' career from a special interpretative perspective:

(a)   God's agents will be rejected by men but vindicated by God.
(b)   All of God's prophets, if they are true prophets, are rejected.
(c)   In fact, the truly honorable persons are they who are treated like prophets with persecution and dishonor.
(d)   True honor and prominence are expected to be hidden and not apparent, but revealed to the truly wise.

Jesus himself embodies this pattern—a king who is rejected by his own and whose life is sought; a ruler who is servant; the first who becomes last; and a prominent whose greatness is lowliness. In short, when it comes to Matthew's labels for Jesus, one would expect prominence to be predicated of Jesus precisely in ironic situations of loss of power and dishonor.

The Passion Narrative, then, affirms that certain prominent labels truly apply to Jesus, even under the deceptive circumstances of trial, dishonor and execution. They should be given to him, moreover, because they embody Jesus' ascribed prominence. They are ascribed to him by God, and they bespeak Jesus' total identity, his master status. For example, as regards the label "Son of God," the evangelist records in his retrospective biography of Jesus how this label was applied to him (a) directly by God, first at his baptismal commissioning (3:17) and again with the revelatory experience of the transfiguration (17:5), and (b) indirectly in God's inspiration of Peter who acclaimed Jesus "the Christ, the Son of the living God" (16:16–17). God, who reads hearts and knows all secrets, acknowledges Jesus' master status as his Son, a holy figure, anointed and authorized to speak on God's behalf.

The audience has been informed from the start of the narrative about Jesus' closeness to God (see 1:20–21; 2:14), an affinity with God that clearly made him the enemy of God's enemies, Satan (4:1–11) and demons (8:29). He is proven to have been all along the "Son of God" by his faithfulness to God in the assaults of God's enemy, Satan (4:3, 6). He is acknowledged by the demon to be its enemy, namely the "Son of God" (8:29). And, after a divinely empowered action such as the stilling of the storm, Jesus' disciples profess him to be "Son of God" (14:33). Consequently, when at Jesus' trial the formal issue is raised of whether he truly is "the Christ, the Son of God," the audience knows that Jesus truly is such and expects the Son of God to be attacked by evil persons—in this case, the high priest Caiaphas and his council. Evil wars on God and God's kingdom; so it has ever been! And the very conflict proves that the contestants belong to two different worlds, thus aiding the audience to perceive the revelation of the hidden agent of God.

The same is true for Jesus as prophet and king. For his truthful confession, Jesus is ironically labelled a prophet, meaning a "false" prophet (26:67–68), but the audience has been conditioned to see in Jesus' rejection and maltreatment the very proof of his being a genuine prophet, for it belongs to prophets to be "killed and crucified" (23:34). When disowned by his own people, Jesus is publicly but ironically acclaimed as their king. But Matthew's audience knows that Israel's king comes to his people meek and humble, even pursued by enemies as David was, first by Saul and later by Absalom. It is, of course, God who ascribes this title, status and honor to Jesus (2:2), in leading Magi to him in fulfillment of the Scriptures, according to the old promise to David (1:22–23; 2:6; 21:5). Hence, when non-Jews acclaim Jesus as king in the Passion Narrative, albeit ironically and sarcastically, this label is intended by the evangelist to be taken literally and seriously.

4.3d Approval.   Approval is to the prominence process what banning is to deviance. Approval consists in (1) interpreting some person, event or thing as good, right and moral and (2) imbuing it with positive judgment, such as merit or honor. This might take place by dissemination and broadening respectability. Dissemination involves giving a high degree of visibility to the meanings developed by the moral entrepreneur. It is best illustrated by the diffusion of that typically Christian innovation, a crucified Messiah, by means of impromptu proclamation, as well as by means of the gospel narrative itself.

The account of the Passion Narrative contains numerous instances where broader respectability was enlisted in support of Jesus' prominence. This notably occurs regarding those who at first glance would not be expected to give this testimony, such as his betrayer, his judge and his executioner. Matthew's version contains a special report about Pilate and his wife that is not found in Matthew's source, Mark, or in any other account of Jesus' trial (Senior 1975:244–46). Matthew relates that Pilate's wife suffered concerning Jesus in a dream (27:19), which in this gospel was a normal form of divine communication prior to Jesus' public activity. Action in the first two chapters of Matthew moves along, thanks to sources of divine communication such as stars, scriptures and especially dreams (see Malina 1967). First Joseph receives a dream concerning Mary's positive sense of shame and Jesus' name and role (1:20–24), a dream that accords with the prophecy of Isa 7:14. The Magi receive a dream from heaven warning them not to return to Herod (2:12), which dream is followed by dreams to Joseph commanding him to flee from Bethlehem (2:13) and to return to Nazareth when safe (2:19–21). Pilate's wife's dream, then, must be taken as another divine communication that affirms Jesus' innocence of all evil, "Have nothing to do with that *righteous man* . . ." (27:19). What is hidden must be revealed, even by improbable witnesses.

Pilate himself is enlisted as a witness on Jesus' behalf (Neyrey 1985:83–84). Like his wife, Pilate cannot find any evil in Jesus; "What evil has he done?" (27:23). He then washes his hands, a gesture rooted in the Old Testament procedure for an unsolved murder (see Deut 21:1–9). If Pilate denies responsibility for the murder of an innocent man by this gesture, then responsibility is assumed by "all the people" (27:25). But Pilate and his wife stand apart from the Jews who call for Jesus' shameful death; together they constitute a double witness to Jesus' innocence (Senior 1975:252–56).

Even as Jesus' fellow Israelites mock him on the cross, his non-Jewish executioner and those with him witnessing the phenomena accompanying Jesus' death proclaim, "Truly this was the Son of God" (27:54). This voice is intended as a contrast to the voices in 27:39–40 and 42–43, which mock Jesus. We then have a non-Jewish voice in opposition to Jewish voices, just as in chapter 2 the obedient Magi following their star stand in opposition to disobedient Herod and the chief priests disregarding their scriptures. Precisely as the Jews mock Jesus for saying "I am the Son of God," the non-Jew acclaims him to be truly "Son of God." On the level of narrative symbolism, Matthew has portrayed the conversion both of Jesus' judge and executioner, a motif found in group accounts of the death of martyrs (Bammel 1968:108–12), enrolling both of them as witnesses on Jesus' behalf.

Furthermore, another of Jesus' adversaries is enlisted on his behalf, his very betrayer, Judas (27:3–10). The narrative reports that "he repented," a technical term in this gospel for a change of heart (see 21:30). He returned the silver pieces with the confession, "I have sinned in betraying *innocent blood*" (27:4). The evangelist would have us interpret "innocent blood" in connection with his earlier remarks on "blood of the prophets," even "the righteous blood of the innocent Abel," which has always been shed especially in Jerusalem (Senior 1975:380–81). This incident signifies for Matthew the fulfillment of scriptural prophecies about "the price of him on whom a price has been set by some of the sons of Israel" (27:9/Zech 11:13). Judas is enlisted under the same rubric as Pilate, yet he declares himself guilty of Jesus' "innocent ($\dot{\alpha}\theta\hat{\omega}ov$) blood," whereas Pilate is "innocent" ($\dot{\alpha}\theta\hat{\omega}os$) of Jesus' blood. Jesus' former betrayer and his judge stand up to testify on his behalf, co-opted as they are by the evangelist to echo his own testimony about Jesus.

Matthew's version, then, clearly indicates a pattern whereby elite non-Jews profess Jesus' innocence and give him honorable status, whereas elite Israelites do not. Those who profess Jesus' innocence, moreover, are precisely those people who should be listened to in any serious consideration of the forensic proceedings against Jesus. Far from labelling him a deviant, his betrayer declared him innocent; his judge found no evil in him; the judge's wife reported a heaven-sent dream about his innocence; and his executioner declared him a holy figure, even God's Son. There seems to be a conscious attempt to have outsiders, non-Jews and even judge and executioner, enlisted to speak the evangelist's point of view, while the Jerusalemite crowd, as well as the elites of Israel, cling to their estimation of Jesus as deviant.

4.3e Retrospective interpretation. In their evaluation of the career of Jesus, those interest groups proposing the prominence of Jesus had to deal with two dimensions of the purity system. First they had to neutralize the assessments of those who labelled Jesus as deviant and then they had to deal with those who claimed that while Jesus was not a deviant, he was in fact simply an ordinary Israelite healer and teacher, caught up in the unstable conditions of the day. Thus, while one group of outsiders insisted that Jesus was a shameless deviant, another would have viewed him as an unfortunate, honorable but ordinary Galilean. In the prominence process, retrospective interpretation would have to underscore the non-ordinary career of the protagonist and thereby neutralize perceptions of ordinariness. Jesus had to be evaluated as an honorable person entitled to prominence.

The five techniques of neutralization noted previously might serve as categories for assessing how the retrospective biography of Jesus and his first followers in Matthew's gospel effectively sought to underscore the non-ordinary quality of Jesus' career, hence his entitlement to prominence.

(1) Denial of aggrandizement: Jesus is described as ultimately having no control over his actions in that he was driven to do what he did (healing, teaching, preaching) by God or God's spirit, or that he acted out of compassion for others, the needs of others and the like. In all the gospels, the baptism of Jesus initially marks this neutralizing function. After all, it is not Jesus who chooses to go public, but God through his spirit impels him. Thus, Jesus is essentially irreproachable because he is more acted upon than acting.

Furthermore, the fact that Jesus' preaching is really not his own, but simply a continuation of John the Baptist's message (3:2; 4:17), points to the same denial of aggrandizement with a view to neutralizing objections. The same holds for the fulfillment of scripture passages sprinkled over the gospel. It comes down to the fact that even though Jesus is a prominent, he did not seek prominence; he did not usurp anything from anyone. Hence, he is honorable and worthy of far more honor than one might initially think.

(2) Claim of benefit: A common gospel theme underscores the perspective that the morality or merit of Jesus' behavior depends upon the benefit or gain to others resulting from those acts. This would entail a demonstration of how

much good happened to so many, such as a report that "the blind receive their sight, the lame walk, lepers are cleansed and the deaf hear, and the dead are raised up, and the poor have the good news preached to them" (11:5). Directly or indirectly, all stories of Jesus' healing point to his benefactions (Danker 1982:393–409). Finally, even his death is "for many for the forgiveness of sins" (26:28). The argument emerges: while Jesus is extraordinarily prominent, it is not to *his* benefit but rather to the actual and real benefit of all. This neutralization technique, then, is a common feature in the gospel.

(3) Affirmation of the beneficiary: In the gospels, Jesus often redefines the status or role of his disciples and followers in such a way as to legitimate his prominent activity. Not only will the core group of his faction, the Twelve, "sit on twelve thrones judging the twelve tribes of Israel" (19:28), but often those whom Jesus helps and/or teaches are told that they are something other than they normally and previously were. Thus, the non-elite who accept Jesus are redefined as better than the elite, as in the beatitudes, for example, where Jesus acclaims the poor in spirit, the meek and so forth, as "blessed." Since it is to babes that "these things" of God are revealed, not to "the wise and understanding" (11:25), Jesus' followers thus outrank the wise and understanding in their knowledge of God's will. Stories and parables of the deserving non-elite who are rewarded serve the same end (e.g., 8:5–10; 21:28–32; 22:1–10), for they neutralize institutionalized envy in the face of prominence, since beneficiaries are affirmed as deserving. The beneficiaries of Jesus' activity, therefore, are redefined as morally prominent, with Jesus as moral benefactor truly meriting his prominent title. Jesus is seen as accepting responsibility for his rule-transcending behavior; the benefits bestowed on others are acclaimed and both are presumed to be fully justified and warranted.

(4) Acclamation of acclaimers: Jesus is reported to have acclaimed those who acclaimed him as prominent on the basis of his activity and the reputation based on it. For example: for Simon's acclamation of Jesus as "Christ," Jesus in turn acclaims him with a title in the form of a nickname: "And I tell you, you are Rock (Πέτρος)" (16:18). While Mark reports that James and John were similarly acclaimed ("Sons of Thunder," Mark 3:17), Matthew keeps the limelight on Simon. On a broader scale, Jesus acclaims his disciples with "Here are my mother and my brothers" (12:49); and again with "But blessed are your eyes for they see and your ears for they hear. Truly I say to you, many prophets and righteous men longed to see what you see and did not see it, and to hear what you hear and did not hear it" (13:16–17). By acclaiming one's acclaimers, it becomes an honor to have been elevated and acclaimed by such "morally irreproachable" people.

As a result of this procedure, attention is shifted from Jesus to his disciples (and other acclaimed beneficiaries), and the disciples' conduct is seen as more irreproachable (see 16:17). Thus, the positive sanctions and acclamation proper to Jesus overflow to the disciples. Of course, the outcome is their central location and prominence in the early Jesus factions, and this not simply because they were witnesses but because they "turned out" morally irreproach-able. Thus, all who had anything to do with Jesus end up "saints," including Pilate in some traditions!

(5)   Appeal to higher loyalties: Jesus' activity is often explained as having taken place "in order to fulfill what was written in the scriptures." Scripture, which is God's will, is *the* higher-level norm in Israel. Jesus' choice to follow God's will in healing and proclaiming the rule of God involved the choice of one set of loyalties with its demands and expectations, and this entailed the transcendence of other loyalties. Thus he explicitly opts for "the command-ment of God" over against "your tradition" (15:3, 6; see also 19:3–7). The violated demands and expectations, notably the traditions of the Pharisees and the norms of the Sadducees, are then defined as being of lesser importance, while the ones followed are defined as being of greater importance. In fact, Jesus' interpretation of God's Torah will be as firm and abiding as heaven and earth themselves (5:18).

Furthermore, because of higher loyalties, Jesus avoids obligations to his family by his public engagement as teacher and healer (12:46). Higher loyalties are involved, "the will of my Father in heaven" (12:50) as it is explicitly and implicitly throughout the narrative (cf. Luke 2:48–49). Leaving home on self-imposed exile "for the sake of the gospel," giving one's goods to the poor to redistribute wealth, giving up one's life for a cause that benefits others and the like are so many instances of behavior that favor one end of a range of obligations in favor of another. As Jesus cites higher-level norms in the course of the narrative, he is portrayed as effectively neutralizing envy or attack on the part of those who would cast doubt on his entitlement to prominence.

4.3f Interrupting the negative labelling process.   Jesus was in fact crucified. In the face of repeated insistence on his entitlement to extraordinary honor and prominence, the mere recollection of his crucifixion would carry in its train overwhelming overtones of successful deviant labelling. Hence, long after Jesus' survivors worked out their retrospective interpretation of Jesus' career in terms of their own interests, resonances of Jesus-as-deviant echoed on. Jesus-movement groups, Matthew's included, felt the continued need to offset the negative labelling of their faction founder. Again, it will be in terms of the techniques of deviance neutralization that we search for clues for revealing the often latent apologetic character of the retrospective biography of Jesus in Matthew's Passion Narrative.

(1) Denial of responsibility: Jesus repeatedly claimed that it was God's will and plan that he go to Jerusalem, be rejected and killed (16:21; 17:22–23; 20:18–19). This will of God is understood by Jesus and embraced in his prayer in the Garden, "Thy will be done" (26:39). This will of God, moreover, is said to be found in the Scriptures, which Jesus claimed to know. At the Last Supper, he acknowledged that "the Son of Man goes as it is written of him" (26:24), appealing to God's will concerning his rejection as found in the lives of

the prophets, the suffering of the righteous in the psalms and other specific texts. This same appeal to the Scriptures appears in Jesus' citation of Zech 13:7 apropos the shepherd's being struck (26:31) and more generally on the occasion of his arrest, that "the scriptures be fulfilled" (26:53). Other passages are either alluded to or said to be fulfilled:

Zech 11:12–13; Jer 18:1–3	Matt 27:9–10
Ps 22:2	Matt 27:45
Ps 22:7–8	Matt 27:39
Ps 22:8	Matt 27:43
Ps 22:18	Matt 27:35

The neutralizing motif of "according to the scriptures" functions in the Passion Narrative to demonstrate that Jesus' arrest, trial and execution were the responsibility of God himself. And in their fulfillment, Jesus is *not* disowned by God or humiliated or dishonored by Him, because like the righteous sufferers of the psalms or the prophets of old, his trial and death are holy acts of obedience to God, not punishments for disobedience. They are precisely acts of loyalty and faithfulness to God, not impiety being requited (Neyrey 1985b: 184–90). The responsibility, then, belongs to God. By responding in obedience, Jesus assumed the most virtuous posture possible in Israel's culture, that of the obedient son (see Heb 3:2, 6; Phil 2:9).

(2) Denial of injury: Although Jesus himself dies, his behavior, which led some to label him a deviant and to destroy him, caused harm to no one. In fact, it is a positive boon to many! God's angel told Joseph to name the child "Jesus," for "He will save his people from their sins" (1:21). That programmatic statement is carefully worked out in the narrative of his ministry, in part by Jesus' exorcism of those possessed by Satan, in part by his own offer of repentance and association with sinners, and finally by a conscious statement that he would give his life in ransom for many (20:28).

The saving quality of Jesus' very name becomes attached especially to his blood. In Matthew's account of the Eucharist at the Last Supper, he records a phrase of interpretation that is not found in his source, Mark.

Matt 26:28	*Mark 14:24*
This is my blood	This is my blood
of the covenant	of the covenant
which is poured out	which is poured out
for the forgiveness	for many.
of sins.	

Jesus' blood is sacrificial blood: (a) *passover* blood effecting liberation from slavery, (b) *covenant* blood effecting a holy covenant people bonded to the covenant Lord and (c) *atonement* blood shed to consecrate God's people. Of the synoptics, only Matthew makes explicit how Jesus, "who will save his people from their sins," sheds blood in "forgiveness of sins."

In our investigation of the beneficial effects of Jesus' trial and death, we should examine the prodigious events that occur after Jesus' death on the cross, for they are life-giving events of great symbolic significance for neutralizing the stigma attached to a shameful death. Mark noted only two extraordinary phenomena: (a) the rending of the temple veil and (b) the confession of Jesus' executioner (15:38–39). Matthew retained notice of these two and added to them a report of several highly unusual phenomena: (a) an earthquake, a traditional symbol of God's presence, and (b) the physical resurrection "of the saints" and their appearing to many (27:51–54).

Irrespective of which scriptural passages Matthew suggests as being fulfilled in these events (Senior 1975:312–29), his reworking of Mark's gospel has great interpretative importance. First, the tearing of the temple veil in two (27:51) demands that the reader re-evaluate the charge in 26:61, linking Jesus' death with the end of the old temple and his resurrection with the claim to "build it in three days." Jesus' death, then, would have effects of ultimate significance, for it occasions and causes a new temple to come into being that is symbolic of the different type of covenant heralded by Jesus. Second, the "resurrection of the saints" (27:52) is explicitly linked with Jesus' death, for as Matthew narrates: "The tombs also were opened (at Jesus' death) and many bodies of the saints who had fallen asleep were raised." Jesus' death, then, directly relates to God's raising the dead on this occasion. These resurrected ones later bear witness to the Resurrected One in the city, for as Matthew narrates, "Coming out of the tomb after *his* (Jesus') resurrection, they went into the holy city and appeared to many" (27:53). The shameful death of Jesus, therefore, harmed no one and produced no injury to others. Rather, it benefited many, resulting in forgiveness of sins, salvation from death, true faith and a new temple.

(3) Denial of the victim: Presumably, the one victimized by Jesus' behavior was God, for the charge of blasphemy would mean that God was dishonored by Jesus' speech. But the story of Jesus' appearance after death (Matthew 28), even without further amplification, would underscore the fact that God approved of him, and that in fact he had never dishonored the God of Israel.

(4) Condemnation of the condemners: Both in Acts 4:19–20; 5:39 and John 3:19–21 we find a complicated motif developed in regard to the trials of Jesus: "the tables are turned." (a) In judging Jesus, the judges of Jesus and his apostles are themselves on trial; and (b) Jesus, the judged one, becomes the judge of his judges (Neyrey 1981:117). We suggest that this common motif, which is part of the telling of the Passion Narrative in other gospels, is also present in Matthew's account. For example, Jesus who is being judged predicts that he will return in glory as judge of his judges under the rubric of the Son of Man (26:64; Dan 7:14).

In another vein, the narrative is at pains to show that Jesus' judges did not judge justly and so are justly judged themselves. As we noted above, numerous acceptable witnesses are brought forward by Matthew to testify to Jesus' innocence. His Roman judge, Pilate, finds no crime in him (27:23), and Pilate's wife reports a dream she had about "that righteous man" (27:19). Judas repents of his base and unjust act of betraying "innocent blood" (27:4), even as his executioner professes him as a holy person, beloved of God (27:54). The people most implicated with the forensic proceedings against Jesus all agree that his death was undeserved and unjustified. The judgment against Jesus, then, was an unjust judgment and those who judged unjustly should themselves be judged.

The narrative, moreover, explicitly builds a case against the unjust judges, detailing their malice and wickedness. First, the reader is informed of a clandestine plot to assassinate Jesus (26:3–5), a plot that had to be carried out "by stealth." This plot apparently received a boost when a base person such as Judas accepted a bribe to betray the teacher of the way of life he espoused (26:14–16). The very assembly of the "whole council" was intended by the evangelist to be seen as a genuine forensic trial: (a) witnesses testify, (b) testimony under oath is taken and (c) a verdict is handed down. Yet, as has been noted (Juel 1973:59–60, 96; Lohse 1971:867–68), this trial is illegal on many counts.

Not only is the process against Jesus unjust and illegal, the evangelist notes as well the base motive that prompted the chief priests and elders to plot against Jesus. Pilate, for example, is reported as knowing "that it was out of envy that they had delivered him up" (27:18). The injustice of the judgment against Jesus is never clearer than when a choice is presented to the people over whether Jesus or Barabbas should be released. Barabbas was a "notorious prisoner," who in Matthew's source was arraigned for murder and insurrection (Mark 15:7). Jesus, of course, is "the one called Christ" (27:17, 22). The injustice lies precisely in the instigation of the people by the chief priests and elders to have the guilty Barabbas released and the innocent Jesus condemned (Bassler 1979:7–17). These same chief priests and elders are reported to have bribed their own guards to lie about Jesus' being raised: "Tell people, 'His disciples came by night and stole him away while we were asleep'" (28:12–13). They are thus presented as resisting the truth in their suborning of false witnesses (26:59–60), rejecting true testimony (26:64–66), and fabricating lies to cover their mistakes (28:12–13).

Although Pilate was nominally the judge at Jesus' condemnation, there is a reversal of roles in the proceedings against Jesus. From being Jesus' judge, Pilate becomes a witness to his innocence (27:23–24). The chief priests and elders start the scene as witnesses against Jesus (27:12–13), but as they persuade the people to seek Jesus' destruction, they and "all the people" become Jesus' judge as Pilate gives them authority to "see to it yourselves." They formally accept this role as they take responsibility for his blood (27:25). In short, while the official judge finds Jesus not guilty, a second process is described in which a plot is hatched by envious, sinful men who subvert the legal process and unjustly condemn an innocent man. These judges should themselves be judged, and so the condemners of Jesus are themselves condemned.

(5) Appeal to higher loyalty: We touched on this aspect earlier in the discussion of the defensive move of evasion. In that regard, Jesus was seen as representative of a kind of covenant different from that of the chief priests and their temple. The actions they condemned, however, were fully justified according to the narrative because Jesus acted in accord with a higher loyalty: God's personal authorization of Jesus and the replication of this in certain aspects of the Scriptures. Jesus' very death, moreover, is presented as obedience to God, and so is taken out of the realm of punishment for sins and crimes. In this vein, the narrative goes to great lengths to present the rejected and dying Jesus as a classically righteous man. For example, the narrative presents Jesus in prayer with God, first in the Garden and then on the Cross.

In Gethsemane, Jesus moved away from his disciples to pray (26:36). The beginning of the prayer is a snippet of a familiar prayer of a suffering righteous person in the Psalms:

Matt 26:38	*Ps 43:5 (LXX)*
My soul is sorrowful (περίλυπος) unto death.	Why are you sorrowful (περίλυπος), O my soul, and why are you disquieted within me (see 42:6).

Matthew narrates that in order to pray, Jesus left even Peter, James and John as they slept. Scholars point out that in the desire to know the text of Jesus' prayer at such a solemn moment, the early church apparently supplied an appropriate prayer, the prayer that Jesus taught his disciples, namely the Our Father. Jesus addresses his prayer in the Garden to "My Father," and prays the major petition of the first half of that prayer, "Not as I will but as you will" (26:39, 42). A line from this premier Christian prayer became Jesus' advice to his sleeping disciples, "Pray that you may not enter into temptation" (26:41). The narrative, moreover, indicates that Jesus prayed this prayer three times, "He went away and prayed for the *third time*, using the *same words*" (26:44). On one level, Jesus is presented as a model for the community in that (a) he prays to God, (b) he prays the perfect prayer, (c) he prays constantly; but on another level, the presentation of Jesus in prayer also serves an apologetic, neutralizing function in portraying Jesus as a righteous person who always sought God's will.

Even when Jesus was crucified, the narrative portrays him at the moment of his death as praying the prayer from the Psalms of a suffering righteous person. Let us look closely at his dying words, "My God, my God, why have you forsaken me?" (27:46). How should these be interpreted? From a form-critical perspective, they are the opening words of a psalm of lament (Ps 22:1), the prayer of a suffering righteous person. As such, they express extreme disappointment and feelings of dishonor, such as were already noted in Jesus' prayer in the Garden based on Ps 43:5.

Matt 27:46 (Ps 22:1)	*Matt 26:38 (Ps 43:5 LXX)*
My God, my God, why have	My soul is sorrowful
you abandoned me?	unto death.

The contention that Jesus is described as praying a scriptural word, a psalm, can be strengthened by noticing that all of the evangelists record Jesus speaking some text from the psalter as his dying words:

Mark 15:35	My God, my God, why have you abandoned me? (Ps 22:1)
Matt 27:46	My God, my God, why have you abandoned me? (Ps 22:1)
Luke 23:46	Father, into your hands I commit my spirit. (Ps 31:5)
John 19:28	To fulfil the Scriptures perfectly, he said, "I thirst." (Ps 22:15)

Jesus' dying words in Matthew, then, are first and foremost a psalm citation directed to God by Jesus and thus imply that he was a typical righteous sufferer who prayed to God in his distress.

The contents of the psalm that is quoted, however, do not seem at first blush to be a prayer, much less a sentiment appropriate to a righteous person. But let us examine the scene further for clues on how to read Jesus' dying words in their full import. It is a commonplace of scholarship that Psalm 22 is being used extensively in the gospel's crucifixion scene (Reumann 1974:39–42):

Matt 27:35	Ps 22:18
Matt 27:39	Ps 22:7–8
Matt 27:43	Ps 22:9
Matt 27:46	Ps 22:1

It is immaterial at this point whether events in the narrative suggested to the evangelist an analogy with Psalm 22 or whether, because Jesus must die in fulfillment of the scriptures, Psalm 22 functioned for the evangelist as a "source" for his narrative. Suffice it to say, Psalm 22 serves a neutralizing function in Jesus' passion, indicating that he dies according to the traditional pattern of suffering righteous people and that every moment of his passion is caught up in God's providential control as the prophecies indicate.

Yet the content of 27:46 would initially seem to suggest that Jesus was *not* modelling a righteous sentiment for edification or imitation. If his words are taken literally, without any critical interpretation, they do not seem appropriate for righteous conduct. However, that is a hasty judgment for two reasons. Matthew has gone out of his way to stress that in Jesus' passion, God neither abandoned nor withdrew from him, nor was Jesus ever described as experiencing such abandonment. For example, Jesus was engaged in deep, intimate communication with God in the garden; three times he professed his faithfulness and obedience to God. Then, at his arrest, only Matthew records Jesus' remark about the immediacy of God's saving presence, "Do you not think that I cannot appeal to my Father, and He will at once send me more than twelve legions of angels?" (26:53). Jesus, then, is portrayed as ever in God's presence, as close to God, who was ever close to him. God's closeness, moreover, is represented by the dream sent to Pilate's wife concerning "that righteous man" (27:19), as well as in the prodigious phenomena that accompany Jesus' death. Most notable among them is the earthquake, a traditional accompaniment to a theophany, an indication of God's presence (27:51–54). Hence, on the level of the narrative, Matthew insists that God has *not* abandoned Jesus. On the contrary!

Second, only Matthew adds to the crucifixion scene a citation from Ps 22:8 as the wording of the chief priests' taunt to Jesus, who ironically attested that Jesus was most faithfully loyal to God: "He trusts in God; let God deliver him if he wants him. For he said 'I am the Son of God'" (27:43). They mock him precisely for his alleged faithfulness toward God, which they could not accept but which the evangelist insists is genuine.

Even the logic of Psalm 22 supports an interpretation of that psalm as a prayer of faith in distress. The psalm is a mixed form, both a lament prayed in distress (22:1–21) and a thanksgiving prayed at worship after deliverance (22:22–31). In the lament half, three strophes repeat a regular pattern of anguished description of suffering balanced with confidence in God's deliverance:

	Psalmist's Anguish	Psalmist's Faith
Strophe 1	22:1–2	22:3–5
Strophe 2	22:6–8	22:9–11
Strophe 3	22:12–18	22:19–21

The psalmist repeatedly insists that even in extreme distress, the righteous person prays: "In thee our fathers trusted; they trusted and you delivered them" (22:4); or "Be not far from me for trouble is near" (22:11); or "O, thou my help, hasten to my aid" (22:19). The opening phrases of the psalm, "My God, my God, why have you abandoned me," are not remarks of *unbelief*, as is shown from the repeated prayers of trust and confidence in God.

The dying words of Jesus, then, should be formally seen as a prayer from the Psalms, a typical prayer of a suffering righteous person. Far from expressing abandonment or despair, the words "My God, my God, why have you abandoned me?" are seen in the context of the narrative to emphasize Jesus' righteousness, his trust in God (27:43), his continual closeness to God (26:53) and his faithfulness to God unto death (26:39, 42).

To return to the model of labelling process, the foregoing features in Matthew's gospel would indicate, therefore, that the negative labelling process had been successfully interrupted. Using typical techniques of neutralization, the evangelist constructs a retrospective interpretation of Jesus' behavior prior to his arrest, trial and execution that demonstrates that all along he was a uniquely faithful, righteous Son of God.

4.3g *Status-elevation rituals*. What specific status elevation rituals are described, directly or indirectly, in Matthew? From the viewpoint of the overall narrative, of course, the premier ritual is God's raising of Jesus. With the resurrection, Jesus is not only vindicated in the face of his enemies but enthroned by God over all. By the time of Matthew's gospel, it had become a commonplace to describe Jesus' resurrection as a royal enthronement in heaven in terms of Psalm 110.

> "The Lord said to my Lord,
> 'Sit at my right hand,
> till I put thy enemies under thy feet'" (Ps 110:1).

According to this psalm, God ("The Lord") will ascribe prominence to Israel's king ("my Lord"). The behavioral paradigm for this is the seating of the new king on a throne ("sit at my right hand"), a position of prominence. At the same time, loyal subjects either stand or bend the knee, while enemies are subjected to him ("under thy feet"). The new king does not sit on just any throne, but according to the psalm he is commanded to "sit at my right hand." Hence, he is installed as God's vice-regent. This is based on the ancient ideology of kingship, whereby the earthly king shares directly in the sovereignty of God (Goodenough 1928; see Feeley-Harnik 1985). God, who is enthroned in the sky, is King of all, and so God's king in Israel, who is enthroned next to God, is Lord of God's realm on earth.

This psalm is first mentioned in the gospel narrative in the context of Jesus' Jerusalem controversies (22:44), an apt place to record a prophecy about Jesus' ultimate triumph over his rivals, antagonists and enemies (". . . till I put thy enemies under thy feet"). With this first citation of the psalm, the reader is prepared to think of Jesus as eventually vindicated over his enemies and enthroned as Lord of God's covenant people, despite the current challenges to his authority and the plots on his life.

The next citation of the psalm occurs at Jesus' trial, itself a ritual aimed at status transformation. There Jesus predicts his eventual status elevation in a remark combining two biblical prophetic texts, both of which describe a status-elevation ritual (26:64):

> "You will see the Son of Man
> seated at the right hand of Power (Ps 110:1)
> and coming on the clouds of heaven" (Dan 7:14).

According to the logic of Matthew's gospel, prophecies, biblical as well as Jesus' own prophecies, simply must be fulfilled. Jesus thus pointed in 22:44 to a prophecy about himself from Psalm 110, a prophecy that he predicts in 26:64 will shortly be fulfilled when his status-degradation ritual is transformed by God into status elevation, an enthronement.

As we noted earlier, the reader is prepared by the narrative not to be put off by the context of Jesus' allusion to Psalm 110 in 26:64; for in this context Jesus is apparently dishonored and degraded. Although the following phrase comes from Luke 24:26, it succinctly describes Matthew's perspective as well, "Ought not the Christ to suffer and so enter into his glory" (see Acts 14:22). The application of this perspective of "glory through suffering" is expressed in Matthew by the application of Ps 118:22 to Jesus in 21:42. Commenting on the parable of the vineyard, where the figure of greatest status, "the Son" of the owner, is dishonored and killed (21:37), Jesus draws a parallel between the parable and himself:

> "The very stone which the builders rejected
> has become the head of the corner;
> this is the Lord's doing,
> and it is marvelous in our eyes" (21:42/Ps 118:22).

It would seem that the condition for being made "head of the corner" is rejection by the builders. Hence, 26:64 and 21:42 communicate and reinforce the message that Jesus is the one prophesied in Scripture to assume prominent status ("head of the corner," "sit at God's right hand") through a ritual that will reverse a previous status of dishonor ("rejected," 22:42; "blasphemy," 26:66).

The status ascribed to Jesus is the most exalted possible next to God, namely Lord and King. The narrative finally dramatizes the fulfillment of the prophecies of Psalms 110 and 118 when in 28:16–20 Jesus appears to his disciples as Messiah with power. At this point the evangelist proclaims that Jesus has already experienced his elevation to God's right hand in heaven and his enthronement. The scene, then, serves to dramatize the prominent status of Jesus, a point that can be noted by following the use of the term "all" in the narrative:

> "*All* authority in heaven and earth has been given to me. Go, therefore, an make disciples of *all* nations . . . teaching them to observe *all* that I have commanded you. And, behold, I am with you *all days*, to the close of the age" (28:18–20).

All authority over *all* nations for *all* time! Jesus indeed has been granted a premier role as one with superior executive power and so enjoys maximum prominent status. There never has nor ever will be a person with his status, role and power.

4.4   Conclusion

Viewing the tradition of Jesus' suffering and resurrection through the prism of the foregoing prominence model has helped us to see a number of things. First of all, it becomes clear why Jesus has to be considered radically different from others in his group. Prominence, like deviance, requires the one being labelled to be placed outside the purview of ordinary humans. Since Jesus was prominent by all criteria available to members of Matthew's group, then he must necessarily stand above and outside their ranks. It would be impossible for him to have been simply human. Furthermore, the prominence perspective would have us focus more sharply on the interest groups and their moral entrepreneurs in whose favor Jesus' status and role were proclaimed. It was their reading of Jesus' death and subsequent appearance that provided the interpretation of those data as a divinely accomplished status-elevation ritual. Thanks to that ritual, Jesus was not simply raised from the dead (that is, simply resuscitated), but transformed. It is the story of Jesus told from the vantage point of his ultimate transformation that controls the retrospective interpretation that is the gospel narrative.

If the resurrection is the ultimate status-elevation ritual, what bearing does this have on our overall reading of the Passion Narrative?

(1) The account of Jesus' passion and death contains predictions by Jesus himself of a reversal of status from shame to honor, from death to life and from powerless victim to powerful lord. These predictions, then, are part of the prominence process, for they set the stage for the ritual that will seal the elevation and vindication of Jesus. For example, even as Jesus predicts his suffering and death, he predicts his vindication: "It is written, 'I will strike the shepherd and the sheep of the flock will be scattered.' But after I am raised up, I will go before you to Galilee" (26:31–32). The datum of Jesus' predicting his vindication belongs with the proclamation of him as a prominent.

(2) According to the narrative, Jesus' closeness to God is never in doubt; there never was a time when he lost status and honor with God. The final instance of this closeness is the elevation ritual of his resurrection by God. For example, he is ever God's obedient son (26:39); even as he is captured, he proclaims that he could ask God and God would "at once send me more than twelve legions of angels" (26:53). Even his enemies mock his righteousness and his claim to God's favor: "He trusts in God; let God deliver him now, if he desires him" (27:43). Jesus dies praying to God (27:46). This suggests that even in his humiliation there was elevation (see Luke 24:25–27).

(3) We have noted the ironic perspective of this gospel that reminds us that the truth is not to be sought in appearances. Just as evil masquerades as good, so true worth and honor may be hidden under rejection, dishonor and death. All of the references to Jesus as "king," then, should be seen as ironically true. Jesus' mockery by the Roman soldiers (27:27–31) is his true investiture as king—crowned, enthroned and acclaimed. His mockery on the cross as "King of the Jews" (27:42) is his true enthronement. The ironic principle that is operative throughout the Passion Narrative leads us to see that Jesus' humiliation is his glorification, his dishonor is his honor, and his status degradation is his status elevation. By the process of redefinition, the rituals of degradation become the very rituals of elevation, and the one honored by this elevation is acclaimed by the author of the text called Matthew.

CONCLUSIONS

Conclusions

As we said in the preface, this book is about several things: the conflict narrated in Matthew 12 and 26–27 and, more precisely, the Christology "from the side" that is contained in those narratives. If successful, this book has provided a set of scenarios adequate for the task of reading and understanding the labels appended to Jesus in conflict situations in Matthew's gospel. We believe these scenarios are adequate because they serve to bring out the cultural communication encoded in the text of Matthew's gospel and so provide the biblical interpreter with needed help in understanding the social system behind the language of the text.

5.1   Christology

From start to finish this book was concerned with "Christology," but not the perspectives in current theology that are known as Christology "from above" and "from below." In one sense, those perspectives differ little from Christology "from the side," in that they all necessarily reflect the agenda and ideology of the group who evaluates Jesus in this or that way, although they are not as conscious of this as is Christology "from the side." In the final analysis, all Christology is "from the side," because it is done by a social group, usually the Church.

Our Christology "from the side," moreover, differs from Christology "from above" and "from below" precisely because it is as interested in the process whereby Jesus was evaluated as in the formulae or labels resulting from the process. This Christology is perhaps less glamorous than other evaluations of Jesus, if only because we came to understand it in terms of the persistent conflict in which Jesus was continually engaged. Our approach to Christology "from the side," then, is more formally a historical approach than Christology "from above" or "from below" because it pays explicit attention to the historical context and social dynamics of the evaluators.

Like other New Testament Christologies, we were concerned with the titles or labels of Jesus. Yet, as we have shown, the presumed *theological* meaning of the titles has to be seen within the perspective of the obvious *ideological* meaning of those same labels. And the *historical* significance of those titles will not stand apart from the *cultural* and *social* underpinnings those titles were meant to maintain. The titles were not ideas or concepts meant to define some abstract divine being but social labels endowed with meaning and feeling

135

meant to mark off the interests of contending groups. As central and focal person, Jesus served as pivotal symbol and ultimate source of the interpretations of life developed by the groups that evaluated him.

As the extensive lists of labels in the Appendices indicate, the use of labelling theory for Christology itself enriches our investigation, for while it attends to "titles," it examines much more data concerning the evaluation of Jesus, especially the contextualization of "titles" in the process of evaluation.

5.2   Need for Models

While we do indeed use social science models to interpret texts, our approach is basically a humanistic, liberal arts approach. As we have developed them here, the models of witchcraft and labelling/deviance theory have been neither reductionistic nor deterministic. But are they necessary to biblical interpretation?

The use of the social sciences is a deliberate attempt on our part to avoid not only ethnocentrism but also disciplinary endogamy. We would keep clear of what Ernest Becker has called fetishist reaction in scholarship, the term he uses to describe the work done by scholars who remain isolated in their respective disciplines, guarding their academic fiefdoms, their journals, their organizations, against the invasion of ideas from other scholarly domains. Such scholarly fetishism arises when one tries "to cope with an overwhelming problem of conceptualization by biting off very tiny pieces of it and concentrating on them alone, even, to push the analogy, deriving all one's sense of self, all one's delight in life and work, from the feverish contemplation of a ludicrously limited area of reality" (Becker 1971:81–82). Disciplines are never discrete, and this *a fortiori* for something such as biblical interpretation. A perusal of the categories in any annual bibliography should quickly dispel any comfortable feelings of disciplinary purity, although the gatekeepers of the "Received View" would have us believe otherwise (see Malina 1986c).

By examining the negative and positive titles of Jesus in Matthew from the viewpoint of the labelling process, we are not attempting to add new names to processes already well understood by exegetes and theologians or to repackage or refurbish a familiar apologetic. We are not attempting to express familiar biblical themes in a new linguistic register. Rather, we are trying to alter those themes quite drastically. Ours is a challenge that purposefully seeks to push beyond the limits of present ways of interpreting biblical texts for historical and/or theological purposes. We believe that studies that take contemporary social science approaches seriously will be able to discover critical ways of uncovering and reconceiving meanings originally imparted by biblical texts to their first generations of hearers. And these ways can enlarge upon established methods of doing biblical interpretation.

We argue that a social science approach is vitally important, if only because it frees biblical study from the tyranny of the spuriously obvious and self-evident. This approach best fits what has already been done in terms of the historical-critical method, but faults those studies, since they have often been guilty of either ignoring or disregarding advances made in other disciplines devoted to the interpretation of human behavior, past and present. Yet, the careful reader will appreciate how we have used social science models closely in conjunction with the findings of the historical-critical method. The best results of biblical interpretation will not come from an exclusive use of any one method or model.

5.3   Etic and Emic

Because we are people capable of abstract thought, we all use models of varying complexity and explicitness in both formal and informal attempts to understand. In this book we have followed the canons of scientific method and from the very beginning made explicit the models we use. These models are themselves etic models, that is, models developed by scholars and social scientists to interpret emic data from cultures long ago and far away. Etic and emic are accepted perspectives in the social sciences that recognize the conceptual gulf between observer and observed (Harris 1976). Although we would all like to describe cultural behavior as favorably as possible on its own terms (emic), if we would understand even any particular segment of human behavior, it needs be interpreted in light of cross-cultural perspectives (etic). A scholar may favor either an emic or etic approach—an aesthetic preference—but both are valid and necessary. Witchcraft and labelling/deviance theory are tested etic models that we have employed to understand conflict in the gospel of Matthew. We will have more to say on their usefulness.

5.4   Labelling Theory and Form Criticism

Christology "from the side" makes explicit what has long been an implicit factor in biblical studies since the articulation of form criticism. Whether one cares to consider it an advance or not, the fact is that using labelling theory immediately places those around Jesus at center stage. In terms of form criticism, the role of the church in developing an understanding of Jesus is highlighted. However, the differences between form criticism and the social science models we are using are significant.

Unlike form criticism, which imagined that all Christological development took place in terms of church liturgy and preaching, the social science models we employ postulate another, different *Sitz im Leben* or "social setting." While the titles of Jesus might be vehicles of revelation about his person, they were nonetheless applied in the crucible of conflict between acclaimers and accusers. Conflict has as valid a claim for the historical setting of Christological development as preaching. Moral entrepreneurs and their interest groups, motivated by a range of interests, were necessarily bound up with the titles of

Jesus, and this is so whether the situation is one of negative or positive evaluation.

A second important difference lies in the precision we can give to the social situation of "conflict" we have studied. Subsequent generations of form critics wrestled with the imprecision of the notions of "preaching" and "liturgy" put forth as the *Sitze im Leben* of the gospels. Our social science models demand and provide for quite specific understandings of "conflict." The witchcraft model indicates both the general cosmological viewpoint of those who employ accusations of demon possession and precise definitions of a "witch," the occasions when these accusations tend to be made and their function. The labelling and deviance model allows us to examine in considerable detail the cast of characters engaged in deviance labeling, their strategies and their maneuverings.

A third difference lies in the social rather than the theological understanding of the groups who evaluated Jesus. While they may in fact be "the Church," their behavior may be analyzed as typical social behavior.

The uniqueness of Jesus for the groups characterized by the Jesus movement seems to have been more a matter of social concern for allegiance and loyalty to a central figure rather than some philosophical or psychological judgment of unrepeatable particularity. Such judgment belongs to Christology "from above." Christology "from the side" is rooted in the anti-introspective, non-psychological, stereotypical thinking characteristic of non-elite Mediterraneans past and present. Our way of doing "Christology" studies the way social groups evaluated Jesus. This means that besides the issue of the status of Jesus, we must attend to the interests and ideologies of his followers and/or opponents, for these interests and ideologies are an integral part of the evaluation itself.

5.5   American versus Mediterranean

As we noted in the preface, contemporary U.S. readers need an adequate scenario to understand the narrative of a first-century Mediterranean evangelist. We believe that our approach in this book satisfies that need in several ways. On the level of a cross-cultural understanding of human behavior, models of witchcraft and labelling/deviance theory offer accurate, plausible and testable scenarios for understanding aspects of conflict in isolated detail and as coherent patterns of behavior. These models are necessarily abstract and drop out of consideration the rich details of specific cultural embodiment that readers always find interesting and satisfying.

Yet we have been singularly conscious of trying to provide as much of that particular detail as possible, as we constantly phrased our comments in terms of Mediterranean culture and categories. For example, we noted why Mediterranean people in particular employ the accusation of demon possession as one of their most potent social weapons. Remarks on "honor" and "shame," on the cultural meaning of "head," Mediterranean personality and the like are intended to supply the particular Mediterranean flavor (emic) to the more abstract, but valid, considerations of behavior (etic). In the Appendix, moreover, we indicate in detail how modern U.S. readers view the world differently from Mediterranean cultures. And we have indicated in our exposition of Matthew 12 and 26–27 how these conflict narratives reflect Mediterranean perspective.

Since modern U.S. readers require scenarios different from their own culture to perceive accurately Mediterranean narratives, we have constantly attended to this problem. In this regard, we call attention to Gallagher (1982), who marshals a range of cultural cues that controlled perception among ancient Mediterraneans and thus facilitated their typical anti-introspective judgments. (1) Genealogy can be deduced from one's subsequent behavior and character (and behavior/character offer solid indication of one's genealogy). (2) Social standing necessarily determines one's abilities or lack of them (and ability or inability is clear proof of one's social standing). (3) A person who does something for all mankind is of divine birth (and divine birth points to benefits for all mankind). (4) Kings necessarily perform valuable actions of benefit to many (hence, actions that benefit many point to some royal agent). (5) Magic is effective only among the ignorant and immoral; the ignorant and immoral are addicted to magic; magicians are fearsome, threatening and suspicious persons; hence, fearsome, threatening and suspicious person are almost certainly magicians. (6) Good and honest persons are preoccupied with continuity and antiquity—they respect the past; hence, those who advocate a break with the past, who advocate something brand new are rebellious, outsiders and deviants.

These generalizations obviously entered into the conflicting assessments of Jesus that emerged in the labels applied to him. These generalizations can certainly help the modern interpreter see what his or her first-century counterpart would have seen because of how they stereotypically viewed the world. They can equally help us understand how Christology "from the side" took root and developed. Again, while such assertions might seem highly irreverent for an ahistorical Christology "from above," they surely are part and parcel of any Christology "from the side."

5.6 Conflict

The four chapters in this study were about conflict in the gospel. But although we focused on Matthew 12 and 26–27, it should be evident that the gospel text tells of a constant situation of conflict in Jesus' village, region and world. What was called for were appropriate models for appreciating that conflict as it pertained to the assessment of Jesus in terms of labels, and these models are available to the biblical interpreter from the social sciences.

At the conclusion of any study using models, it is always necessary to reflect on the models, to see if they have been appropriate and adequate to the task. In the case of this investigation of conflict, it would seem that the models of witchcraft and labelling are useful, accurate and adequate models. As we noted at the end of chapter two when the models used to interpret Matthew 12 were compared, witchcraft modeling allows us to make sense of language patterns and conflictual dynamics that are common to Mediterranean culture, but that are foreign to the contemporary United States. Through the use of such a model, we came to appreciate why the worst label that could be used against someone in Jesus' world is precisely the accusation of demon possession, and how that label was intended to function in the highly contentious society of Jesus' Galilee and Palestine. The model, moreover, offered an "exploration in cosmology," as the subtitle in Mary Douglas's *Natural Symbols* indicates; the model indicated a series of redundant attitudes whereby the cosmos is interpreted in such a way that accusations of demon possession make sense in that cosmos.

Furthermore, as we indicated, this model becomes a welcome and necessary tool in the interpretation of other New Testament passages in which Christians repeatedly accuse rival Christians of demon possession (e.g., John 8:44 and 1 John 4:1–3; 2 Cor 11 and Gal 3:1). The model can be tested on other documents deriving from the first-century Mediterranean. This feature indicates that it is not an idiosyncratic suggestion, but a valid, adequate and necessary aid in biblical interpretation.

Labelling theory and the deviance model rooted in it allowed us to take a different look at familiar passages. This different approach highlighted terms, persons and activity in the narrative in ways that simply are not possible without such modeling. Although not as culturally specific as the witchcraft model, labelling and deviance modeling nevertheless aided us in interpreting the Passion Narrative so that we were able to appreciate the dramatis personae, the almost necessary coherence of the plot line, the conflictual dynamics and the offensive and defensive strategies described in the story. As with the witchcraft model, labelling and deviance modeling can be tested, so that its validity and applicability are made salient.

Labelling and deviance modeling, moreover, would seem applicable to the pervasive sense of conflict in the New Testament. In particular it would offer welcome and fresh insights into (1) the accounts of Jesus' conflicts and trials in the other gospels, (2) Paul's conflict in Galatians and his trials in the Corinthian correspondence, (3) the polemics in the Pastoral and Catholic Epistles, (4) the forensic proceedings against Peter and Paul throughout Acts of the Apostles and (5) the bitter internal conflict recorded in 1 John. Conflict is a pervasive, major social condition in which the Christian documents were written; and the models developed here are appropriate ways of understanding that conflict.

The overlapping of witchcraft and deviance models for understanding conflict is surely a plus in the interpretation of Matthew 12. No one perspective can exhaust our perception of the world, but the redundancy of these two models on the principal features of the conflict in Matthew 12 served to confirm their adequacy and give us an adequate approximation of the scenario depicted in the narrative. Likewise, the interpretation of the Passion Narrative as describing both deviance and prominence processes served to confirm our understanding of the typical features of any labelling situation of conflict. In short, the models would seem to be valid and adequate to their task.

We have sketched the models adequately; we have indicated other important texts in the New Testament where these models seem appropriate. It is our hope that our colleagues engaged in the task of biblical interpretation will find the models useful and apply them to other texts and narratives. Matthew 12 and 26–27 hardly exhaust the scope of texts that may be enlightened by the use of these models. The very attempt to apply them further cannot help but give a greater sense of their accuracy and utility, even as it will enrich the understanding of those texts by biblical interpreters.

5.7   Prominence

Deviance theory, moreover, offered us the possibility of understanding how someone might be proclaimed a prominent. Although prominence need not start as a reaction to a deviance process (for example, candidates for public office; hype for entertainers), in the case of Jesus it would appear that the first attempts at proclaiming him as a prominent were occasioned by successful manipulation of attempts to label him a deviant. And so, by a mirror reading of the deviance process, we were able to sketch the essential elements and dynamics of a process whereby someone is acclaimed a prominent.

The importance of this prominence model for interpreting New Testament Christology should be apparent. Whatever the followers of Jesus would say of him, either in remembering his own words or in preaching and interpreting him, an adequate Christology must include the perspective "from the side," from the social group that proclaimed him a prominent, whether this be his immediate followers, the early church, the gospel writers or subsequent patristic Christian groups. Labelling and prominence modeling, then, can become a most useful and needed addition to the task of biblical interpretation.

5.8   Adequate for Understanding

If we judge the models used here to be "adequate," that judgment needs further precision. The charter of modern New Testament scholarship is the claim that it is "historical" rather than "dogmatic." It seeks to step aside from church or any other modern biased interpretation of the ancient texts and to investigate the meanings that the original authors intended. Although it has been immensely enriched by a wealth of archeological and linguistic material, the discipline of biblical interpretation has not always been able to free itself from ethnocentric interpretations of ancient cultures and texts. As we have repeatedly noted, the evangelists are "inconsiderate" authors who do not imagine that their modern readers do not share their scenarios; how could they? This becomes the task of the scholar, consciously to step apart from ethnocentric scenarios appropriate to modern Western culture and to develop scenarios more appropriate to the cultures that gave birth to the New Testament documents. We believe that in principle our use of witchcraft and labelling/deviance models aids us in detaching ourselves from modern ethnocentric understanding of the gospel of Matthew, a task immeasurably aided by the constant attention to the way these models are couched in terms of Mediterranean culture and perceptions. The models used in this book are our attempts at being "considerate" readers.

5.9   Historical?

Yet how "historical" is this approach? And how might this relate to the axiom that biblical interpretation must be radically historical? "Historical" can mean many things to many people. It describes the perspective of people who focus on details, dates, so-called "facts," as well as the approach of people who inquire about processes or sequences of events. Definitions, then, of what is a validly "historical" inquiry depend on the disposition of the historian and/or the current canons of historiography. The models used here, while not intended to manufacture historical details, are "historical" in the sense that they provide an accurate way of *understanding* the particular details narrated. After all, history concerns itself not just with "facts" but the meaning of facts and the interpretation of detail.

The issue of what is "historical" unfortunately is not clarified by reference to the discussion of the Gospels as "historical," although we can make the following clarifications. In regard to the use of labelling/deviance theory and the Passion Narrative, at least it is appropriate to Matthew's version of those events. The extent to which Matthew's version depends on earlier tradition and memory, even "historical facts," is another question. In regard to witchcraft modeling and the Beelzebul controversy, it is adequate to the conflict located in the Q tradition. This begs the question of whether Jesus actually engaged in the events narrated in this snippet of the Q tradition, but at least we can evaluate that story in the context of its distinctive stratum of the tradition through this perspective.

We think that our use of social science models falls within the accepted "historical" concerns of form and redaction criticism as currently practiced by biblical interpreters. The models, while abstract, offer a heuristic framework for the many individual details found in the narratives we have examined. They offer ways of understanding and perceiving that are historically specific to the author of the text but that may elude a modern historian unfamiliar with such perspectives. They offer, moreover, a sense of the coherence of a process, a grasp of the interrelation of incidents and details that is otherwise not available.

One unsettled "historical" issue remains. Can these models be used in retro-diction? Can they be used to "reconstruct" the history narrated in the text? No simple answer can be given yet. At least they allow us to postulate what typically tends to happen in conflictual situations such as accusations of demon possession and arrests, trials and executions. The possible categories and perspectives that the models make salient provide a correct focus through which one can then recognize in a narrative those very elements that might otherwise pass unobserved and not understood. Once art students are taught about perspective, then they can readily recognize it in Renaissance painting. The models we have used do not predict what a historian will necessarily find, but they indicate where to look for typical materials, thus making possible the accurate identification and understanding of information and data. In this sense, the models contribute to an adequate historical reconstruction of the scenario of the narrator and suggest as well the plausibility of the events narrated.

The witchcraft model, for example, offers an understanding of details that is appropriate to the time and culture of the document being interpreted; it suggests how the natives would have perceived their world and what emotional effect they would have given to certain materials. The labelling and deviance model seems quite appropriate, not so much to reconstruct the history of Jesus' actual arrest, trial and execution, but to understand the version of those events narrated by an evangelist writing many years later. *His* perception is clarified. It remains a question as to the relationship of his redaction of Jesus' Passion Narrative to what might actually have happened. But in terms of *his* perception of the events, the model provided adequate and coherent under-standing of the individual events narrated.

The development and use of these models for biblical interpretation as presented in this book can itself serve as a model for contemporary interest by the biblical guild in using social science models for interpretation. The models and their presuppositions must be stated in advance and in detail. Only then can they be used to make sense of some features of behavior described in the narrative. Like all social science modeling, these models also remain open to correction and modification. And so it is that we end this study, inviting further testing of the models and continued use of them for the important task of developing scenarios for accurate, non-anachronistic interpretation of bibli-cal texts.

Appendices

Table 1
Comparing U.S. Values with the Mediterranean View

As noted in the preface, the purpose of this comparative listing is to provide a set of comparative cultural perspectives for readers unaccustomed to taking seriously the cultural dimensions involved in biblical study. It is impossible to build an adequate reading scenario without such cross-cultural perspectives. Here Mediterranean cultural anthropology is basic.

On the other hand, we would caution against the use of sociology for biblical study, even the sociology of religion, a presumably logical partner in biblical interpretation. The fact is that any use of U.S.-based sociology is highly questionable for the task of understanding another society. Sociology, including the sociology of religion, has been developed to explain social interaction only within the society of the sociologists. Furthermore, sociology often gives some of its practitioners illusions of universal validity. At most, sociological models would tell us what the people we study would be like had they lived in our contemporary society. However, with some adequate set of cross-cultural filters, a useful comparative model with which to apply sociological perspectives can be developed.

The U.S. View	*The Mediterranean View*
Self Perspectives	
Emphasis on autonomy and individualism, with adults presumed to be equal with regard to law and custom; adult children dissociated from parents, husband and wife in egalitarian relationship, siblings treated equally.	Emphasis on sociality and group orientation, with adults in patron-client relation, sons and fathers interacting over a lifetime, wives subject to husbands, younger brothers subject to the elder.
Friends are expected to provide emotional support and companionship; chosen from both sexes and a range of social groups.	Friends are expected to readily provide material and emotional support; chosen from males only within a limited group, e.g., village, neighborhood.

145

The U.S. View	*The Mediterranean View*
Emphasis on rights and the right to experiment and change individually and socially.	Emphasis on duty and loyalty with the obligation to remain in one's group(s) and abide by its decisions.
Preference for majoritarian decision making, with the willingness to abide by the will of the majority.	Preference for consensual decision making, with dissatisfaction should one be omitted from the consensual process of one's peers.
Respect for efficiency, ability, success.	Respect for hierarchy, seniority, family.
Quality of life assessed in terms of individual success, achievement, self-actualization, self-respect.	Quality of life assessed in terms of family/group success, achievement, respect of others for the group.
Quality of work life judged by a task's challenge to the individual and the intrinsic needs of the individual that it meets.	Quality of work life judged by degree to which a job allows the individual to fulfill obligations to the family/groups.
Satisfaction comes from a job well done.	Satisfaction comes from a job well recognized.
Students are motivated by a need to master the subject and the desire to get good grades for some future occupation.	Disciples are motivated by a need to acquire the status that a discipleship can provide.
Avoiding guilt, either internalized or applied by another for some infraction, is a fundamental concern.	Avoiding being shamed by others, and thus maintaining one's family's/group's honor, is a fundamental concern.
Preserving self-respect is basic.	Preserving face, i.e., respect from one's reference groups, is basic.
Children learn to think of themselves as "I."	Children learn to think of themselves as "we."
Just as children are socialized to think of themselves as individualists,	Just as children are socialized to think of themselves as dyadic group

The U.S. View	*The Mediterranean View*
they are taught to relate to others as individuals.	members, they are taught to relate to others in terms of the stereotypes characteristic of the groups to which others might belong.

Relations with Others

Fairness or justice refers to treating each person according to what is his or her due on the basis of some universalistic set of norms equally applicable to all.	Fairness or justice refers to treating each person according to what is due to his or her social group and the ranking or social location of that group in society at large; the norms that apply are group- or rank-specific.
Success and wealth belong to the individual alone, to be distributed as the individual sees fit.	Success and wealth belong to the group; relatives and friends are to share in it.
The world of work, i.e., one's job, and one's private world, are sharply distinguished both in time and mind; job is kept out of family/private concerns, and employer has no obligation to one's family duties and problems.	The world of work and one's private world are fused: job may invade private life; employer is to take the family/group duties and problems into account.
In work organization, the task comes before the relationship; the reason for this is that since an "I" is the agent of a task, the individualistic person needs no time to develop a relationship with another in order to form a "we"; teams consist of individuals doing their individual best in their individual roles, thus assuring a "victory." Individuals can quit teams that do not fit their individual needs for competitive challenge and self-respect.	In work organization, the relationship comes before the task; the reason for this is that since a "we" is the agent of a task, the dyadic individual must have time to develop a relationship with another in order to perform a task or do business with that other, thus allowing the other into the group. Time to develop such a relationship is an essential precondition for achieving a task.

The U.S. View	*The Mediterranean View*
The norm of subjecting oneself to the power of others is undesirable.	The norm of subjecting oneself to the power of others is desirable.
Laws and rules are expected to apply to superiors and subordinates alike.	Laws and rules are expected to apply quite differently to superiors than they do to subordinates.
Subordinates allow themselves into that position for pragmatic reasons only, i.e., for better competitive advantage.	Subordinates have strong, culturally instilled dependence needs.
Subordinates expect superiors to behave as team managers in consultation with their players.	Subordinates expect superiors to behave autocratically and not to consult them.
Ideal superiors are capable managers who facilitate the expertise and abilities of team members.	Ideal superiors are benevolent autocrats or paternalists, good "fathers" on whom subordinates like to depend.
The functioning of the social system is determined by multiple persons in small power positions; individuals thus can accept new and less powerful roles and still continue to function.	The functioning of the social system is determined by a few persons in distant power positions; these few powerful individuals determine the effective functioning of the system.
Weak uncertainty avoidance, i.e., tolerance of situations that are considered to be unstructured, unclear or unpredictable; hence persons tend to be patient problem solvers, less aggressive, unemotional, accepting of individual risk, relatively tolerant.	Strong uncertainty avoidance, i.e., intolerance of situations that are considered to be unstructured, unclear or unpredictable; hence persons tend to be active, aggressive, emotional, security-seeking and intolerant.
A person-based culture: there are relatively overlapping social roles for males and females, with no explicit sexual division of labor. Yet dominant values are those of males,	A gender-based culture: a sexual division of labor with no overlapping roles. Men are to be assertive, ambitious and competitive; they are to strive to

The U.S. View

The Mediterranean View

with institutionalized concern for a range of types of quality of life, for interpersonal relationships and concern for the weak (those who cannot compete due to no fault of their own).

acquire goods/services of others, including their honor; they are to respect what is big, powerful, fast. Women are to care for the nonmaterial qualities of life, for children and for the weak. Dominant values are those of males, with females embedded or encysted in males. Institutionalized concern is for material acquisition and assertiveness.

Everyday Affairs

Main form of resolving the problems of everyday life is individual self-reliance, with mastery of technological skills needed to "get the job done."

Main form of resolving the problems of everyday life is networking, i.e., by means of "friends" or "friends of friends" with whom the person with a problem may form at least a temporary alliance.

The individualist, technological problem solver needs the resources, usually in terms of money, to solve his or her problems, hence devotes large amounts of time to "the job."

The dyadic, networking problem solver needs to maintain his (rarely and secondarily, her) network, hence devotes most of the "working" day to this task.

Success or promotion in one's job requires time to develop proficiency, a place to work, a willingness to change jobs for something better and a choice of types of work one is willing to do.

Success at network maintenance requires time to service the network, a place to do so, a willingness to rearrange network parts and a choice of size of network parts.

The daily round of activities (cooking, washing, baking, eating) takes place in private.

The daily round of activities (cooking, washing, baking, eating) takes place in public.

Shopping takes place weekly.

Shopping takes place daily.

The U.S. View	*The Mediterranean View*
Social contacts requiring attention to the persons met are infrequent, based on previous commitments, formal, focused in time and place (i.e., by formal or informal appointment).	Social contacts requiring attention to the persons met are frequent, noncommital, casual, ubiquitous (one is obliged to speak with everyone in one's family/neighborhood when met; to ignore others is both impolite and shameful).
People visit each other, but infrequently and by appointment, i.e., threshold crossings into the home of another are prearranged, usually only for special relations at special times.	People do not make formal visits very frequently; i.e., threshold crossings into the home of another are for special relations at special times. Since the round of daily activities takes place outdoors, people meet frequently and by chance.
Due to climate, housing styles and the social activity patterns that these replicate, the requisite skill is an inner-oriented social personality.	Due to climate, housing styles and the social activity patterns that these replicate, the requisite skill is an outer-oriented social personality.

Political Organization

Characterized by voluntarism and voluntary associations.	Characterized by coalitions and lack of voluntary associations.
Central government guarantees and regulates the rights of business enterprises.	Central government offers no guarantees or regulations relative to business enterprises.
Corporate associations (corporations) organize productive and other activities, and utilize government agencies for protection.	Small coalitions in which kinsmen play a predominant part organize productive activity and provide self-protection.
Individuals regard themselves as citizens of a Nation-State, are highly integrated into it and participate in its institutions.	Individuals regard themselves as subjects of a Nation-State, are poorly integrated into it and avoid its institutions as much as possible.

The U.S. View	*The Mediterranean View*

The State is something reasonable human beings create to facilitate their freedoms, something to which each citizen must contribute (taxation) and in which they must participate (voting).

The State is something imposed by others, something apart from the individual to which the individual does not contribute (if possible), and in which the individual does not participate.

High formal interdependence of people on each other (specialization of roles), and few differences in relative power (not wealth).

Low formal interdependence of people on each other (little specialization), and great differences in relative power.

Since the rule of law is accepted, the State can guarantee the interests and values of the entrepreneur in particular, and the members of the community in general.

Since the rule of law is not accepted, the State does not guarantee the interests and values of anyone except bureaucrats and those in patronage relationships with bureaucrats.

Coalitions such as action sets and factions can develop into corporate associations because of the overall security provided by the rule of law and a relatively impartial State bureaucracy.

Coalitions cannot develop into corporate associations because of lack of security, no rule of law and bureaucratic favoritism.

(This list has been composed from data provided by Boissevain 1974; 1982/3; Hofstede 1984; and Malina 1981; 1985; 1986).

Table 2
List of Negative Labels in Matthew

Passage	Label followed by Source and Addressees
3:7	"brood of vipers," by John the Baptist, of Pharisees and Sadducees
4:16	"people who sat in darkness . . . who sat in the region and shadow of death" (quoting Isa 9:1–2), by evangelist, of Galilee
5:19	"least in the kingdom of heaven," by God, of those relaxing the least of these commandments
5:22	*Raka* ("fool"), by hypothetical brother, of another brother
6:2	"the hypocrites," by Jesus, of those who flaunt almsgiving
6:5	"the hypocrites," by Jesus, of those who pray for publicity's sake
6:16	"the hypocrites," by Jesus, of those who fast for publicity's sake
7:5	"you hypocrite," by Jesus in a parable, of one whose eye is full of debris, yet would take the speck out of his brother's eye
7:11	"you being evil," by Jesus in Sermon on the Mount, of his disciples
7:23	"evildoers," by Jesus, of those who prophesy, cast out demons, and do many mighty works in his name, yet who do not do the will of the Father who is in heaven
7:26	"foolish man," by Jesus, of one who hears Jesus' word but does not do it
9:3	"blaspheming," by some of the scribes, of Jesus
9:4	"thinkers of evil in the hearts," by Jesus, of some of the scribes, after "seeing their thoughts"
9:34	"he casts out demons by the prince of demons," by the Pharisees, of Jesus
10:3	"Matthew the Tax Collector," traditional name, of disciple
10:4	"Judas Iscariot who betrayed him," traditional name, of disciple
10:25	"Beelzebul," presumably by Pharisees of 9:34, of Jesus
11:11	"lesser," by Jesus, of John the Baptist in comparison with "the least in the kingdom of heaven"
11:18	"he has a demon," by this generation (the crowds of 11:7), of John the Baptist because he fasted continually
11:19	"glutton," by "this generation" (the crowds), of Jesus "drunkard," by "this generation," of Jesus "friend of tax collectors those with him and sinners," by "this generation," of Jesus
11:22	"worse than Tyre and Sidon," by Jesus, of the populace of Chorazin and Bethsaida
11:23	"you shall be brought down to Hades," by Jesus, of the populace of Capernaum

11:24	"worse than Sodom," by Jesus, of the populace of Capernaum
12:2	"profaners of the Sabbath," by the Pharisees, of Jesus' disciples
12:4	"profaner of Temple bread," by Jesus, of King David and those with him
12:5	"guiltless profaners of the Sabbath," by Jesus, of priests' activity in the Temple on the Sabbath
12:7	"condemners of the guiltless," by Jesus, of the Pharisees
12:24	"exorcises by Beelzebul, prince of the demons," by the Pharisees, of Jesus (see 10:25; 9:34)
12:31	"blasphemers against the Spirit," by Jesus, indirectly of the Pharisees (see 12:28)
12:34	"brood of vipers," by Jesus, of the Pharisees (see 3:7; 23:33)
12:34f.	"evil hearted . . . evil speaking," by Jesus, of the Pharisees (see vs 37)
12:39	"an evil and adulterous generation," by Jesus, of some of the scribes and the Pharisees
12:41f.	"worse than non-Jews," by Jesus, of some of the scribes and the Pharisees
12:43–45	"a once exorcised, repossessed person with eight unclean spirits," by Jesus, of some of the scribes and the Pharisees
12:45	"this evil generation," by Jesus, of some of the scribes and the Pharisees
14:31	"man of little faith," by Jesus, of Peter
15:2	"transgressors of the tradition of the elders," by Jerusalem Pharisees and scribes, of Jesus' disciples
15:3	"transgressors of the commandment of God," by Jesus, of the accusing Jerusalem Pharisees and scribes
15:7	"hypocrites," by Jesus, of Pharisees and scribes
15:14	"blind guides," by Jesus, of Pharisees and scribes
15:26	"dogs" (lit. "pups"), by Jesus, of Gentiles
16:4	"an evil and adulterous generation," by Jesus, of Pharisees and Sadducees who test him
16:6	"leaven," by Jesus, of the teaching of Pharisees and Sadducees (see vs 12)
16:8	"men of little faith," by Jesus, of all the disciples
16:23	"Satan," by Jesus, of Peter
17:17	"faithless and perverse generation," by Jesus, of the crowd, disciples and parents of moonstruck boy
17:20	"little faith," by Jesus, of disciples unsuccessful in healing
18:17	"non-Jew and tax collector," by Jesus, of the sinning and recalcitrant brother
21:31	"lower than tax collectors and harlots," by Jesus, of chief priests and elders of the people in Jerusalem, because of their lack of faith in John the Baptist and lack of repentance

21:43	"less than 'a nation producing fruits of the kingdom,'" by Jesus, of chief priests and Pharisees (see vs 45)
22:8	"unworthy invitees of God's wedding banquet," by Jesus, of chief priests and Pharisees (see vs 1)
22:18	"hypocrites," by Jesus, of Pharisees and Herodians who test him
22:29	"ignorant of Scripture and of the power of God," by Jesus, of mocking Sadducees
23:13, 15, 23, 25, 27, 29	"hypocrites," by Jesus, of scribes and Pharisees in Jerusalem (see vs 37)
23:13	"excluded and excluders from the kingdom of God," by Jesus, of scribes and Pharisees of Jerusalem
23:16, 24	"blind guides," by Jesus, of scribes and Pharisees of Jerusalem
23:17	"blind fools" (see 5:22), by Jesus, of scribes and Pharisees of Jerusalem
23:19	"blind men," by Jesus, of scribes and Pharisees of Jerusalem
23:23	"neglecters of the weightier matters of the law, justice and mercy and faith," by Jesus, of scribes and Pharisees of Jerusalem
23:25	"full of extortion and rapacity," by Jesus, of scribes and Pharisees of Jerusalem
23:27	"full of dead men's bones and all uncleanness," by Jesus, of scribes and Pharisees of Jerusalem
23:28	"full of hypocrisy and iniquity," by Jesus, of scribes and Pharisees of Jerusalem
23:31	"sons of those who murdered the prophets," by Jesus, of scribes and Pharisees of Jerusalem
23:33	"serpents, brood of vipers," by Jesus, of scribes and Pharisees of Jerusalem
25:2	"foolish," by Jesus, of maidens in parable who run out of oil
25:26	"wicked and slothful," by Jesus, of servant in parable who buries the hard master's wealth instead of investing
25:32	"goats," by Jesus, of those in parable on left hand, judged negatively
25:41	"accursed," by Jesus, of goats in parable destined for eternal fire prepared for the devil and his angels
26:2	"Simon the leper," traditional, fixed name, of host of Jesus
26:46, 48; 27:3	"the betrayer," by author, fixed name (see 26:25) of Judas who betrayed Jesus
26:65	"blasphemer," by high priest, of Jesus
27:63	"that imposter," by chief priests and Pharisees, of Jesus

Table 3
List of Positive Labels in Matthew

Passage	*Label followed by Source and Addressees*
1:1	"Jesus Christ," by narrator, of Jesus
1:1	"Son of David," by narrator, of Jesus
1:1	"Son of Abraham," by narrator, of Jesus
1:6	"David the King," by narrator, of David
1:16	"Jesus . . . who is called Christ," by narrator, of Jesus
1:17	"the Christ," by narrator, of Jesus
1:18	"the Christ," by narrator, of Jesus
1:18	"Mary his mother," by narrator, of Mary
1:19	"Joseph, being a just man," by narrator, of Joseph
1:20	"angel of the Lord," by narrator, of dream messenger
1:20	"Joseph, Son of David," by angel of the Lord, of Joseph
1:20	"Mary, wife (of Joseph)," by angel of the Lord, of Mary
1:21	"he will save his people from their sins," by angel of the Lord, of Jesus
1:23	"Emmanuel (God with us)," by angel of the Lord and narrator, of Jesus
1:24	"angel of the Lord," by narrator, of angel
2:1, 3	"Herod the king," by narrator, of Herod
2:2	"king of the Jews," by wise men from the East, of new born
2:4	"the Christ," by narrator, of Jesus
2:11	"Mary his mother," by narrator, of Mary
2:13	"angel of the Lord," by narrator, of angel
2:19	"angel of the Lord," by narrator, of angel
3:1	"John the Baptist" (lit. "Dipper"), by narrator, of John
3:17	"my beloved Son," by God, of Jesus at his baptism
4:3	"Son of God," by tempter, of Jesus
4:6	"Son of God," by tempter, of Jesus
4:18	"Simon who is called Peter," by narrator, of Simon
4:19	"fishers of men," by Jesus, of Simon, Andrew, James and John
7:21	"Lord, Lord," by anonymous disciple, of Jesus
8:2	"Lord," by leper, of Jesus
8:6, 8	"Lord," by centurion, of Jesus
8:19	"Teacher," by scribe, of Jesus
8:21, 25	"Lord," by disciple, of Jesus
8:29	"Son of God," by demoniacs, of Jesus
9:6	"Son of man," by Jesus, of himself
9:8	"one authorized by God," by crowd, of Jesus

9:11	"your Teacher," by Pharisees, of Jesus
9:27	"Son of David," by two blind men, of Jesus
9:28	"Lord," by blind men, of Jesus
10:2	"Simon who is called Peter," by narrator, of Simon
10:2	"James the Son of Zebedee," by narrator, of James
10:3	"Matthew the Tax Collector," by narrator, of Matthew
10:3	"James the Son of Alphaeus," by narrator, of James
10:4	"Simon the Canaanaean," by narrator, of Simon
11:2	"the Christ," by narrator via John the Baptist, of Jesus
11:3	"he who is to come," by John the Baptist, of Jesus
11:19	"Son of man," by narrator, of Jesus
12:8	"Son of man," by narrator, of Jesus
12:23	"Son of David," by the people, of Jesus
12:32	"Son of man," by narrator, of Jesus
12:38	"Teacher," by scribes and Pharisees, of Jesus
12:49	"my mother and brothers," by Jesus, of his disciples
14:2	"John the Baptist raised from the dead," by Herod the tetrarch, of Jesus
14:5	"Prophet," by Herod the tetrarch, of Jesus
14:28	"Lord," by Peter, of Jesus
14:30	"Lord," by Peter, of Jesus
14:33	"Son of God," by those in the boat, of Jesus
15:22, 25, 27	"Lord," by Canaanite woman, of Jesus
15:22	"Son of David," by Canaanite woman, of Jesus
15:26	"children of the house," by Jesus, of the lost sheep of the house of Israel
16:13	"Son of man," by Jesus, presumably of himself
16:14	"John the Baptist," by the people, of Jesus
16:14	"Elijah," by the people, of Jesus
16:14	"Jeremiah," by the people, of Jesus
16:14	"one of the prophets," by the people, of Jesus
16:16	"the Christ," by Simon Peter, of Jesus
16:16	"Son of the Living God," by Simon Peter, of Jesus
16:22	"Lord," by Peter, to Jesus
16:27, 28	"Son of man," by Jesus, presumably of himself
17:4	"Lord," by Peter, of Jesus
17:5	"my beloved Son," by God, of Jesus at transfiguration
17:12	"Elijah," by Jesus, of John the Baptist
17:12	"Son of man," by Jesus, presumably of himself
17:15	"Lord," by the father of the epileptic son, of Jesus
17:22	"Son of man," by Jesus, presumably of himself
17:24	"Teacher," by Capernaum tax collector, of Jesus
18:21	"Lord," by Peter, of Jesus
19:16	"Teacher," by one who came up, of Jesus

19:28	"Son of man," by Jesus, presumably of himself
20:18	"Son of man," by Jesus, presumably of himself
20:28	"Son of man," by Jesus, presumably of himself
20:30, 31, 33	"Son of David," by two blind men at Jericho, of Jesus
21:3	"the Lord," by Jesus, of himself
21:9	"Son of David," by the crowd, of Jesus
21:11	"the prophet Jesus from Nazareth of Galilee," by Jerusalem crowd, of Jesus
21:15	"Son of David," by children in the temple, of Jesus
21:46	"prophet," by crowds, of Jesus
22:16	"Teacher," by Pharisees' disciples and Herodians, of Jesus
22:24	"Teacher," by Sadducees, of Jesus
22:36	"Teacher," by one of the Pharisees, of Jesus
22:41–46	"Christ . . . son of David . . . Lord," by Jesus, of himself
23:8	"one Teacher," by Jesus, presumably of himself
23:10	"one Master (καθηγητής), the Christ," by Jesus, presumably of himself
23:34	"sender of prophets, wise men, scribes," by Jesus, of himself
23:39	"he who comes in the name of the Lord," by Jesus, of himself
24:30	"sign of the Son of man," by Jesus, presumably of himself
24:30, 39	"Son of man," by Jesus, presumably of himself
24:42	"your Lord," by Jesus, of himself
25:31	"Son of man in glory," by Jesus, of himself in a parable
25:34	"king," by Jesus, of himself in a parable
26:2, 24	"Son of man," by Jesus, presumably of himself
26:25, 49	"Rabbi," by Judas, of Jesus
26:63	"the Christ, the Son of God," by High Priest, of Jesus
26:64	"Son of man," by Jesus, presumably of himself
26:68	"you, the Christ," by Sanhedrin, of Jesus
27:11	"King of the Jews," by Pilate, of Jesus
27:17, 22	"Christ," by Pilate, of Jesus
27:29	"King of the Jews," by soldiers of governor, of Jesus
27:37	"King of the Jews," by Pilate, of charge over Jesus' cross
27:40	"Son of God," by passersby at cross, of Jesus
27:42	"King of Israel," by chief priests, scribes, elders, of Jesus
27:43	"he said: 'I am the Son of God,'" by chief priests, scribes, elders, of Jesus
27:54	"this was the Son of God," by centurion and others, of Jesus
28:2	"angel of the Lord," by narrator, of messenger at tomb
28:18	one with "all authority in heaven and earth," by the raised Jesus, of himself

Works Consulted

Bammel, Ernst
  1970   *The Trial of Jesus*. London: SCM.
Barton, Stephen C.
  1986   "Paul's Sense of Place: An Anthropological Approach to Community Formation in Corinth." *New Testament Studies* 32:225–46.
Bassler, Jouette M.
  1981   *Divine Impartiality: Paul and a Theological Axiom*. Society of Biblical Literature Dissertation Series 59. Chico, CA: Scholars Press.
Baumbach, G.
  1963   *Das Verständnis des Bosen in den synoptischen Evangelien*. Berlin: Evangelische Verlagsanstalt.
Becker, Ernest
  1971   *The Lost Science of Man*. New York: George Braziller Inc.
Becker, Howard S.
  1963   *Outsiders: Studies in the Sociology of Deviance*. New York: Free Press.
Beckwith, Roger
  1985   *The Old Testament Canon of the New Testament Church and its Background in Early Judaism*. Grand Rapids: Wm. B. Eerdmans.
Beer, Lawrence W.
  1984   *Freedom of Expression in Japan: A Study in Comparative Law, Politics and Society*. Tokyo, New York, San Francisco: Kodansha International, Ltd.
Blinzler, Joseph
  1959   *The Trial of Jesus: The Jewish and Roman Proceeding against Jesus Christ Described and Assessed from the Oldest Account*. Trans. I. and F. McHugh. Westminster, MD: Newman Press.
Boissevain, Jeremy
  1974   *Friends of Friends: Networks, Manipulators and Coalitions*. New York: St. Martin's Press.
  1982/83   "Seasonal Variations on Some Mediterranean Themes." *Ethnologia Europaea* 13:6–12.
Borhek, James T. and Richard F. Curtis
  1975   *A Sociology of Belief*. New York: John Wiley & Sons, Inc.
Boring, M. E.
  1976   "The Unforgiveable Sin Logion Mark III 27–28//Matt XII 31–32//Luke XII 10: Formal Analysis and History of Tradition." *Novum Testamentum* 18:258–79.
Brown, Peter
  1970   "Sorcery, Demons, and the Rise of Christianity from Late Antiq-

uity." Pp. 17–45 in *Witchcraft Confessions and Accusations*. Ed.
Mary Douglas. New York: Tavistock Publications.

Brown, Raymond E.
1973   *Peter in the New Testament*. New York: Paulist Press.
1977   *The Birth of the Messiah*. Garden City: Doubleday & Co.

Cadbury, Henry
1937   "Rebuttal, A Submerged Motif in the Gospels." Pp. 99–108 in
        Quantulacumque. Ed. R. P. Casey and Silva Lake. London: Chris-
        tophers.

Cassidy, Richard
1983   "Luke's Audience, the Chief Priests, and the Motive for Jesus'
        Death." Pp. 146–67 in *Political Issues in Luke-Acts*. Maryknoll, NY:
        Orbis Books.

Catchpole, R. R.
1971   *The Trial of Jesus*. Leiden: E. J. Brill.

Chouinard, Larry
1987   "Gospel Christology: A Study of Methodology." *Journal for the
        Study of the New Testament* 30:21–37.

Cicourel, Aaron V.
1985   "Text and Discourse." *Annual Review of Anthropology* 14:159–85.

Clements, R. E.
1967   *Abraham and David*. Naperville, IL: Alec R. Allenson.

Coser, Lewis A.
1956   *The Functions of Social Conflict*. New York: Free Press.

Dabrowski, E.
1968   "The Trial of Jesus in Recent Research." *Studia Evangelica* 4:21–27.

Danby, H.
1919   "The Bearing of the Rabbinical Criminal Code on the Jewish Trial
        Narratives of the Gospel." *Journal of Theological Studies* 21:151–76.

Danker, Frederick W.
1982   *Benefactor*. St. Louis: Clayton Publishing House.

Daube, David
1973   *The New Testament and Rabbinic Judaism*. New York: Arno.

Davis, Fred
1961   "Deviance Disavowal: The Management of Strained Interaction by
        the Visibly Handicapped." *Social Problems* 9:120–32.

De Beaugrande, Robert
1980   *Text, Discourse and Process: Toward a Multidisciplinary Science of
        Texts*. Advances in Discourse Processes, Vol. 4. Norwood, NJ: Ab-
        lex Publishing Co.

Demos, John Putnam
1982   *Entertaining Satan*. New York: Oxford University Press.

Derrett, J. Duncan M.
1979   "'Where two or three are convened in my name . . .': A Sad
        Misunderstanding." *Expository Times* 91:83–6.

Donahue, John R.
1973   *Are You the Christ?* Society of Biblical Literature Dissertation Series
        10. Missoula, MT: Scholars Press.

Douglas, Mary T.
1963   "Techniques of Sorcery Control in Central Africa." Pp. 123–41 in *Witchcraft and Sorcery in East Africa*. Eds. John Middleton and E. H. Winter. London: Routledge and Kegan Paul.
1966   *Purity and Danger*. London: Routledge and Kegan Paul.
1967   "Witch Beliefs in Central Africa." *Africa* 37:72–80.
1970   "Introduction: Thirty Years after *Witchcraft, Oracles and Magic*." Pp. xiii–xxxviii in *Witchcraft Confessions and Accusations*. Ed. Mary Douglas. London: Tavistock Publications.
1982   *Natural Symbols*. New York: Pantheon Books, Inc.
Douglas, Mary and Aaron Wildavsky
1983   *Risk and Culture*. Berkeley: University of California Press.
Downing, F. G.
1964   "Towards the Rehabilitation of Q." *New Testament Studies* 11:170–81.
Dunn, James D. G.
1980   *Christology in the Making*. London: SCM.
1984   "In Defence of a Methodology." *Expository Times* 95:295-99.
Elliott, John H.
1981   *A Home for the Homeless*. Philadelphia: Fortress Press.
Erikson, Kai T.
1966   *Wayward Puritans*. New York: John Wiley & Sons, Inc.
Evans-Pritchard, E.E.
1937   *Witchcraft, Oracles and Magic Among the Azande*. Oxford: The Clarendon Press.
Feeley-Harnik, Gillian
1985   "Issues in Divine Kingship." *Annual Review of Anthropology* 14:273–313.
Fensham, F. C.
1967   "The Good and Evil Eye in the Sermon on the Mount." *Neotestamentica* 1:51–58.
Forkman, Göran
1972   *The Limits of Religious Community*. Lund: Student-litteratur.
Gager, John G.
1983   "Culture as the Context for Meaning." *Interpretation* 37:194–97.
Gallagher, Eugene V.
1982   *Divine Man or Magician? Celsus and Origen on Jesus*. Society of Biblical Literature Dissertation Series 64. Chico, CA: Scholars Press.
Garfinkel, Harold
1956   "Conditions of Successful Degradation Ceremonies." *American Journal of Sociology* 61:420–24.
1967   *Studies in Ethnomethodology*. Englewood Cliffs, NJ: Prentice-Hall.
Gese, Hartmut
1968   "Psalm 22 und das Neue Testament." *Zeitschrift für Theologie und Kirche* 65:1–11.
Gilmore, David D.
1982   "Anthropology of the Mediterranean Area." *Annual Review of Anthropology* 11:175–205.

Goffman, Irving
1963   *Stigma: Notes on the Management of Spoiled Identity*. Englewood Cliffs, NJ: Prentice-Hall.
Goode, William J. and Paul K. Hatt
1952   *Method in Social Research*. New York: McGraw Hill Book Co.
Goodenough, Erwin R.
1928   "The Political Philosophy of Hellenistic Kingship." *Yale Classical Studies* 1:55–102.
Goody, Esther
1970   "Legitimate and Illegitimate Aggression in a West African State." Pp. 207–44 in *Witchcraft Confessions and Accusations*. Ed. Mary Douglas. New York: Tavistock Publications.
Halliday, Michael A. K.
1978   *Language as Social Semiotic: The Social Interpretation of Language and Meaning*. Baltimore: University Park Press.
Hare, Douglas A. R.
1967   *The Theme of Jewish Persecution of Christians in the Gospel According to Matthew*. Society for New Testament Studies Monograph Series 6. Cambridge: Cambridge University Press.
Harris, Marvin
1976   "History and Significance of the Emic/Etic Distinction," *Annual Review of Anthropology* 5:329–50.
Harvey, A. E.
1976   *Jesus on Trial*. Atlanta: John Knox Press.
Hiers, R. H.
1974   "Satan, Demons and the Kingdom of God." *Scottish Journal of Theology* 27:35–47.
Hofstede, Geert
1984   "The Cultural Relativity of the Quality of Life Concept." *Academy of Management Review* 9:389–98.
Hollenbach, Paul W.
1981   "Jesus, Demoniacs, and Public Authorities: A Socio-Historical Study." *Journal of the American Academy of Religion* 49:567–88.
Horbury, Will
1982   "The Benediction of the *Minim* and Early Jewish-Christian Controversy." *Journal of Theological Studies* 33:19–62.
Hubbard, Benjamin
1974   *The Matthean Redaction of a Primitive Apostolic Commissioning: An Exegesis of Matthew 28:16–20*. Society of Biblical Literature Dissertation Series 19. Missoula, MT: Scholars Press.
Hummel, Reinhart
1963   *Die Auseinandersetzung zwischen Kirche und Judentum im Matthäusevangelium*. Munich: Christian Kaiser Verlag.
Isenberg, Sheldon and Dennis E. Owen
1977   "Bodies, Natural and Contrived: the Work of Mary Douglas." *Religious Studies Review* 3:1–16.
Jewett, Robert, Larry Hurtado, and Patrick Keifert (eds.)
1984   *Christology and Exegesis: New Approaches (Semeia: 30)*. Decatur, GA: Scholars Press, 1985.

Juel, Donald
 1977   *Messiah and Temple.* Society of Biblical Literature Dissertation Series 31. Missoula, MT: Scholars Press.
Kähler, Martin
 1964   *The So-Called Historical Jesus and the Historic Biblical Christ.* Philadelphia: Fortress Press.
Keck, Leander E.
 1986   "Toward the Renewal of New Testament Christology." *New Testament Studies* 32:363–77.
Kelber, Werner
 1976   *The Passion in Mark.* Philadelphia: Fortress Press.
Kolenkow, Anitra Bingham
 1976   "A Problem of Power: How Miracle Doers Counter Charges of Magic in the Hellenistic World." Pp. 105–10 in *Society of Biblical Literature 1976 Seminar Papers.* Ed. George MacRae. Missoula, MT: Scholars Press.
Krige, J. D.
 1947   "The Social Function of Witchcraft." *Theoria* 1:8–21.
Kruse, H.
 1977   "Das Reich Satans." *Biblica* 58:29–61.
Lane, Dermott A.
 1975   *The Reality of Jesus: An Essay in Christology.* New York: Paulist Press.
Lieberman, Saul
 1965   *Greek in Jewish Palestine: Studies in the Life and Manners of Jewish Palestine in the II–IV Centuries C.E.* New York: Philipp Feldheim, Inc.
Lightstone, Jack
 1984   *The Commerce of the Sacred.* Chico, CA: Scholars Press.
Lohse, E.
 1971   "Synedrion." Pp. 860–71 in *Theological Dictionary of the New Testament Vol. VII.* Ed. G. Friedrich. Grand Rapids: Wm B. Eerdmans.
McCorkle, Lloyd and Richard Korn
 1954   "Resocialization Within Walls." *The Annals of the American Academy of Political and Social Science* 293:88–98.
Mair, Lucy
 1969   *Witchcraft.* New York: World University Library.
Malina, Bruce J.
 1967   "Matthew 2 and Is 41, 2–3, A Possible Relationship?" *Studii Biblici Franciscani Liber Annuus* 17:260–302.
 1971   "The Literary Structure and Form of Matt. XXVIII. 16–20." *New Testament Studies* 17:87–103.
 1978   "The Social World Implied in the Letters of the Christian Bishop (Named Ignatius of Antioch)." Pp. 71–119 in *Society of Biblical Literature Seminar Papers Vol. II.* Ed. Paul J. Achtemeier. Missoula, MT: Scholars Press.
 1981   *The New Testament World: Insights from Cultural Anthropology.* Atlanta: John Knox.

1985   *The Gospel of John in Sociolinguistic Perspective.* 48th Colloquy of the Center for Hermeneutical Studies. Ed. Herman Waetjen. Berkeley: Center for Hermeneutical Studies.

1986a   *Christian Origins and Cultural Anthropology: Practical Models for Biblical Interpretation.* Atlanta: John Knox.

1986b   "Normative Dissonance and Christian Origins." Pp. 35–59 in *Social-scientific Criticism of the New Testament and Its Social World.* Ed. John H. Elliott. *Semeia* 35.

1986c   "The Received View and What It Cannot Do: III John and Hospitality." Pp. 171–94 in *Social-scientific Criticism of the New Testament and Its Social World.* Ed. John H. Elliott. *Semeia* 35.

1986d   "Religion in the World of Paul: A Preliminary Sketch." *Biblical Theology Bulletin* 16:92–101.

Marwick, M. G.
1952   "The Social Context of Cewa Witch Beliefs." *Africa* 22:120–35; 215–33.

1965   *Sorcery and Its Social Setting: A Study of the Northern Rhodesian Cewa.* Manchester, England: Manchester University Press.

Mayer, Anton
1983   *Der zenzierte Jesus: Soziologie des Neuen Testaments.* Olten: Walter Verlag.

Meier, John P.
1979   *The Vision of Matthew.* New York: Paulist Press.

Middleton, John and E. H. Winter
1963   *Witchcraft and Sorcery in East Africa.* London: Routledge and Kegan Paul.

Murdock, George P.
1980   *Theories of Illness: A World Survey.* Pittsburgh: University of Pittsburgh Press.

Nader, Laura and Harry Todd
1978   *The Disputing Process—Law in Ten Societies.* New York: Columbia University Press.

Neusner, Jacob
1973a   *The Idea of Purity in Ancient Judaism.* Leiden: E. J. Brill.

1973b   *From Politics to Piety.* Englewood Cliffs, NJ: Prentice-Hall.

1978   "Map Without Territory: Mishnah's System of Sacrifices and Sanctuary." *History of Religions* 19:103–27.

Neyrey, Jerome H.
1980   "The Apologetic Use of the Transfiguration in 2 Peter 1:16–20." *Catholic Biblical Quarterly* 42:504–19.

1981   "John III—A Debate over Johannine Epistemology and Christology." *Novum Testamentum* 23:115–27.

1985a   *Christ is Community.* Wilmington: Michael Glazier, Inc.

1985b   *The Passion According to Luke.* New York: Paulist Press.

1986a   "Witchcraft Accusations in 2 Cor 10–13: Paul in Social-Science Perspective." *Listening* 21:160–70.

1986b   "The Idea of Purity in Mark." Pp. 92–123 in *Social-scientific Criticism of the New Testament and Its Social World.* Ed. John H. Elliott. *Semeia* 35.

1986c "Body Language in 1 Corinthians: The Use of Anthropological Models for Understanding Paul and His Opponents." Pp. 129–70 in *Social-scientific Criticism of the New Testament and Its Social World.* Ed. John H. Elliott. *Semeia* 35.

1988 "Bewitched in Galatia: Paul and Cultural Anthropology." *Catholic Biblical Quarterly* 50:72–100.

Nolan, Brian M.

1979 *The Royal Son of God.* Göttingen: Vandenhoeck and Ruprecht.

O'Collins, Gerald

1977 *What Are They Saying About Jesus.* New York: Paulist Press.

Pamment, Margaret

1981 "Witch-hunt." *Theology* 84:98–106.

Pfuhl, Erdwin H.

1980 *The Deviance Process.* New York: Van Nostrand Reinhold Co., Inc.

Reagan, Ronald

1983 Address to the National Association of Evangelicals. *New York Times* March 9, 1983, A 18.

Reumann, John

1974 "Psalm 22 at the Cross: Lament and Thanksgiving for Jesus Christ." *Interpretation* 28:39–58.

Rogers, Joseph and M. D. Buffalo

1974 "Fighting Back: Nine Modes of Adaptation to a Deviant Label." *Social Problems* 22:101–18.

Sanford, A. J. and S. C. Garrod

1981 *Understanding Written Language: Explorations of Comprehension Beyond the Sentence.* New York: John Wiley & Sons, Inc.

Scheff, Thomas J.

1968 "Negotiating Reality: Notes on Power in the Assessment of Responsibility." *Social Problems* 16:1–17.

Schur, Edwin M.

1971 *Labeling Deviant Behavior: Its Sociological Implications.* New York: Harper & Row.

1980 *The Politics of Deviance: Stigma Contests and the Uses of Power.* Englewood Cliffs, NJ: Prentice-Hall.

Selby, Henry A.

1974 *Zapotec Deviance: The Convergence of Folk and Modern Sociology.* Austin: University of Texas Press.

Senior, Donald

1975 *The Passion Narrative According to Matthew: A Redactional Study.* Leuven: University Press.

1977 "The Death of God's Son and the Beginning of the New Age." Pp. 29–53 in The *Language of the Cross.* Ed. A. Lacomara. Chicago: Franciscan Herald Press.

1985 *The Passion of Jesus in the Gospel of Matthew.* Wilmington: Michael Glazier, Inc.

Simon, Marcel

1967 *Jewish Sects at the Time of Jesus.* Philadelphia: Fortress Press.

Smallwood, Mary

1976 *The Jews under Roman Rule.* Leiden: E. J. Brill.

Smart, Ninian
1987   *Worldviews: Crosscultural Explorations of Human Beliefs.* New York: Charles Scribner's Sons.
Snow, David A., Louis A. Zurcher Jr. and Sheldon Ekland-Olson
1980   "Social Networks and Social Movements: A Microstructural Approach to Differential Recruitment." *American Sociological Review* 45:787–801.
Soler, Jean
1979   "The Dietary Prohibitions of the Hebrews." *The New York Review of Books* 26/10 (June 14) 24–30.
Sykes, Gresham and David Matza
1957   "Techniques of Neutralization: A Theory of Delinquency." *The American Sociological Review* 22:664–70.
Theissen, Gerd
1977   *Sociology of Early Palestinian Christianity.* Philadelphia: Fortress Press.
Thompson, Michael
1979   *Rubbish Theory: The Creation and Destruction of Value.* Oxford: Oxford University Press.
Thrall, M. E.
1980   "Super Apostles, Servants of Christ, and Servants of Satan." *Journal for the Study of the New Testament* 6:42–57.
Turner, Ralph
1972   "Deviance Avowal as Neutralization of Commitment." *Social Problems* 19:307–21.
Turner, Victor
1969   *The Ritual Process: Structure and Anti-Structure.* Chicago: Aldine Publishing Co.
van Unnik, Willem C.
1974   "The Death of Judas in St. Matthew's Gospel." *Anglican Theological Review* (supplement series) 3:44–57.
Vanhoye, Albert
1967   *Structure and Theology of the Accounts of the Passion in the Synoptic Gospels.* Trans. C. H. Giblin. Collegeville, MN: The Liturgical Press.
Weidman, Hazel Hitson
1968   "Anthropological Theory and the Psychological Function of Belief in Witchcraft." Pp. 23–35 in *Essays on Medical Anthropology.* Ed. Thomas Weaver. Athens, GA: University of Georgia Press.
Weinfeld, M.
1976   "Covenant, Davidic." *Interpreters Dictionary of the Bible, Supplement* 188–92.
Wilson, M. H.
1951   "Witch Beliefs and Social Structure." *American Journal of Sociology* 56:307–13.
Winter, Paul
1963   "The Markan Account of Jesus' Trial by the Sanhedrin." *Journal of Theological Studies* 14:94–102.
1974   *On the Trial of Jesus.* 2d ed. Rev. and ed. T. A. Burkill and G. Vermes. (Studia Judaica 1) New York: Walter de Gruyter, Inc.

Worsley, Peter
    1982   "Non-Western Medical Systems." *Annual Review of Anthropology*
                 11:315–48. 14:273–313.
Wrede, William
    1971   *The Messianic Secret.* Greenwood, SC: Attic Press.

Indices

167